Daniel Bukszpan

CONTENTS

Introduction 6

ONE
THREE TRAVELERS FORD THE RIVER

01 / Prologue 10
A young power trio goes 45 rpm

02 / The fourth man 12
"Terry really fixed that record"

03 / Working men 14
A seven-minute song blows up on WMMS

04 / "He pounded the crap out of them" 16
Toronto power trio ISO drummer, lyrics a plus

05 / "Led Zeppelin with lobotomies" 18
Rush avoid the sophomore slump

06 / Let them eat cake 20
The band get the cold shoulder

07 / There's always the farm equipment business 22
The heartbreaking tale of the "Down the Tubes Tour"

08 / The rule of the red star 24
No single, no Top 40, no problem

09 / "The end of the beginning" 26
Rush record their *Double Live Gonzo*

TWO
A QUANTUM LEAP FORWARD

10 / A few weeks in Wales 32
A band takes their artistic freedom out for a spin

11 / Sound and fury 34
Heading for the heart of Cygnus

12 / Have you chaps heard of editing? 36
Geddy Lee has the worst two weeks of his life

13 / Book II 38
Lee, Lifeson, and Peart lose their minds

14 / Realignment 42
Leaving the formula behind

15 / The future is now 44
Rush step into the 1980s

16 / "A miasma of moronism" 48
The band deviate from the norm

17 / "Three people playing like ten people" 52
Rush close out 1981 with a stellar live set

THREE
IN CONSTANT MOTION

18 / Is that a fire hydrant? 58
Rush get the seven-year itch

19 / It's not you, it's me 64
Rush break up with their fourth man

20 / In a big country 66
"Mr. So-and-so" hates odd time signatures

21 / "A lumbering metal anachronism" 68
Rush make a dark and stormy record

22 / Yes + The Sex Pistols = *Power Windows* 72
We really hope you like keyboards

23 / What's that smell? 74
Rush eat themselves

24 / "The emotional emptiness of bad jazz fusion" 78
I can't believe it's a live album!

25 / Out with the old 80
Where's the synthesizer off-ramp?

FOUR
A LIMITED TIME

26 / Scissors, paper, stone   86
A tight three-piece band and a tight two-piece production team

27 / Why are we here?   88
Rush rap, chaos ensues

28 / R-E-S-P-E-C-T   90
Unlikely Rush fans come out of the closet

29 / Feels like the first time   92
Neil Peart learns all about traditional grip

30 / Is that a bong?   94
Let's get mediocre

31 / An evening with Rush   96
News flash: No one wants to see Rush's opening acts

32 / Afterimage   98
A drummer enters limbo

33 / Four studio, one live   102
The walking wounded try to press on

FIVE
THE TIME IS NOW AGAIN

34 / Out of the cradle   110
A wounded trio ponders their return

35 / "A very fragile representation of the band"   112
The hiatus ends

36 / "Holy sh*t, this is Rush!"   118
A performing entity comes roaring back to life

37 / Recording in Rio   122
Rush endure a grade-A Charlie Foxtrot

38 / A rough night for agoraphobes   126
The Rio crowd sings all the lyrics to "YYZ"

39 / For what it's worth   128
The band's first EP and least essential release

40 / Happy birthday to you   130
What do you get for the band that have everything?

41 / Middle East, Middle West   132
Another unique entry in the Rush catalog

42 / New world men   136
Pop acceptance on the thirty-five-year plan

SIX
TURN AROUND AND SAY GOODBYE

43 / "They loved sound checking"   142
Another live album, yet again

44 / Planet Olivia   146
Peart becomes a father again

45 / A bout of nostalgia   150
Rush take a glorious look backward

46 / "I do believe it's our best work"   152
Rush make their favorite album

47 / Different strings   156
Why add one member when you can add nine?

48 / Life begins at forty   160
10-4, good buddy, over and out

49 / In praise of Neil Ellwood Peart (1952–2020)   164
"I miss him even to this day"

50 / Epilogue   168
"It's what we do"

Discography   174
Bibliography   187
Photo Credits   188
Acknowledgments   189
About the Author   189
Index   190

INTRODUCTION

Alex Lifeson, Neil Peart, and Geddy Lee at New York City's Palladium on May 11, 1980. The club's punk rock regulars must have loved hearing both books of "Cygnus X-1" back-to-back.

Rush released their self-titled debut album in 1974. Since then, the band have been the subject of countless books, podcasts, documentaries, fan websites, journalistic articles, scholarly articles, and dissertations. What could there possibly still be to say about them fifty years later?

As it turns out, plenty. It's not just that Rush don't sound like anyone else, and it's not just that they've never made the same record twice. This music refuses to go away, it remains as relevant as ever, and it has continued to connect with listeners, regardless of external fads.

Rush stopped touring and recording in 2015, but if YouTube is anything to go by, kids eighteen and younger are fully on board. They react to "Tom Sawyer" the same way their parents did when they first heard it on eight-track tape. The music inspires the same wonder and affection, and nothing has really changed but the playback format.

Initially, I didn't really hear them much until high school in the 1980s, when MTV played the videos for "Distant Early Warning" and "The Big Money" fairly often. I liked what I heard, but not enough to part with eight of my weekly allowance dollars and invest in a cassette.

Then, one great and glorious day, I heard "Freewill," and when Alex Lifeson played that magnificent guitar solo, I was on board. That was decades ago, and I've had a chronic, inoperable case of Rush Fever ever since. No matter how much I listen to them, I never suffer from Rush Fatigue.

Once I was a fan, it took almost no time to see that Rush have devoted haters, people who think nothing of telling you to your face how much they hate the band. They hate Geddy Lee's voice. They hate Neil Peart's lyrics. They hate the ten-minute songs about black holes. Journalists and civilians alike have flung raw bile at the band since their formation, and it's persisted to this day.

Interestingly, the haters are as intensely committed as the fans and for the same reason: The music is impossible to ignore while it's playing. It will either draw you in immediately and make you a lifer, or you will hate it instantly and shut it off mid-song, even if you're not in your own home and it's not your stereo. There is no "in-between" response to this trio—only irrational love or irrational hatred.

I had to take some things into consideration when I wrote this book. Rush are one of the most documented bands on earth, so serious fans already know their history. Books like *Visions*, by Bill Banasiewicz, and *Contents Under Pressure*, by Martin Popoff, are comprehensive and lay out the sequence of events definitively, so I left out stuff like how the band formed, the early lineup changes, and other things that have been covered thoroughly by others before me.

I also could not possibly compete with the books the band members themselves have written. No one is going to have more insight into Neil Peart's life than Neil Peart, and he wrote several books that should be considered the last word on his personal life.

That being the case, I decided to focus on how I feel personally about the band, my opinion of their music, and the parts of the Rush story that I found emotionally affecting or otherwise interesting. I also tried to get a sense of what the band members were like as individuals by interviewing people who had worked alongside them for years.

I also wrote this book to process the 2020 passing of drummer Neil Peart, which hit me like a ton of bricks. It upset me as if it had happened to someone I knew, especially after his daughter Selena and common-law wife Jackie passed away in

In prog rock, you haven't made it until you have your own director's chair. These were photographed in the dressing room of the Civic Auditorium in Bakersfield, California, on September 26, 1977, during the *A Farewell to Kings* tour.

the 1990s. That news affected me deeply, so I was relieved to learn he had remarried and become a father again. I thought he was "all better." So, when the news came through that he had passed, it just seemed so unbelievably cruel.

I've been sitting with that feeling ever since, and I think a lot of fans are still reeling from the news. I hope reading my take on all that is somehow helpful to them. Writing it was helpful to me.

I feel like I can never say enough about Rush, and I've learned that expressing intense love with words while still sounding coherent is really difficult. Most of the time, what I really wanted to say was, "Oh, my God! Did you hear that drum fill? This is awesome!" I mean, those are my true feelings, but they wouldn't make much of a manuscript any more than typing "SCREW FLANDERS" over and over again will make a good restaurant review. So, hopefully, despite my shameless, undignified, and worshipful fanboying, I wrote something coherent.

Rush's music continues to matter to me, and it's been there for me in difficult times. It centers me. It's been a real friend to me and continues to be. As I said, I never knew Neil Peart, but when I heard the lyrics to "Subdivisions," "Circumstances," and "Secret Touch," they succinctly expressed thoughts and emotions I didn't even realize I was feeling. This is why I say that, even though I never knew Neil Peart, his lyrics made it feel like he knew me.

In the 1976 song, "Something for Nothing," he gave timeless advice to anyone who was listening: "Let your heart be the anchor and the beat of your song." That's guided me throughout my life, and all the misfit kids in the immediate and distant future will also feel spoken to directly when they hear it. He'll live on through them. He'll live on through the kids who hear him play one time and immediately get hooked for life. In that sense, we can say about Neil Peart what he wrote in the obituary for his drum instructor Freddie Gruber: "He will be missed, but he is not gone."

INTRODUCTION / 7

ONE
THREE TRAVELERS FORD THE RIVER

Alex Lifeson, Geddy Lee, and John Rutsey, when Rush were just a young and underfed power trio in dire need of a sandwich.

01 PROLOGUE
A young power trio goes 45 rpm

In their earliest days, Rush were inspired by late-1960s bands that played what the late Frank Zappa once called "Quaalude Thunder"—Iron Butterfly, Blue Cheer, and Vanilla Fudge, to name a few.

Rush's self-titled debut album was released in 1974, featuring bassist and vocalist Geddy Lee, guitarist Alex Lifeson, and drummer John Rutsey.

Initially, they were a Toronto bar band emulating acid rock groups like Cream and The Jimi Hendrix Experience. Those bands made the loudest and heaviest music of the 1960s, and the members of Rush had been paying attention. Now, it was their turn, and they wanted in.

The three band members had all gone to school together, and those years had made them close. However, Lee and Lifeson had always been closer. The pair hailed from immigrant families, making them perennial outsiders at school to everyone but each other.

"We were sons of Eastern European immigrants who had left Europe after the Second World War to start a new life in Canada," Lee told *Classic Rock* in 2016. "We understood where each other came from, culturally."

Lee's parents were Polish Jews who had survived the Holocaust. Born Gershon Eliezer Weinrib, the name "Geddy" derived from his mother saying "Gary" in a Polish accent. The moniker had stuck since his school days, and when he turned sixteen, he took it as his legal name. Lifeson, meanwhile, was born Aleksandar Živojinović to Serbian parents.

"I grew up in a very Serbian home," Lifeson told the podcast *Make Weird Music* in 2021. "I didn't speak English until I started kindergarten."

The band formed in 1968, and the lineup shifted multiple times, finally stabilizing in 1972. In 1973, after five years of playing the local circuit, they recorded their first single.

The A-side was a cover of Buddy Holly's "Not Fade Away," and the mix hopelessly neutered it. The song had been a fixture of their live set, but this sounded less like the turbocharged Rolling Stones tribute they intended and more like Bow Wow Wow's cover of "I Want Candy."

Side B featured the Lee-Rutsey original, "You Can't Fight It," which fared slightly better than side A. The mix was still lifeless and flat, but the individual performances stood out a little better. You can hear Rutsey's drumming clearly, and Lifeson's status as a world-class guitarist is already on display, even at this early stage. But as far as the A-side was concerned, it was a crushing disappointment.

"I was embarrassed by how it came out," Lee said. "It was so . . . dinky."

Record labels wanted nothing to do with the fledgling trio and refused to sign them. The band members and their comanagers, Ray Danniels and Vic Wilson, responded by taking matters into their own hands, dubbing themselves Moon Records, and pressing five hundred copies of "Not Fade Away" / "You Can't Fight It."

The single got a decent review from Peter Taylor of *RPM Weekly*, who wrote that it "manages to capture the excitement that they can whip up in a live performance."

The single was intended to bring them to a broader audience and maybe even get them a U.S. record deal. It did nothing for them, and when you listen to it, you can hear why. It wouldn't be until their sound was captured correctly that they would get the wider notice they were looking for.

Alex Lifeson, John Rutsey, and Geddy Lee extend a warm welcome during their early days, when Rutsey was the leader of the group, according to Lee.

Moon Records 001, better known as the first Rush single, "Not Fade Away." The band didn't like how it sounded, but if you're curious, you can get a copy off of Discogs for a mere $1,000. It's even suitable for framing!

ONE: THREE TRAVELERS FORD THE RIVER / 11

02
THE FOURTH MAN
"Terry really fixed that record"

After their single failed to make an impact, the members of Rush began thinking about their next step. They decided to go big and make a full album, but the resources to do so were scarce.

"Our manager Ray Danniels put up the money," Lee told *Classic Rock* in 2016. "We had to do it cheap, recording late at night, after hours."

Even though they hadn't liked how their single sounded, they re-enlisted the same recording engineer to helm their debut LP. Recorded at Toronto's Eastern Sound, Lee said the sound wasn't any better than it was on their first single, and they couldn't live with it.

Terry Brown, a British engineer who had worked on *Axis: Bold as Love* by The Jimi Hendrix Experience, took the helm as the trio worked to salvage the recording. He told *Sonic Perspectives* in 2022 that he took to their music instantly upon hearing it.

"I'd never heard anything like it," he said.

He understood the sound they wanted and knew how to get it. They rerecorded three tracks from the Eastern Sound sessions—"Finding My Way," "Need Some Love," and "Here Again"—and added overdubs to the tracks they were keeping. The whole process took about a week, and Brown faithfully got the band's raw hard-rock sound to tape.

"Terry really fixed that record," Lee said. "It sounded great."

One problem remained, and it was a big one. The lyrics were written primarily by Rutsey, who withdrew them just as Lee was about to step into the vocal booth and record them. Lifeson told *Rolling Stone* in 2016 that this left him and Lee to write entirely new lyrics from scratch at the last minute.

"Here Again" and "Working Man" fared the best, but the lyrics on the other six songs aren't up to snuff. The band needed a dedicated lyricist, and they didn't have one.

Luckily, the music on *Rush* more than makes up for it. "Finding My Way" is as energetic an opener as anyone could hope for, while "Here Again," the band's lone foray into slow blues, evokes the melancholy vibe of "Ready for Love." Rutsey's drumming recalls that of Bad Company's Simon Kirke, one of his biggest influences.

After the almost Sabbath-heavy side 2 opener, "What You're Doing," comes "In the Mood," a throwaway filler tune reminiscent of Diet KISS. The LP closes out with "Working Man," and anyone who had to drag themselves out of bed every morning to get to a tedious, soul-destroying day job could easily get behind the lyrics.

The lineup on *Rush* didn't last beyond the debut album (more on that later), but one has to imagine what might have been in an alternate universe where Lee, Lifeson, and Rutsey stayed together. They could have had a respectable career as a straight-ahead hard rock band in the vein of Nazareth or Humble Pie, and there's certainly no shame in that. But ultimately, Lee and Lifeson wanted more than that.

At New York City's Beacon Theater on November 5, 1974, Alex Lifeson and Geddy Lee perform with drummer Neil Peart, who had joined the band just a few months earlier.

ONE: THREE TRAVELERS FORD THE RIVER / 13

03

WORKING MEN
A seven-minute song blows up on WMMS

Rush may be a fundamental entry in the band's catalog, but when it was released, no record label would go near it. Luckily, one of the 3,500 copies Moon Records pressed was sent to Donna Halper, then music director for WMMS radio in Cleveland.

It was sent to her by A&M Canada promoter Bob Roper. Had the album come out on a major U.S. label, there might have been an aggressive publicity push to get it airplay, but Rush had nothing of the sort. When Roper sent the LP, Halper characterized it as "an act of kindness."

She put on "Working Man," the last song on the record, and it immediately struck her as an ideal song for Cleveland's radio listeners. The city was a manufacturing hub full of blue-collar workers, and she believed many of them would relate to the lyrics. Her instincts were right, and upon playing the song on the air, listeners flooded the phone lines to say they loved it.

The only hitch was that Lee's high-pitched vocal led many callers to ask which new, unheard Led Zeppelin album WMMS was premiering. Brad Madix, the band's front-of-house engineer from 2002 through 2015, thought the same thing when he first heard the song.

"I literally thought it was Led Zeppelin the first time I heard it," he said.

That small error aside, *Rush* connected with audiences directly through the music, bypassing the recording industry entirely. Halper said it was a testament to the quality of the song, and she's not surprised people today still listen to it.

"'Working Man' sounds as good now as it sounded in 1974," she said.

Meanwhile, the critics hated both the album and the band that made it. The trio became the subject of scathing reviews, which started a long tradition of journalists excoriating the group every chance they got. One could say without resorting to hyperbole that critics hated *Rush* and Rush to a degree that was utterly deranged.

"*Rush* is like so many hundreds we have heard before, rock without melody, unintelligible lyrics, songs we have heard though the name and the band remain anonymous," wrote Gary Tannyan in the June 6, 1974, edition of the *Saskatoon Star-Phoenix*. "Music without a face, music without any distinction, and most of all music that does not fill any void in the music scene."

Journalists may have reviled them, but the positive response *Rush* got from radio listeners throughout the United States was too strong to ignore. It forced American record labels to pay attention, and *Rush* ultimately received a worldwide release from Mercury Records later in 1974.

The Mercury reissue featured two changes to the album jacket. The band's red logo on the front cover was rendered in a hideous shade of magenta, and a small acknowledgment was added to the album credits: "A special thank you to Donna Halper for getting the ball rolling."

Shortly after the album's release, Rush parted ways with Rutsey, and U.S. tour dates were booked and imminent. Lee and Lifeson would need to find someone new to take over, and the clock was ticking.

Alex Lifeson puts his Gibson ES-335 and Marshall cabinets through their paces at New York City's Beacon Theater on November 5, 1974.

04

"HE POUNDED THE CRAP OUT OF THEM"

Toronto power trio ISO drummer, lyrics a plus

When Neil Peart was a kid, he was obsessed with rhythm. He would bang out percussive patterns with his hands, with chopsticks, on any nearby surface. He couldn't help it.

His teachers and classmates didn't see him as a great artist discovering his destiny. They saw him as an annoying weirdo who wouldn't stop banging on his desk.

"A girl named Donna once threw a book at me," he wrote in the *St. Catharines Standard* in 1994. He also said his science teacher called him "some kind of retard."

His parents were more understanding and signed him up for drum lessons. Many aspiring percussionists get sick of practicing paradiddles and give up after a week, but Peart could practice all day and never get sick of it.

In short order, he became a very in-demand drummer, playing with several local groups. He had too much ambition to stay local, so in 1971, he proposed to his bandmates in J.R. Flood that they leave Ontario behind and move to an urban hub—one with a major music scene and larger audiences.

There were no takers, so Peart went off to London by himself to do it on his own. It was one of many solo trips he would take during his life to parts unknown.

As the reality of becoming a professional musician abroad set in, his optimism faded along with his mercenary instincts. He quickly learned from doing session work that he didn't want to be a hired gun. It simply wasn't in him to put his creativity aside for commerce. He wanted to make music that mattered to him, even if there wasn't much money in it—or any money, for that matter.

After eighteen frustrating months overseas, he returned home in 1973 with a plan. He would earn a living selling tractor parts alongside his father and play music he liked in a band called Hush (with an "H"). Creativity and commerce would be kept separate, a sensible and hard-won strategy. He told *Drum!* magazine it only lasted a year.

"One day that July, as I stood behind the parts counter, a man drove up in a white Corvette," he said. It was Rush comanager Vic Wilson, who had come to tell him the band he represented had just lost its drummer and needed a replacement. It had to be a quick learner who could jump right on board because U.S. tour dates were rapidly approaching.

In 1989, Alex Lifeson told the radio show *In the Studio with Redbeard* that when Peart came down to audition and started playing his drums, "he pounded the crap out of them." For a lot of bands, that would be enough to win the gig, but he brought a lot more to the table than just volume. Brent Carpenter, Rush's monitor engineer from 2002 through 2015, said the drummer had a unique and instantly recognizable sound that distinguished him from other players.

"I don't know how he did it, but you knew it was him," Carpenter said.

Neil Peart makes the kit do his bidding in Tulsa, Oklahoma, October 1975.

Robert Scovill, the band's live sound engineer from 1989 through 1997, said Peart had a perfect "kit mix." In engineering parlance, that means all the drummer had to do was sit down and play, and it sounded phenomenal.

"You could have put up one microphone on that guy and probably gotten away with it," Scovill said.

Peart became a member of Rush on July 29, 1974, and just sixteen days later, they were in front of eleven thousand people at the Pittsburgh Civic Arena, opening for Uriah Heep and Manfred Mann's Earth Band.

Lee told *Canadian Musician* in 1990 that he and Lifeson didn't even consider that their new drummer might also be a lyricist. When he auditioned, it was for the drum position only, but it didn't take long for them to notice that he had an extensive vocabulary. Maybe he could take a crack at writing a few lyrics.

"We did notice his incredible appetite for books and for reading," Lee said. "He also spoke English better than anyone we knew."

Donna Halper, former music director for WMMS radio in Cleveland, eventually got to know him as he integrated himself into the band. She said it didn't take long for her to come to the same conclusion.

"Neil was a reader, and he read just about everything you could imagine," she said. "He read philosophy, he read poetry, he read literature. I mean, you name it, he read it."

While Peart had the qualifications, neither he nor anyone else in the band remembered a conscious decision to appoint him to the official lyricist position. He told *Canadian Musician* that he was never asked to take the role. He just took it.

"I don't think anybody ever asked me," he recalled. "I saw a vacuum and worked on a couple of things that I submitted and were accepted."

ONE: THREE TRAVELERS FORD THE RIVER / 17

05

"LED ZEPPELIN WITH LOBOTOMIES"
Rush avoid the sophomore slump

When Rush embarked on their 1974 U.S. tour, it was their first opportunity to be heard by American music journalists. The critics of this great nation were unanimous in their assessment of the band.

Dennis Hunt of the *Los Angeles Times*, reviewing their concert at the legendary Whisky a Go Go, described the trio as "one of those fledgling groups with an alarming disregard for originality."

Another gig was at Cleveland's Agora Theater and Ballroom, a concert that made the rounds on the bootleg circuit for years. Mark Kmetzko wrote in the local publication *Scene* that the Led Zeppelin comparison Rush frequently received was "ludicrous" because of the trio's "too-simple compositions and lack of dynamics." However, he conceded that "the crowd ate it up."

Rush came off the road in December 1974. According to *Circus Raves*, the band had all of five days off, then entered the studio to record their sophomore LP. Terry Brown, who had salvaged the band's debut, returned as coproducer.

Little material carried over from the John Rutsey era. "Best I Can" and "In the End" were written before Peart joined, but the other six songs on their second album were largely worked out on tour, sometimes from the back seat of the car driving them to their next gig.

Despite the pressure cooker situation, *Fly by Night* came out very well and featured a transformed version of the group's sound. "Anthem" starts the record off in aggressive 7/8 time, and the lyrics are many steps up from the placeholder stuff on the debut.

On "Beneath, Between, and Behind," Peart delivers a pummeling straight out of the Ginger Baker playbook, and there's even some predisco four-on-the-floor for a hot minute. The title track is based around a contemplative guitar riff, and you can almost imagine the lyrics acting as Peart's kiss-off to London after his frustrating experience there. If that's the case, it's the loveliest middle-finger salute ever recorded.

18 / RUSH AT 50

The album also features "Rivendell," a heartfelt rumination on the works of J.R.R. Tolkien. It's easy to imagine the song winning lifelong fans among the "Dungeons and Dragons" set, just as it's easy to imagine it inspiring others to go out and buy Stooges records. Rush may never have set out to be divisive, but you either loved that they sang unironically about Gollum's misty mountains, or ran away as fast as your legs could carry you.

Upon hearing *Fly by Night*, Donna Halper, former music director for WMMS radio in Cleveland, said her first impression was that it was an ambitious expansion of what had come before.

"There were still flashes of what made them a really good rock and roll band in the first record, except now the lyrics were going to be a little bit more involved, a little bit deeper," she said.

Reviewing the album, John Mendelssohn wrote in *Phonograph Record* that Rush sounded "like Led Zeppelin with lobotomies." Pam Simon wrote in the March 29, 1975, edition of North Carolina's *Statesville Record & Landmark* that side 1's "By-Tor and the Snow Dog" was an outrageous affront to the human ear, calling the guitar sounds "grotesquely ugly."

"I can only hope that *Fly by Night* will do exactly that," she wrote.

Geddy Lee, Neil Peart, and Alex Lifeson sit for an early Mercury Records promo photo.

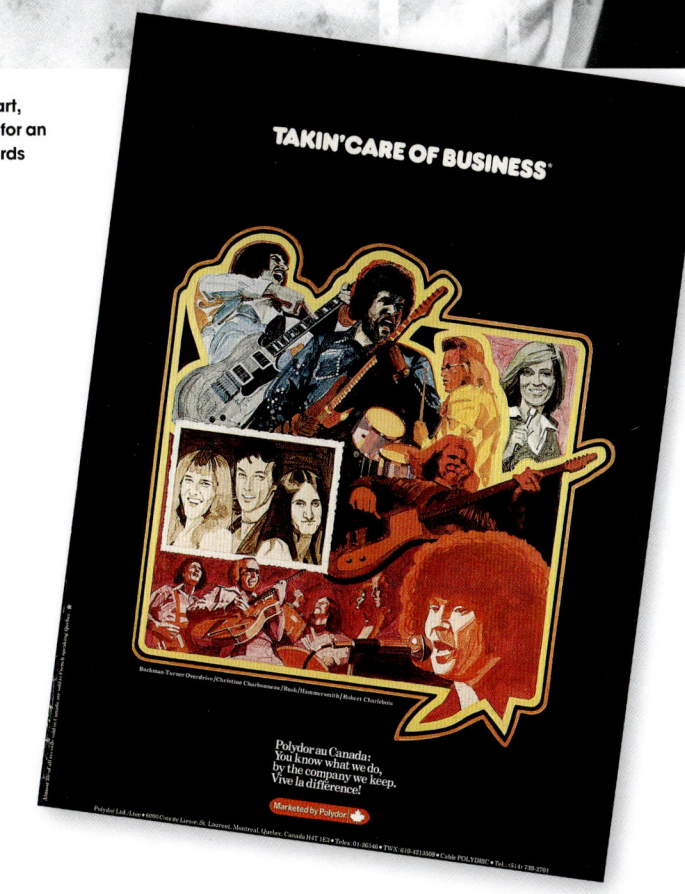

06
LET THEM EAT CAKE
The band get the cold shoulder

After the *Fly by Night* tour, Rush came home as conquering heroes. According to a Mercury Records press kit, the title track had made Canada's Top 10, and the album stayed in the Top 30 for six months.

Thus emboldened, the trio walked into Toronto Sound to chart a daringly progressive course on their next album, *Caress of Steel*. In 2023, Lee revealed that so much hash oil was consumed during the sessions that he heard reverb that wasn't there, affecting the final mix. He described that outcome as "cautionary."

"You can't be a serious musician if you're f*cking around with these drugs when it comes to work," he said.

Auditory hallucinations aside, *Caress of Steel* has a lot going for it. The opener, "Bastille Day," has a punk-rock-meets-Queen vibe that starts things off grandly, and Peart's autobiographical "Lakeside Park" is a gem.

The three-part suite, "The Necromancer," is the highlight of the album. The first section, "Into Darkness," is almost Pink Floydian in its moodiness, and Lifeson wrings palpable agony out of his Les Paul. In the middle section, "Under the Shadow," the band locks into a heavy mid-tempo groove and rides it for a couple of minutes before switching to a faster, more frantic section. Lifeson solos furiously over all of it while Lee and Peart show they're already a completely locked-in rhythm section. It's a tornado of controlled chaos.

There are also some blunders. "The Fountain of Lamneth" takes up all of side 2 and drags in many places, and "I Think I'm Going Bald" adds nothing to the album and shouldn't even have been recorded.

The critics were again consistent in their assessment of the band's music.

"'Lakeside Park' could be a tremendous tune if someone else performed it," Stan Tepner said in the November 21, 1975, *Kingston (Ontario) Whig-Standard*.

There were also issues with the cover art. It was designed by Hugh Syme, an illustrator who played keyboards with the Ian Thomas Band. That group had the same record label and management as Rush and opened for them frequently across Canada. When he designed a cover for his own band that caught Peart's eye, he was asked to create one for his labelmates.

The album cover he created was silver, per the "steel" in the title, but the label changed it to an ugly, muted gold. The illustrator said at the time, neither he nor the band were aware that a record label could step in and unilaterally change an artist's work.

"Mercury didn't think it had enough 'shelf appeal,'" he said. "They saturated my illustration with this really heavy-handed sepia brown, then added this chromium lettering, which looks like something from the Fillmore East. It just had nothing to do with what we intended."

Syme said after that experience, it was written into Rush's contract that he must be invited to the printing press to approve the artwork for all releases from that point on. While he was happy to regain control over his work, he wasn't bitter about what Mercury did to the *Caress of Steel* cover.

"Nobody meant any harm," he said. "It just began the process of making sure that nothing was ever presumed in the future."

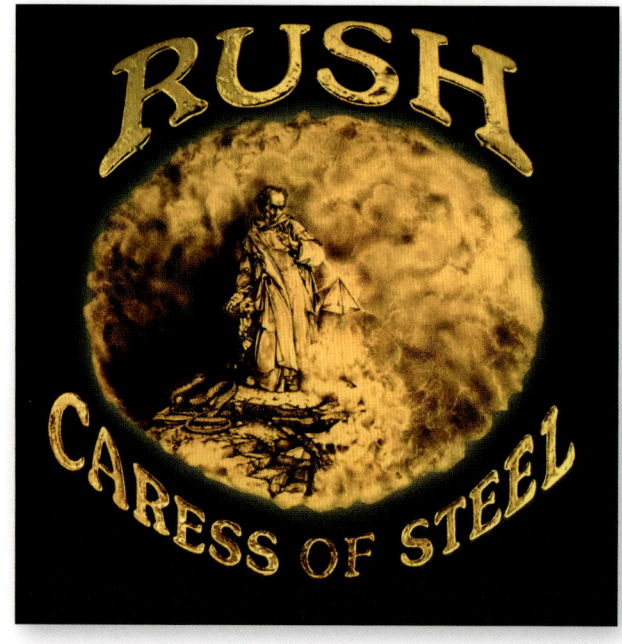

Alex Lifeson channels his inner Motor City madman in Detroit.

ONE: THREE TRAVELERS FORD THE RIVER / 21

07

THERE'S ALWAYS THE FARM EQUIPMENT BUSINESS

The heartbreaking tale of the "Down the Tubes Tour"

If Geddy Lee, Alex Lifeson, and Neil Peart weren't aware that *Caress of Steel* wasn't selling, they found out repeatedly on tour, night after night. They played sixty-seven concerts between August 24, 1975, and January 10, 1976, and during that time, they became demoralized by all the half-empty halls.

"We named it the 'Down the Tubes Tour,'" Lee told *Mojo* in 2016. "We joked about Neil going back into the farm equipment business."

Much of the excursion was spent opening for KISS, and the two bands formed an unlikely friendship. KISS bassist Gene Simmons told *Classic Rock* in 2012 that, despite the *Caress of Steel* tour's reputation as a humiliating bust, he thought that Rush had been well received by KISS fans.

"They didn't really have their own fans turning up to see them in any numbers at that stage, but they weren't all that different to us, so they appealed," Simmons said. "It was all riff-based blues rock with a lot of bombast."

He added that if Rush had a real ace in the hole, it was their commitment to touring, which he described as a "grueling" exercise that could give even the most gung ho aspiring musician second thoughts. But Simmons said the trio's ironclad commitment was plain to see. They meant business, and it would take a hell of a lot more than sluggish record sales and empty seats to stop them.

"They were 'all for one and one for all,'" he said.

The *Caress of Steel* tour put Rush in a precarious financial position. Peart told *Classic Rock* in 2004 that it had gone so poorly that they couldn't afford to pay their crew—or even themselves.

The record company wasn't happy either, but rather than drop the band, Mercury would allow them to make one more record, preferably one brimming with radio-friendly hits. This was something they couldn't consciously do.

Lee told *Louder* in 2023 that he, Lifeson, and Peart felt "the very idea of compromise was offensive." Rather than play it safe and court the Top 40, they decided to make their potential final album one for the ages. It stood an excellent chance of achieving "pearls before swine" status and going over every listener's head, but hey, Vincent van Gogh wasn't appreciated in his lifetime either.

"We thought this would probably be the last record we make," Lee told *Mojo*. "So we were like, 'F*ck you, Mercury. If we're going to go out, we'll go out doing our crazy sh*t, not failing at what you want us to be.'"

The trio made good on their pledge. They got to work on their next twenty-minute opus, a science fiction space opera based in a futuristic totalitarian state. It was seventeen minutes too long for pop radio and featured the phrase "I love you" nowhere in its lyrics. Still, despite the possibility that it was an act of commercial suicide, coproducer Terry Brown told *Mojo* in 2016 that he was convinced the album they had recorded was a work of genius.

"I felt that this was a huge leap forward for the band," he said. "I thought they'd nailed it, totally."

Alex Lifeson and Geddy Lee deliver the goods at the Tulsa, Oklahoma, Civic Center, on October 24, 1975.

08
THE RULE OF THE RED STAR
No single, no Top 40, no problem

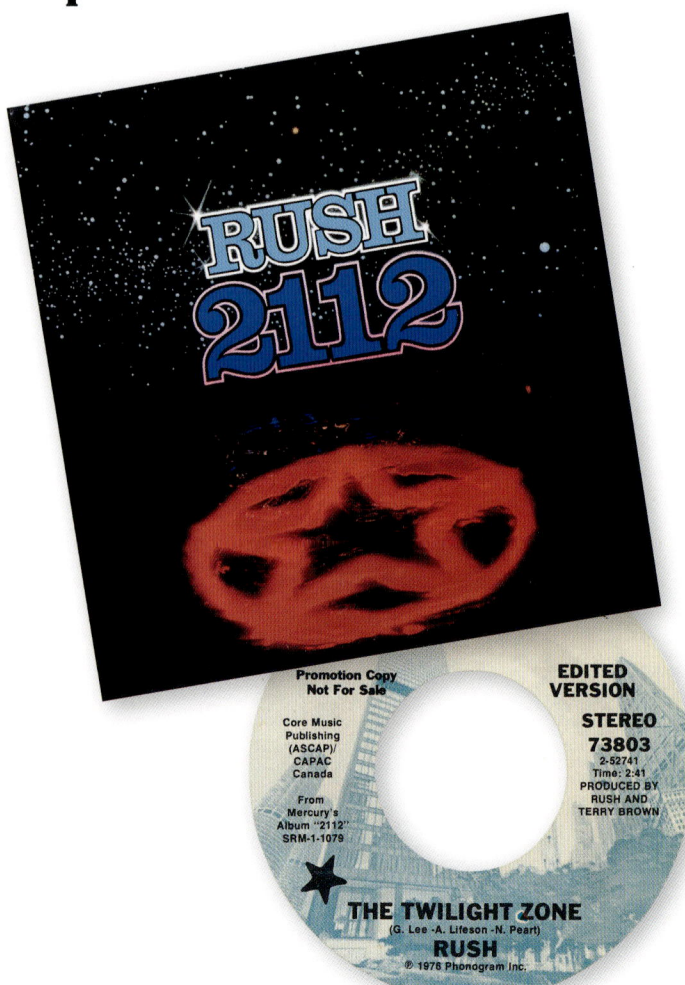

The album *2112* is Rush's first outright masterpiece. It may have a couple of lulls here and there on side 2, but it's an otherwise fascinating listen from start to finish.

It's also notable for featuring cover artist Hugh Syme's first musical contribution to a Rush album. It came about spontaneously.

"I visited them in the studio and Terry Brown said, 'Hugh plays keyboards. We should have him play something on the album,'" Syme said. "I opened up the 'Overture' on '2112,' and then got a beautiful song on the flip side called 'Tears.' I went down the hall for a few hours and worked up all the Mellotron parts."

The title track takes up all of side 1. If you didn't fully grasp the story, a concise synopsis appeared in the program for Rush's three-night engagement at Toronto's Massey Hall in June 1976.

"In the year 2062, a galaxy-wide war results in the union of all planets under the rule of the Red Star of the Solar Federation," it read. "The world is controlled by computers, called Temples, which determine all reading matter, songs, pictures . . . everything connected with life during the year 2112."

The twenty-minute suite was borderline autobiographical. Just as Rush had presented *Caress of Steel* to Mercury Records, the main character in "2112" presents the priests of the Temples of Syrinx with a guitar. In both cases, the protagonists were proud of what they had delivered, and in both cases, the response from the powers that be was, "Don't annoy us further."

The suite ends with what sounds like the end of the world. It was fitting for a band that would have the plug pulled on them if *2112* didn't shift enough units.

Side 2 isn't the home run that "2112" is, but there's plenty of solid material anyway, such as "The Twilight Zone" and "A Passage to Bangkok," a weed travelogue describing all the places where the sticky icky is grown. But the album closer, "Something for Nothing," is one of the best songs the band ever recorded. Its lyrics characterize being true to yourself as the ultimate act of defiance: "What you love is your own power/What you live is your own story."

The artistic risk Rush took with *2112* paid off. Boyd Tattrie of *RPM Weekly* wrote in the April 24, 1976, issue that "American sales have been outstanding," something that had to put a lot of minds at ease among the band and the people around them.

He also said that *2112*'s status as a concept album made it easy to promote, as the jacket's "grabbing graphics" were perfect for trade paper advertisements. The popularity of *2112* had even boosted sales of the much-maligned *Caress of Steel*, since kids who went to record stores to buy the new album would often pick up the last one, too.

Decades later, it's worth asking what it was about this record that brought Rush to a broad audience. In 2013, *Rolling Stone* critic Rob Sheffield said that its sound and fury had kept it permanently relevant decades after its release.

"The abrasively distinctive sonics, from Peart's busy tempo shifts to Lee's squawk of doom, keep it from ever fading into the background," he wrote. "Nobody will ever turn it into a Broadway show."

Sorry, Corey Hart. It may only be 1977, but Geddy Lee is already wearing his sunglasses at night.

ONE: THREE TRAVELERS FORD THE RIVER / 25

09
"THE END OF THE BEGINNING"
Rush record their *Double Live Gonzo*

After the success of *2112*, the naysayers had to concede that Rush might have been onto something. No one but Lee, Lifeson, and Peart could know what that might have been, but Boyd Tattrie of *RPM Weekly* gave it his best guess.

"Rush seem to have a sense for anticipating and understanding their audience," he wrote. "The majority of their audience are teens in the 15–17 year old bracket, who are naturally attracted to antiestablishment concepts and philosophies that they can call their own."

The trio barely had time for a Molson before returning to Massey Hall for a string of dates in June 1976. These concerts were recorded and used for the band's first live album, *All the World's a Stage*. It had the good fortune to be released during the mid-1970s when every self-respecting band was expected to have a live double album in its arsenal. It also gave the trio a little breather before they had to start work on their next record.

All the World's a Stage features furious readings of "Bastille Day" and "Anthem," as well as a slightly trimmed version of "2112." It's wild to hear them play the whole thing—well, maybe 85 percent of it—and if it's missing anything, it's the discipline of the studio version. However, that's been exchanged for an almost-explosive rage that's surprising to hear from these guys. It's the sound of three young people who had nearly been denied their vision and were now going to be as 100 percent Rush as possible.

The sound quality is not at the audiophile level many fans expect from this band, but the performances have a savagery that appears nowhere else in their catalog. Both Lifeson and Peart have solo turns in which they showcase their undeniable chops, but even without a solo of his own, Lee's playing is all over the neck—his entire performance is basically an eighty-minute bass solo.

The record has none of the flubbed notes or other imperfections that make live albums feel like genuine concert artifacts, but the energy comes through loud and clear. It doesn't feel like a perfectly replicated collection of studio songs with applause piped in. Instead, it's a well-executed performance that's still really raw—the best of both worlds.

Not everyone was sold on the Rush live experience. A few months after the release of *All the World's a Stage*, Stephen Ford of *Detroit News* attended a concert at Cobo Arena and registered his disgust at parting with $6.50 to attend the "monstrosity."

"Lead singer Geddy Lee continues to sound as though he played one football game too many without ample equipment, guitarist Alex Lifeson studies the stage charisma of the great guitarists without ever noticing their craft, and drummer Neil Peart should take a long, hard look at learning computer programming," he wrote.

All the World's a Stage became the first Rush album to break into the U.S. Top 40 album charts. The band must have sensed that they were already at a mile marker, as the liner notes contain a statement revealing their commitment to leaving the past behind. It was very clearly written by Neil Peart: "This album to us, signifies the end of the beginning, a milestone to mark the close of chapter one, in the annals of Rush."

Alex Lifeson helps put Jim Marshall's kids through college on the *All the World's a Stage* tour.

IN PRAISE OF JOHN HOWARD RUTSEY (1952–2008)

Pour one out for Rush's O.G. drummer

For most of the trio's existence, the name "Rush" has meant "Lee-Lifeson-Peart." Period, full stop. However, their original drummer was John Rutsey, who had to leave the band after recording the debut album.

He left for two reasons. One was purely a matter of taste—Lee and Lifeson wanted to take the music in a more progressive direction, and he didn't. The other factor was diabetes, which he suffered from and which made it next to impossible for him to tour.

His truncated tenure has led some to believe his contributions to the band were minimal. This is incorrect. According to those who knew him, he was as vital to the band as anybody and was instrumental in getting it off the ground.

"In those early days, John was the leader of the band," Lee told *Classic Rock* in 2016.

When "Working Man" got an overwhelmingly positive response from WMMS listeners, they won their first gig in the United States at Cleveland's Allen Theater. Former WMMS radio music director Donna Halper met them in person when they came to town for the show and described their emotional state as a mixture of youthful enthusiasm and raw terror.

"They were kids, nineteen, twenty years old," she said. "They had never been prepared for this."

She said that it quickly became clear to Lee and Lifeson that if they were going to tour—and they had to if they wanted to graduate from Toronto's bar circuit—they needed a different drummer. The subject had come up privately before, but now it was in sharp relief and needed to be addressed.

"They were going to go and perform in other cities, and John Rutsey couldn't do that," Halper said. "His health problems were going to make that impossible."

In the twenty-first century, medical technology has enabled diabetic musicians to manage the illness on the road—see Poison's Bret Michaels, for example. Halper said that in 1974, that wasn't possible.

"Today, you take out your little pen, do your little finger prick, and go on with your life," she said. "That isn't how things were for people with severe diabetes in the 1970s. You needed to find a hospital, and you needed to have things administered to you. It could take half a day."

She added that Rutsey's youth didn't help either. Like many people just a few years removed from adolescence, he didn't prioritize his health. He didn't always consider the consequences if he wanted to eat sugar-infused buttercream cake and wash it down with a beer.

"He didn't want all those restrictions," she said. "It was going to lead to them replacing him, but the fact that suddenly they were about to perform in Cleveland, Pittsburgh, and a couple of other cities made it much more urgent."

Lee and Lifeson knew change was inevitable, but it was heartbreaking when the time came to part ways for good. They had grown up with Rutsey and played music together for years. They had paid their dues with him as their drummer, and just as their hard work began to bear fruit, they had to show him the door.

"They still cared deeply about each other," Halper said. "On a professional level, they knew that it needed to happen, but on a personal level, they felt terrible about it."

After leaving the band, Rutsey pursued bodybuilding. Original roadie Ian Grandy told *Guitar International* in 2009 that he hadn't seen the drummer for about a year after he departed from the group. When he did, the former drummer was in peak physical condition.

"I was happy that he was into something healthy," Grandy said.

Original Rush drummer John Rutsey, without whom none of this would have been possible.

Rutsey's enthusiasm for pumping iron also came in handy in the late 1980s when his former bandmate Alex Lifeson wanted to shed some pounds. According to *Music Express*, the guitarist would regularly come to the gym where Rutsey exercised, and the former drummer would motivate his old bandmate with some good-natured competitiveness.

John Rutsey died on May 11, 2008, at fifty-five. The *Toronto Star* attributed the death to "complications from his lifelong affliction with diabetes," causing a fatal heart attack as he slept. Shortly afterward, Lee and Lifeson released a statement warmly recalling their days with him as a hardworking bar band that dreamed of bigger things.

"Our memories of the early years of Rush when John was in the band are very fond to us," the statement read. "Those years spent in our teens dreaming of one day doing what we continue to do decades later are special. Although our paths diverged many years ago, we smile today, thinking back on those exciting times and remembering John's wonderful sense of humor and impeccable timing. He will be deeply missed by all he touched."

Despite acknowledging that the change was necessary for Lee and Lifeson, Halper remains adamant that Rutsey's tenure was crucial to the group and he was a lot more than just the drummer Neil Peart replaced. She said there would have been no Rush without him.

"We would not even be having this conversation if it weren't for that first album," she said. "If people didn't fall in love with 'Working Man,' with 'Finding My Way,' it wouldn't have generated the interest that led to them getting a management deal in the States and a contract with a U.S. record company. None of it would have happened."

TWO
A QUANTUM LEAP FORWARD

Alex Lifeson (center) refrains from smoking backstage at the Springfield Civic Center in Massachusetts on December 9, 1976. Geddy Lee and Neil Peart are happy to take up the slack.

10
A FEW WEEKS IN WALES
A band takes their artistic freedom out for a spin

For many groups, releasing a successful album and completing a well-attended tour signifies that it's time to take a few months off and recharge. The tour Rush had just finished to promote *All the World's a Stage* had kicked off a few weeks before the album's release on August 8, 1976, and ended on June 13, 1977. That's a punishing ten months on the road, enough to test any musician's resolve.

Rather than try to preserve their emotional states, Lee, Lifeson, and Peart packed their bags and headed for Rockfield Studios in Wales to start recording their next album. It would be their first time doing so outside of Toronto, and coproducer Terry Brown had handpicked the facility.

After the success of *2112*, they could have chosen a more high-profile producer than the man they had nicknamed "Broon." However, he had proven himself time and again since rescuing their debut LP, he understood what sound they wanted, and most of all, they respected him. His input carried a great deal of weight, so much so that Peart described him to *Circus* magazine in October 1977 as "our fourth man in the studio." There was no reason to have anyone else come in and twiddle the knobs.

The band members added new instruments to their sonic arsenals in an attempt to expand their sound. Lee took up the Mini Moog, and he and Lifeson started playing bass pedal synthesizers and double-neck guitars and basses.

The man with the most new toys was Peart, who incorporated such nonrock percussion instruments into his drum kit as the triangle, the glockenspiel, and the vibra-slap. Most importantly, unlike many other bands who start incorporating exotic instruments into their repertory, these three musicians actually played them instead of positioning them somewhere onstage to make their gear look bigger.

Not content to rely solely upon esoteric musical instruments to develop their expanding sound, the trio went outdoors to record the birds that chirped idyllically outside the studio. That may not have been a particularly indulgent use of studio time, but it meant the trio knew they didn't have to worry about someone from the label coming in and pulling the plug on them.

The new album was recorded in three weeks and mixed in two. Despite the relatively quick turnaround time, the record they came up with would be their most ambitious yet. It covered more sonic territory, offered a more finely tuned version of what had come before, and featured ideas that were well and truly their own.

Just as *Fly by Night* was an expansion of the ideas on *Rush*, this newest album wasn't a rejection of their past. It was something built upon it, a progression from what had come before. If *All the World's a Stage* had been the end of chapter one, as its liner notes proclaimed, it was very easy to see how this new album was charting a bold course for chapter two.

An historical artifact from the pre-Ticketmaster era, when you could see Rush in Tulsa, Oklahoma, for a mere $6.50. People probably complained about the price then, too.

Alex Lifeson, Neil Peart, and Geddy Lee display their hirsute chests. But what's with that Instagram filter?

TWO: A QUANTUM LEAP FORWARD / 33

11

SOUND AND FURY
Heading for the heart of Cygnus

It's an understatement to say that *A Farewell to Kings* was a progression from *2112*. When you listen to it for the first time, it's the same band—Geddy Lee's voice will always make Rush instantly recognizable—but everything, from the performances to the lyrics to the songwriting, shows a band determined to conquer new musical terrain.

It features "Xanadu," one of their most outstanding achievements. Its lyrics are inspired by Samuel Taylor Coleridge's poem "Kubla Khan" and features an extended instrumental introduction that lasts a full five minutes. That may sound like a chore, but in this case, the music is so engrossing that when you finally get to the lyrics, you may have forgotten that someone was supposed to be singing in the first place.

Lee's vocal is easily one of his best. Few singers can handle lyrics like "To stand within the pleasure dome, decreed by Kubla Khan," but coming from him, it works perfectly. He also pushes the synthesizer to the forefront, although it's only used sporadically to create space-age noises and doesn't become a full-time resident of the song.

Once "Xanadu" is over, it doesn't feel like eleven minutes have passed. If anything, it makes you wonder what could be in store for you when you flip the record over. The answer is "Closer to the Heart." Clocking in at just under three minutes, the bittersweet major-key music is the perfect setting for its affecting lyric (an example that Spinal Tap's Nigel Tufnel did not follow when he wrote "Lick My Love Pump" in D minor, the saddest of all keys).

"Cinderella Man" is an excellent deep cut featuring lyrics from Lee and Lifeson, who may not have been interested in the job full time but could turn in good stuff when the spirit moved them. Its guitar solo finds Lifeson wringing all manner of unnatural sounds out of his wah pedal while Lee and Peart percolate beneath him. Lifeson also turns in some tremendous acoustic playing. Every change in instrumentation is well thought out and never feels gratuitous.

"Cygnus X-1" closes out the record, and it's completely and absolutely bonkers. Another epic exceeding the ten-minute mark, it's the harsh and dissonant counterpart to the uplifting and inspiring "Xanadu." It also answers the question, "Who influenced Voivod?"

The song tells the story of a space traveler in his ship, the "Rocinante," which readers of seventeenth-century Spanish literature will recognize as the name of Don Quixote's horse. For everyone else, it was one of many literary allusions made by Peart that was lost on the audience.

As the song's narrator realizes he's perilously close to becoming antimatter, the music launches into an abrasive, high-speed battery of anxiety-provoking minor chords that recalls the first Dirty Rotten Imbeciles record. It ends with Lee unleashing his most extreme, pained, high-pitched howl, so here's hoping that when the band's critics die and go to hell, their punishment is to be trapped in an elevator with that part of the song piped in for eternity.

Once the song ends and the record goes silent, you may find yourself wondering what the hell you just experienced. As baffling and confounding as "Cygnus X-1" is, a closer look at the track listing shows that it's actually "Cygnus X-1 Book I: The Voyage," which meant there was at least one more book coming.

A Farewell to Kings finds Rush at the height of their prog powers. It deserves a place alongside *Close to the Edge* by Yes, King Crimson's *Red*, or *Ys* by Il Balletto Di Bronzo, an example of how far the progressive rock form can be pushed when the artist takes all the guardrails away.

Alex Lifeson and Neil Peart observe as Geddy Lee gets his Moog on. Should the guitarist be worried about getting edged out of the mix by this gizmo?

TWO: A QUANTUM LEAP FORWARD / 35

12
HAVE YOU CHAPS HEARD OF EDITING?
Geddy Lee has the worst two weeks of his life

Rush fans had last heard from their heroes in 1977 with the release of *A Farewell to Kings*. All they knew was that the narrator of "Cygnus X-1 Book I: The Voyage" had been sucked into a black hole, with details to follow in "Book II."

While many may have believed that "Book II" was already a thing when they wrote and recorded "Book I," they were wrong. Peart told *Music Express* in 1978 that it was only half-written when they entered the recording studio.

"I hadn't even begun to write it until three weeks before we went back to Wales," he confessed.

The band eventually got it together and completed their next record. It would have a somewhat cryptic album jacket featuring two dudes—one naked and one in a suit—standing atop the two hemispheres of the human brain. It would also feature "Cygnus X-1 Book II: Hemispheres," which would follow the "2112" template and take up all of side 1.

Since it was their sixth studio album in four years, it's tempting to assume that these consummate professionals only needed to show up at Rockfield, hit "record," and go home. In reality, all three band members described the sessions as pretty hellish and something they wouldn't want to repeat.

"Looking back, we all acknowledge that it was the record that 'nearly killed us,'" Peart told *Drum!* magazine.

This was partially because the trio had yet to embrace approaches that might have made their lives easier. One would have been to find keys in which Lee could sing comfortably, then write the song in those keys. Instead, they wrote and recorded everything first, and Lee only found out the keys were too high when he stepped into the vocal booth. He got it done, but in 2015, he told *Rolling Stone* that the process added up to "the worst two weeks of my life."

On the plus side, the difficulty of the recording caused them to embrace editing, a concept they had previously rejected. Other prog bands, such as Yes, recorded the different sections of a suite at different times, edited them together, and ended up with "The Gates of Delirium," no muss, no fuss.

For Rush, it was an unwritten rule that you record a song in a single pass all the way through no matter how complex a task that might be. You may not get it in one take, or even in twenty takes, but splitting it up into more easily recorded separate parts and then stitching them together after the fact was, they felt, taking the easy way out.

Peart told *Drum!* magazine that the complex instrumental rounding out their forthcoming album made them finally break down and embrace editing. They had tried for four days to nail it in a single pass, to no avail. Finally, their coproducer decided to be the voice of reason and intervene.

"Terry Brown tried editing together three takes into one, it sounded great, and I had to cry, 'Uncle,'" Peart said.

The band were in a ragged state. Apart from the considerable creative demands they placed upon themselves, they had been touring relentlessly for four years with little time off before heading back into the studio and going back on the road. It was time to embrace new ways of doing things.

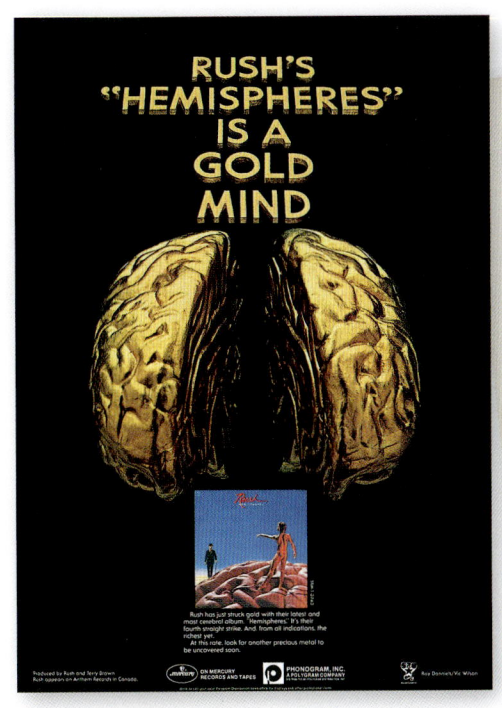

Alex Lifeson and Geddy Lee play something with an A major chord at Memorial Coliseum in Fort Wayne, Indiana, during the *All the World's a Stage* tour on April 14, 1977.

TWO: A QUANTUM LEAP FORWARD / 37

13

BOOK II
Lee, Lifeson, and Peart lose their minds

Albums are a lot like children. If you make enough of them, problems are inevitable.

This is where Lee, Lifeson, and Peart found themselves when they made *Hemispheres*. The record is full of excellent performances, and where it works, it really works. But some of it (okay, "Cygnus X-1 Book II: Hemispheres") meanders quite a bit, and it's a problem.

"Cygnus X-1 Book II: Hemispheres" takes up all of side 1, as "2112" did two albums prior. The difference is that "2112" was a coherent piece, fully mapped out and thought through. It may not have been necessary to include two minutes of someone tuning a guitar by a waterfall, but in the context of the suite, it worked.

The same cannot be said for "Book II." There are good ideas throughout, but structurally, it buckles under its own weight. It seems less like a single, coherent piece and more like a loose accumulation of starts and stops, winding riffs, and needlessly exotic time signatures, with only Roman numerals to light the way.

There are, of course, fans who love every note and will gladly sing its praises, but even some die-hard fans will concede that it sometimes overstays its welcome. Bluntly, during its eighteen-minute running time, there might be eight minutes of real meat on the bone. Maybe ten.

Side 2, meanwhile, is solid all the way through. "Circumstances" tells the story of Peart's disappointing eighteen months in London, but what jumps out at you is Lee's vocal, the highest-pitched ever to appear on a Rush studio album. The song gets right to the point, which is welcome after listening to "Cygnus X-1 Book II: Hemispheres" take its sweet time to cycle through all the various bits.

It's followed by "The Trees," a whimsical song about short, stubby maple trees deprived of sunlight by the much taller oaks with whom they must share the forest. The lyrics may be a little esoteric, but Robert Scovill, Rush's live sound engineer from 1989 to 1997, said the music was even more out there in certain spots.

"Listen to that bridge leading up to the solo and tap along with it," he said. "Try to stay on the beat. You won't be able to do it, yet it feels perfect."

He added that coproducer Terry Brown's lack of interference during such complex musical passages was just what the doctor ordered. Part of the job of co-producing Rush was knowing when to stay out of their way, even when they wrote music that defied the Top 40. Scovill said that Brown would never have told Peart just to play a straight beat and stick to the two and four.

"It would have killed it," he said.

Donna Halper, former music director for WMMS radio in Cleveland, also had an observation about "The Trees," but it wasn't about the music. She took issue with the lyrics, which she interpreted as a swipe at the feminist movement.

"Neil was very traditional back then," she said. "I took 'The Trees' to be a song where it was like, 'You're not satisfied with being in the shadow of man? Why can't you be happy with a little bit less light?'"

Given Peart's libertarian views at the time, it's also tempting to think the song may be a warning against socialism, a system in which every person standing in line for state-dispensed toilet paper is made equal by being put in last place. He told *Modern Drummer* in 1980 that the song was not intended that way either.

"I was working on an entirely different thing when I saw a cartoon picture of these trees carrying on like fools," he said. "I thought, 'What if trees acted like people?' So I saw it as a cartoon really and wrote it that way."

The instrumental "La Villa Strangiato (An Exercise in Self-Indulgence)" rounds out the album, and while no one wants to abuse the word "masterpiece," it's a masterpiece. "Circumstances" and "The Trees" are absolutely high points, but this ten-minute instrumental is easily the best thing on the record.

While much agony went into its recording, "La Villa Strangiato" sounds effortless. The fact that it goes through multiple sections and textures without seeming like they're just trying to fill time is remarkable. But while Lee and Peart play like demons throughout, the piece belongs to Lifeson. It has meaty riffs for days, and the quieter middle section with volume swells creates a dreary mood in the best possible way. Rush mostly get credit for their technical expertise, but they had an uncanny ability to create a real sense of gloom when it suited them.

While there are some issues on side 1, this record is redeemed by the almost-flawless side 2. If Rush had chosen to continue in this vein, few fans would have complained, but recording *Hemispheres* proved so unpleasant to the guys who made it that they would wipe the slate clean and start fresh in the next decade.

Geddy Lee, Neil Peart, and Alex Lifeson, chilling in their limo during the *A Farewell to Kings* tour.

TWO: A QUANTUM LEAP FORWARD / 33

Above: Alex Lifeson, Neil Peart, and Geddy Lee, none of whom were particularly fond of the whole "rock star" thing, give it their Sears Portrait Studio best anyway.

Below: Flight cases, Geddy Lee, and more flight cases, deep in the bowels of Shepperton Studios in April 1979.

Alex Lifeson ponders whether there might be unrest in the forest at Shepperton Studios in April 1979.

14
REALIGNMENT
Leaving the formula behind

After the release of *Hemispheres*, Rush embarked on a nine-month tour to promote it. It ended on June 4, 1979, at Holland's Pinkpop Festival, a heavily bootlegged concert so popular with fans that it was released on the bonus disc of the *Hemispheres* fortieth-anniversary edition in 2018.

Time has been kind to *Hemispheres*. It achieved platinum certification in the United States in 1993. In 2012, it came in eighth place in *Rolling Stone* magazine's readers' poll of favorite prog rock albums of all time, sharing space with King Crimson, Genesis, and Yes, all undisputed masters of the genre.

Despite the album being embraced by fans, the individual members of Rush were dissatisfied. Sure, they could have undoubtedly rested on their laurels if they wanted to and stuck with the "twenty-minute epic on side 1 and shorter songs on side 2" formula until retirement. However, being the people they were, that would never happen. They never made the same album twice, and they had come as close to doing that as they cared to with *Hemispheres*.

They unanimously agreed that it was time to modify the formula, and even though that meant shorter songs and the incorporation of new musical styles, none of it was a sop to the mainstream. It was a decision made out of artistic necessity by people not afraid to abandon their old ways or try new ones.

First and foremost, the band afforded themselves a luxury that had gotten away from them for a few years—taking time off after coming off the road. In "*Personal Waves*—The Story of an Album," an essay written by Peart in the *Permanent Waves* tour book, the drummer said that taking some time off had never really been "economically possible" for them before. It still wasn't, but they did it anyway and took a then-unprecedented six weeks to decompress.

Geddy Lee, Neil Peart, and Alex Lifeson record *Permanent Waves* at Le Studio in Morin-Heights, Quebec, in October 1979.

Alex Lifeson, Neil Peart, and Geddy Lee work out the bugs during the October 1979 *Permanent Waves* sessions at Le Studio.

The trio had also decided that rather than return to Rockfield Studios, they would make their next record closer to home in Canada. First, they went to Lakewoods Farm in Ontario to write and rehearse the new material. A few weeks later, they had their new songs in hand and decamped to Le Studio in Quebec to record them. Peart told *Drum!* magazine that the experience was so positive they would do it that way again for the next several albums.

"That became our pattern for a long time," he said. "It was much less crazy, and much more fun."

The album that eventually emerged showed the band writing more concise songs and, in so doing, attracting popular appeal. While the "sell out" accusation was hurled at them from some quarters for committing this unforgivable crime, Donna Halper, former music director for WMMS radio in Cleveland, said that the evolution was a natural part of the band's overall approach.

"They never wanted to sell out to do it, but they did want to reach a wide audience," she said. "You're not going to reach one if you're stuck in one particular thing and never change."

TWO: A QUANTUM LEAP FORWARD / 43

15
THE FUTURE IS NOW
Rush step into the 1980s

Permanent Waves was the first Rush album of the 1980s. It consisted of six songs that showed them embracing new sounds and technologies, particularly those used by the era's New Wave groups.

It wasn't an attempt to rebrand themselves. They genuinely liked the music they heard from bands like Talking Heads and The Police and wanted to incorporate those sounds into their music. They weren't afraid of the new sounds or the shifting times.

"The Spirit of Radio" kicks the record off with an attention-grabbing guitar introduction, punctuated by Lee and Peart playing a bizarre counterpart in lockstep. Once the song gets underway, it has a much more straightforward hard rock vibe than anything on their past few records. It's not dumbed down but streamlined, and it shows that the band were committed 100 percent to their new direction.

"Freewill" features lyrics some have interpreted as a knock against religion, thanks to the line, "You can choose a ready guide in some celestial voice." The lyrics also seem like an indictment of passive-aggressive people who can't or won't make a decision, particularly the line, "If you choose not to decide, you still have made a choice."

The middle instrumental section features one of the best guitar solos of Lifeson's entire career, with Lee and Peart once again going nuts on their respective instruments but never losing the plot. These guys could get way out there musically when they wanted to, but they never lost control of the song and always kept it grounded.

"Jacob's Ladder" still has one foot in the band's progressive rock past, but it's more economical, and it spends its seven-and-a-half-minute running time building suspense and reaching a crescendo. By the way, how the hell did Peart do these weird fills in alternating measures of 6/8 and 7/8 time without getting confused and messing it up? Seriously, how?

If you're Alex Lifeson and it's May 23, 1980, then you must be at Nassau Coliseum in Uniondale, New York.

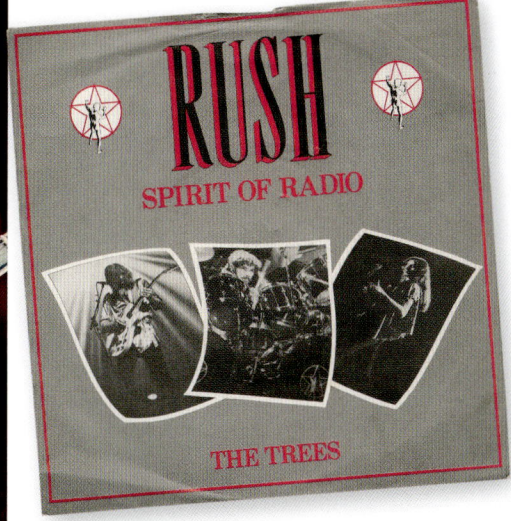

Geddy Lee brings the throbbing bottom end to Nassau Coliseum in Uniondale, New York, on May 23, 1980.

Contrary to popular opinion, the deceptively straightforward ballad "Different Strings" is the highlight of the record's second side. Featuring some rare Lee-penned lyrics, the music is moody without being overwrought and doesn't fight for the listener's attention. The ending is perfectly restrained, with all three musicians turning in sophisticated performances that quietly dazzle.

The album closes with "Natural Science," which shows Rush still shaking off some of its 1970s prog-isms. At over nine minutes, it's not trimmed quite as meticulously as "Jacob's Ladder," and it suffers a bit for that. There's plenty of good stuff, but it could have used a little more tightening.

Not that it's bad, mind you. Lifeson turns in yet another outstanding guitar solo, leaving one to wonder yet again why he's never called one of the greatest rock guitarists of all time. Are people just stupid? Is that why? And those lyrics—"Science like nature must also be tamed with a view towards its preservation." Has anyone besides Neil Peart ever even attempted to write something like that? And if they did, did it come out in the form of a compelling lyric as it did here, or did it emerge in the form of half-baked garbage that shouldn't have been written?

Rush rarely got credit for being a topical band, but *Permanent Waves* is a topical record nonetheless, "The Spirit of Radio" in particular. Rush had

TWO: A QUANTUM LEAP FORWARD / 45

Neil Peart on a relatively small (for him) drum kit at the Palladium in New York City on May 11, 1980.

won their initial fan base through airplay from local stations like KSHE in St. Louis, WMMR in Philadelphia, and, of course, WMMS in Cleveland. Increasing corporatism was making it harder for local stations to operate independently and champion artists they liked.

"You're starting to get into the era of deregulation, you're getting the end of the fairness doctrine in America," former WMMS radio music director Donna Halper explained. "Pretty soon, you're going to have six or seven giant conglomerates owning most of the stations, and what WMMS did would no longer be possible."

Permanent Waves did very well upon its release, selling one million copies in the United States in just two months. The band's decision to evolve musically hadn't hurt them with their fans. If anything, it won them new ones.

Rush were still not critics' darlings at this point, but a few journalists, such as *Rolling Stone*'s David Fricke, started to give them a little more of a fair shake. In his review of *Permanent Waves*, he observed that his profession simply wasn't a factor for the band's fan base. They loved the music, and they didn't care what *CREEM*, the *New York Times*, or even, yes, *Rolling Stone* had to say about it.

"They simply don't play fashionable music," he wrote of the band. "If they couldn't cut it on their own terms, that'd be different. But this band is among the very best in its genre. And if the Top 5 status of *Permanent Waves* is any example, it's a genre wherein critics don't count at all."

TWO: A QUANTUM LEAP FORWARD / 47

16
"A MIASMA OF MORONISM"
The band deviate from the norm

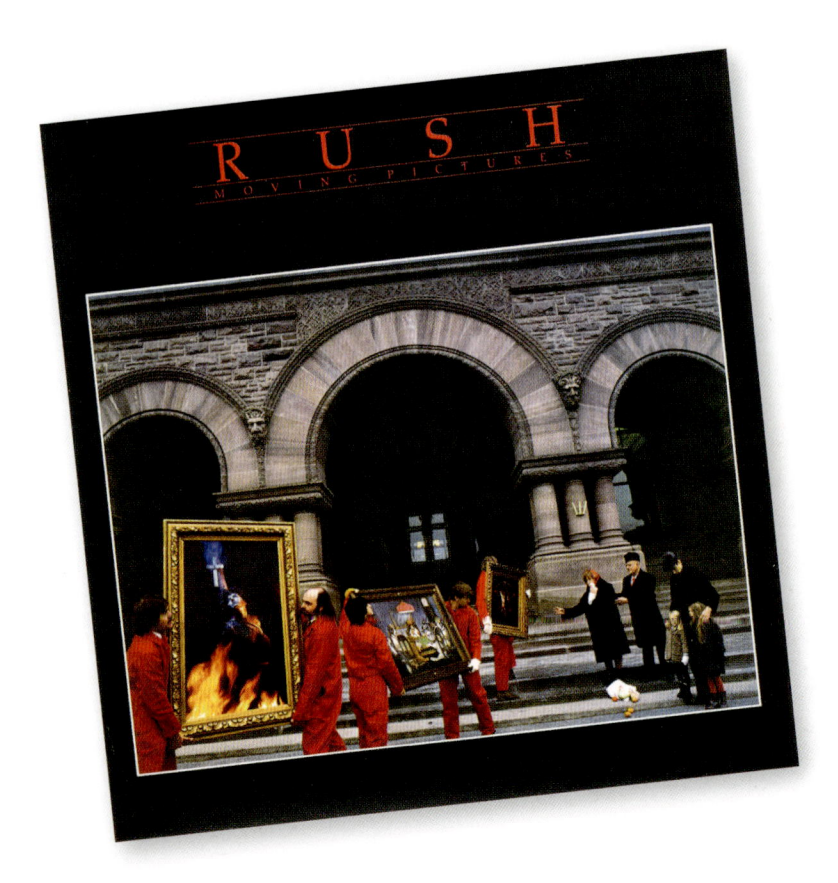

Moving Pictures turned Rush into a mainstream institution. In the 2010 documentary *Rush: Beyond the Lighted Stage*, Peart called it the album with which "we became 'us.'" It had taken seven studio albums and a live album to get there, but the long years of toil had paid off. Today, you'd be hard-pressed to find a better example of who they were as a band.

In a 2021 interview with the podcast *Make Weird Music*, Lifeson revealed that the band members considered it their finest hour.

"*Moving Pictures* was by far the greatest record that we made, from our perspective," he said. "When we went to the studio and started recording it, everything about it fell into place."

The proceedings get underway with "Tom Sawyer," which features Peart's tour de force performance. It's easy to envision millions of teenagers hearing it and immediately demanding drum lessons. In fact, every teenager with a YouTube reaction channel is currently losing their mind as they listen to it for the first time.

A heavy guitar riff propels the song, which only breaks out of its irresistible groove when it reaches its middle section. Based around an exotic keyboard figure recalling something out of the *Space: 1999* television series, Lifeson solos over the catchiest 7/8-time hook in existence. If any other band tried this, it would sound fussy and robotic, but Rush did it, so it sounds utterly natural.

"Red Barchetta" has a similarly approachable sound that stops short of crossing the line into pop. It makes you feel the authentic joy of tearing down the road in a fast car, even if you mainly associate driving with bumper-to-bumper rush-hour traffic among idiots who don't know how to merge.

"Limelight," Peart's meditation on fame, contains the lyric, "I can't pretend a stranger is a long-awaited friend," perfectly demonstrating his ambivalence toward being a public figure. The song's underlying structure is relatively complex, as the meter and time signature keep changing and shifting. Despite its unusual structure, it also hits undeniable pop notes that helped it get on the radio. And how about that opening riff?

"I remember I bought a new stereo, and the first thing I put on was 'Limelight,'" said former Rush monitor engineer Brent Carpenter. "That guitar intro is one of my favorite guitar intros of any record on the planet."

"Witch Hunt (Part III of Fear)," a song about mob justice, is one of the best things on the record and one of the best things the group ever recorded. Everyone turns in an excellent performance—Peart's lyrics are eerily timeless, and the groove is irresistible. Slow and deliberate but not plodding, it's based around a simple but devastating repeating riff. The song also

Geddy Lee gives a master class in how to play the bass correctly to a lucky audience in 1981.

TWO: A QUANTUM LEAP FORWARD / 49

Alex Lifeson gets with the new wave skinny-tie program at Madison Square Garden in 1981.

Geddy Lee, a mere human conduit for the enthralling sound of the Rickenbacker bass, no matter how many necks it has.

Neil Peart, Alex Lifeson, and Geddy Lee on the Moving Pictures tour at New York City's Madison Square Garden on May 18, 1981.

features another keyboard contribution from Hugh Syme, who played his parts on an Oberheim PPG and kept layering it until it became suitably epic.

He said his presence on the record was a by-product of the analog era. In those preinternet days, he had to deliver album art to the band in person at the studio, and since he was physically present, he could tickle the ivories for the band at a moment's notice.

"I would fly up to Montreal and hang out at Le Studio in Morin-Heights for anywhere from four to six days, just because we were having a good time," he said. "It wasn't like I was imposing by sitting beside Terry [Brown] in the control room."

The album concludes with "Vital Signs," another track that shows the influence of New Wave on the band. Some fans may have scratched their heads at some of the new sounds, but Syme said it was all just part of the band's commitment to ongoing evolution.

"Very early on, Neil coined the phrase, 'Got to deviate from the norm,'" he said. "They always aspired to deviate, grow, and keep their fans guessing. They always wanted to be sure what they delivered each time was interesting and unique."

After its release, *Moving Pictures* saw the band get more radio airplay. Lee told *Circus* magazine in 1981 that this may have been because the band had written the songs for *Moving Pictures* in a lower key than in the past, making his singing voice lower. Radio programmers who hadn't wanted to put a high-pitched Geddy vocal on the radio were more willing to play the group now that the bassist's voice had been dialed back.

"We had a very raw sound, and a lot of people didn't want to put that sound on the radio," Lee said of the group's earlier music. "Also, I had a very weird voice that people didn't think was suitable."

Sadly, not everyone was sold on the new Rush album, or any Rush album, for that matter. John Kordosh of *CREEM* magazine referred to the band's music as a "miasma of moronism" and observed upon meeting him that Peart had no sense of humor. Meanwhile, Lee refused even to be interviewed by him, and the journalist ended the article with a whole paragraph about how much he had enjoyed not talking to Lee. No sour grapes there!

Kordosh's missive notwithstanding, *Moving Pictures* was embraced by fans and brought the group quite a few new ones, too. Decades after its release, it's still gaining the band new listeners, and it will likely continue to do so a hundred years from now. So suck it, haters.

17

"THREE PEOPLE PLAYING LIKE TEN PEOPLE"

Rush close out 1981 with a stellar live set

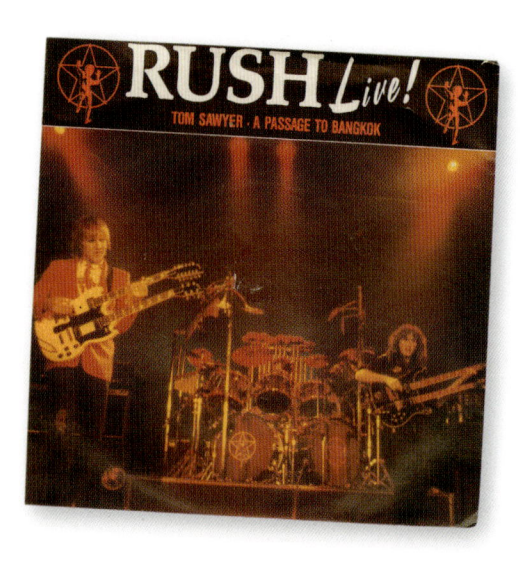

Rush have a lot of live albums, and a case can be made for more than a few of them that they're the band's best. While there will never be a definitive answer to the question, "Which one?" a persuasive case can be made for 1981's *Exit . . . Stage Left*.

Recorded in June 1980 in Glasgow and March 1981 in Montreal, it underwent some surgery in post-production. In 1993, Lee told the United Kingdom's *Guitar Magazine* that the band "had a lot of trouble with out-of-tune guitars," necessitating numerous overdubs. He also noted that the decision to dampen the audience microphones made the recording "too sterile and not very live."

Listening to the finished product, you can see his point. However, the measures taken in the studio to bring the songs up to code do nothing to diminish the power of the performances. In fact, a few of them may well be the definitive recordings of the songs.

That goes for the version of "The Spirit of Radio" that opens the record. There's nothing wrong with the studio version, but this one jumps out of the speakers a little more. Lee turns in a fantastic vocal, and Lifeson's wah pedal solo is a stunner.

The band does a note-perfect reading of "Jacob's Ladder," followed by the acoustic guitar interlude, "Broon's Bane." It would not sound out of place at a Renaissance fair, and after about a minute and a half, it segues into a version of "The Trees" that's a little heavier and more aggressive than its studio counterpart.

It's followed by a version of "Xanadu" that's arguably the definitive one. There are no significant deviations from the studio version, but it's just a little "extra." The band are clearly not satisfied just churning out the songs, so all three musicians throw in a few little bonus bits to add variety to the proceedings. The original is still a masterpiece, but this is a more-than-worthy companion, at the very least.

The record concludes with "La Villa Strangiato." The acoustic guitar introduction is almost as furious as Van Halen's "Eruption," albeit on nylon strings. Lifeson also goes utterly mad in the middle section, again leading us to wonder why he's not on the cover of every guitar magazine ever published.

Most of the songs were recorded in Montreal with Le Mobile studio by what the liner notes referred to as "Tech-man" Guy Charbonneau. He recalled being bowled over by the band's ability to sound like more than just a power trio.

"It was interesting to see three people playing like ten people," he said.

Rush would go back to the live-recording well numerous times in the future, especially late in their career. But *Exit . . . Stage Left* may well be their live desert island disc. *All the World's a Stage* may be more raw, and the 1978 Hammersmith concert included in the fortieth-anniversary edition of *A Farewell to Kings* may have a more authentic "you are there in the audience" vibe, but *Exit . . . Stage Left* is overflowing with excellent readings of the band's finest songs. If you only have seventy-seven minutes to acquaint yourself with their work up to that point, the record is the ideal crash course in Rush circa 1981.

Geddy Lee and Alex Lifeson literally exiting stage left at London's Wembley Arena on November 4, 1981, on the *Exit . . . Stage Left* tour.

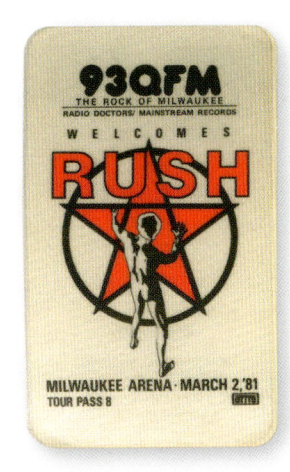

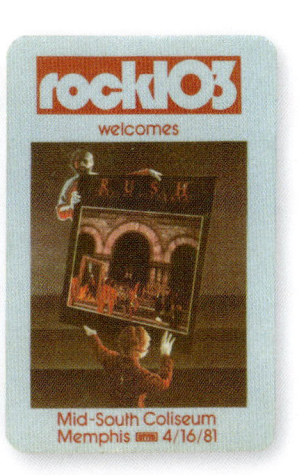

"WITH ACKNOWLEDGMENT TO THE GENIUS OF AYN RAND"

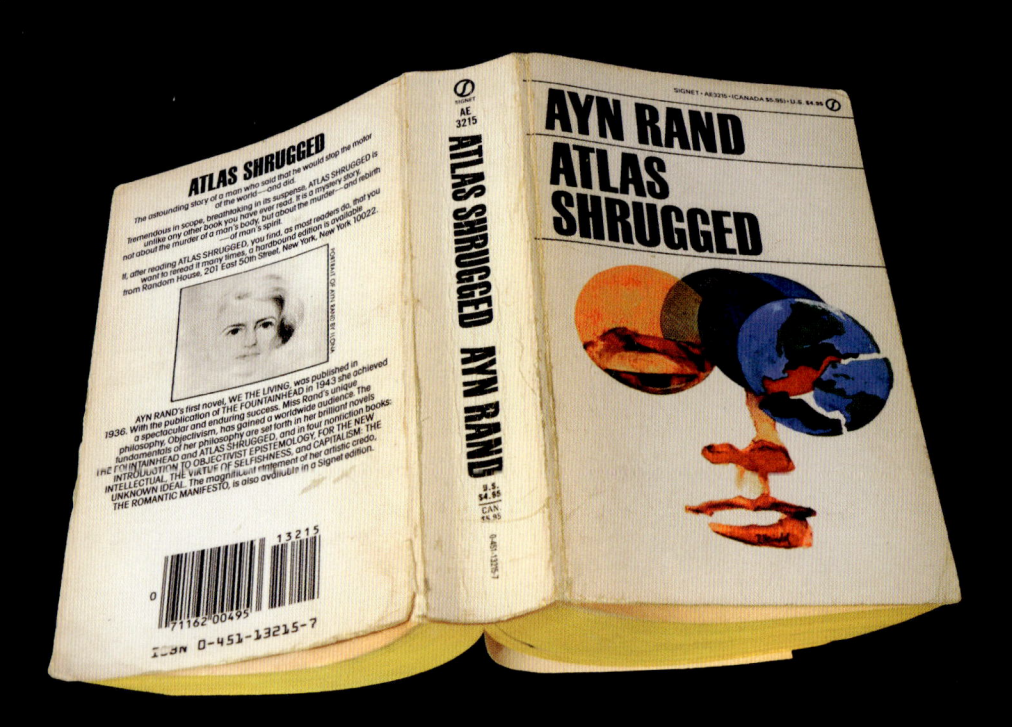

In 2010, ophthalmologist Rand Paul ran for a U.S. Senate seat and played Rush music at his campaign rallies. The Kentucky Republican incorporated their lyrics into his stump speeches, particularly the line "glittering prizes and endless compromises shatter the illusion of integrity" from "The Spirit of Radio."

On May 25 of that year, his campaign received a cease-and-desist letter from Robert Farmer, director of legal affairs for Anthem Entertainment Group. It advised him to stop using the band's music, saying it infringed upon their copyrights and trademarks.

Paul can be forgiven for thinking he had a common cause with the band, particularly its lyricist. Peart had discovered the works of author Ayn Rand as a youth, and they had resonated with him. "Anthem," the first song on 1975's *Fly by Night*, was based on the Ayn Rand book of the same name, and it put a libertarian philosophy front and center (e.g., "Live for yourself, there's no one else").

The group took it further on *2112*. In the epic title track, the collective is revered, and the individual is *persona non grata*, a recurring theme in the works of both Ayn Rand and Rush. The band put "With acknowledgment to the genius of Ayn Rand" in the album's liner notes, and a stubborn and persistent misconception was born.

"We were labeled Nazi fascists, which was interesting to Geddy seeing as his mother spent five years in Auschwitz during the war," Lifeson told *Sounds* magazine in 1989.

"TODAY, THE CONFLICT HAS REACHED ITS ULTIMATE CLIMAX. THE CHOICE IS CLEAR-CUT. EITHER A NEW MORALITY OF RATIONAL SELF-INTEREST, WITH ITS CONSEQUENCES OF FREEDOM, JUSTICE, PROGRESS AND MAN'S HAPPINESS ON EARTH— OR THE PRIMORDIAL MORALITY OF ALTRUISM, WITH ITS CONSEQUENCES OF SLAVERY, BRUTE FORCE, STAGNANT TERROR AND SACRIFICIAL FURNACES."

— AYN RAND

Author and chain-smoking enthusiast Ayn Rand, whose early influence on Neil Peart's lyrics got him in a bit of a pickle with journalists.

So how did this happen? In 1978, journalist Barry Miles from the *New Music Express* interviewed the group at their Hammersmith concert. He asked Peart about Ayn Rand, leading to an animated exchange in which drummer and journalist had a political discussion best suited to Reddit, forty years before Reddit.

Based on this exchange, Miles insinuated that Peart—and, by extension, the band—advocated a "Work Makes Free" philosophy suited to "the Thousand Year Reich." He also described Rush's lyrics as dangerous propaganda.

"These guys are advocating this stuff on stage and on record, and no one even questions it," Miles wrote. "Rush would like to return to the survival-of-the-fittest jungle law, where the fittest is of course the one with the most money. Make sure that next time you see them, you see them with your eyes open, and know what you see. I, for one, don't like it."

Journalists have been taking this misrepresentation and running with it ever since. As recently as 2021, an article appeared in *Literary Hub* titled "How an Iconic Canadian Rock Band Lured Angry Teens to the Dark Arts of Ayn Rand." The writer, Jonny Diamond, signs off with, "So, in closing, f*ck you, Rush."

Sadly, Diamond wasted all that perfectly good bile for nothing. The guy who wrote the lyrics in question had abandoned Rand's philosophy decades earlier and was no longer, in his own words, a "Randroid." Peart told *Rolling Stone* in 2012 that was all forty years behind him when he "was a kid" in his early twenties. However, he still credited her writing with helping him stick to his artistic vision, no matter what.

"[Her writing] was an affirmation that it's all right to totally believe in something and live for it and not compromise," he said.

In 2017, Peart revisited the conflict for *Classic Rock*. He recalled it not as an argument but as a good-natured intellectual debate. He and the band were shocked to see it depicted differently in *New Music Express* when the feature was published.

"As far as I was concerned, we were just having an intellectual conversation," he said. "But these things are wide open to misinterpretation, and that was a classic case."

Donna Halper, former music director for WMMS radio in Cleveland, said that even when Rand was being acknowledged in the band's liner notes, Peart was never dogmatic about her philosophy. She also said as the years passed, his views evolved. He found that, contrary to Objectivist doctrine, the playing field wasn't level, and if someone had fallen on hard times, it wasn't always a simple case of "They should have worked harder."

"I don't want to put words in Neil's mouth, but basically, he was like, 'I reached a point where it became obvious to me that Ayn Rand's philosophy no longer fit where I was,'" she said.

If the band consistently adhered to any part of the Objectivist philosophy, it was through their aversion to conformity and their embrace of individualism. Furthermore, Halper said that each band member respected other people's lifestyles and choices, so if they were fascists, they were pretty bad at it.

"They didn't feel like that was their decision," she said. "They felt like you need to decide for yourself."

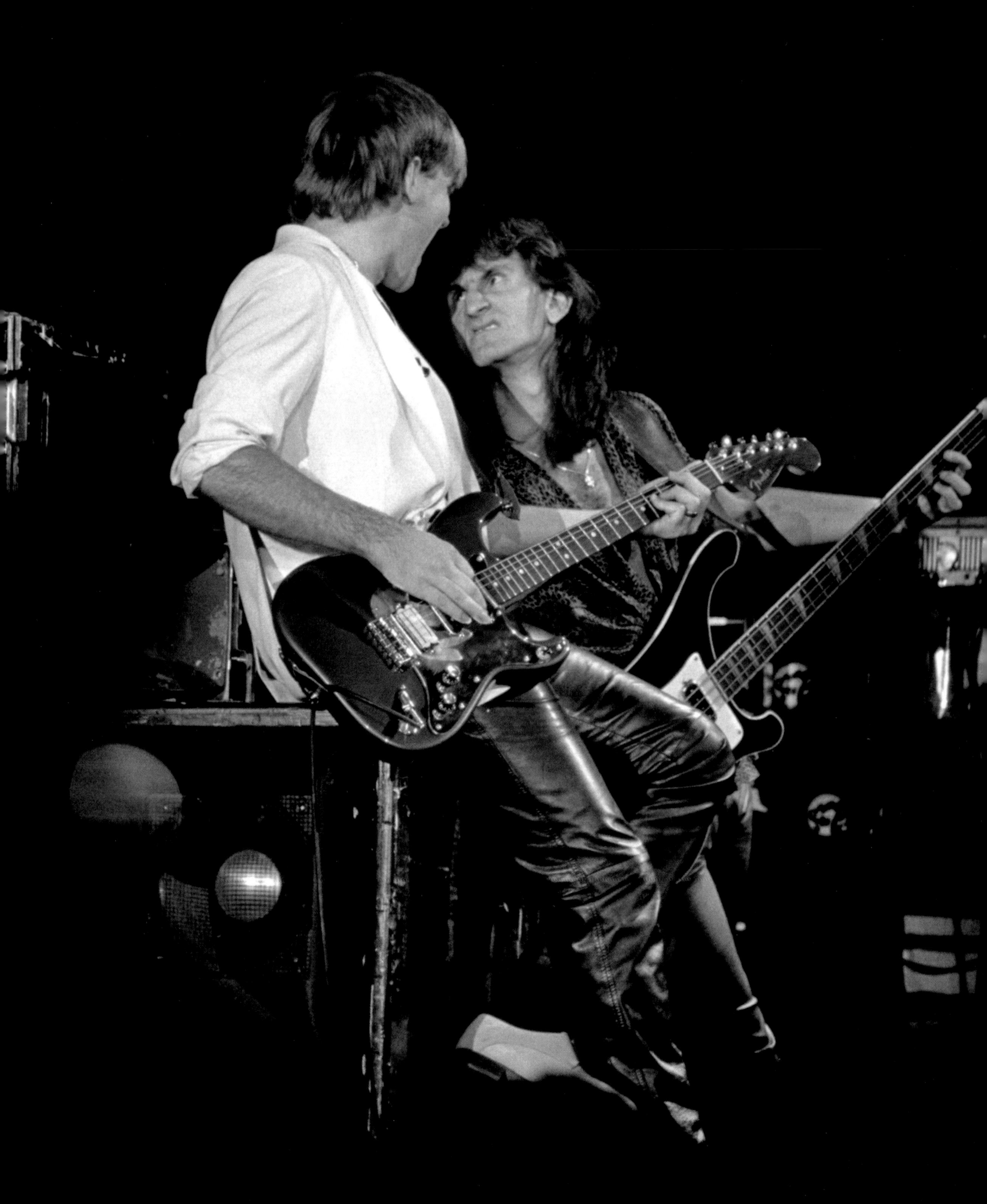

THREE
IN CONSTANT MOTION

Geddy Lee appears disgruntled as Alex Lifeson disrespects a piece of equipment at London's Wembley Arena in May 1983.

18
IS THAT A FIRE HYDRANT?
Rush get the seven-year itch

For some fans, Rush's 1982 album *Signals* was a misstep. They felt the band were changing their sound too much and the synthesizers were intrusive. Those fans could handle the keyboards if they provided the occasional flourish or some padding in the background, but those infernal synths were moving to the forefront now. For some fans, it was too much.

In reality, *Signals* is a masterpiece. Every track is uniformly strong, and there's no filler. There isn't a bum note or throwaway song on it anywhere, even in the case of "New World Man," which was written specifically to fill up four minutes on side 2 for mastering purposes.

"Subdivisions" showed that Rush had moved beyond fantasy as a lyrical topic. The lyrics are about the oppressive conformity of the suburbs, and Peart told *Rolling Stone* in 2015 that it was his first attempt to write about something approximating everyday life.

"I realized what I most wanted to put in a song was human experience," he said.

While you could argue that he had done so already on *Hemispheres* with "Circumstances," there's no denying that "Subdivisions" hit close to home with listeners. The music has an icy chill that matches the subject perfectly. While the grousers are correct that Lifeson's guitar is more rhythm than lead here, he turns in a lyrical solo that pushes hummable melodies to the fore.

The same goes for "The Analog Kid," which opens with fiery licks and has a solo that jumps right out at you. Honestly, there's tons of excellent guitar playing on this record. Too much has been made of *Signals* being the album where Rush turned into The Human League.

"Chemistry" is one of the band's best deep cuts, and it's baffling that it isn't among their more popular songs. The only Rush song to feature lyrics by all three members, it's heavy on the keyboards, but again, you can't say Lifeson was sidelined, since he does some excellent lead work in the first minute of the song.

Then there's that flawless prechorus section. If you don't love it, something is wrong with you: "Eye to I, reaction burning hotter/Two to one, reflection on the water."

The keyboards during this section are exquisite—there's no other word for it. All the instruments are also perfectly balanced, including Lifeson's rhythm guitar and Peart's more restrained drumming.

"Digital Man" shows the band getting their Police on, Peart especially. Lifeson uses striking open chords, and Lee goes into total berserker mode on the bass, flying all over the neck. The faux reggae might have caused some side-eye among change-averse fans, but the playing is so good that hating on it is impossible.

If playing double-neck guitars and basses is wrong, Alex Lifeson and Geddy Lee don't want to be right.

THREE: IN CONSTANT MOTION / 53

Alex Lifeson, one of a handful of people in all of recorded history to actually deserve a double-neck Gibson SG.

60 / RUSH AT 50

The song also features another engaging lead from Lifeson, even though the album allegedly has no guitar on it.

Rush never wrote a lot of ballads, but of those they did, "Losing It" may be the best. The subject matter—losing the ability to do something you used to be good at—is heartbreaking, and the lyrics lay it out in an unforgiving manner. Very few songs remind you as starkly of your mortality as this one.

Ben Mink's violin solo is extraordinary, and Peart's complex playing beneath it is somehow as driving as it is perplexing. He navigates its treacherous 11/8 time signature like it's nothing.

The album ends with "Countdown," a song that neither the band nor the fans have had very kind things to say about. One wonders why, since it's a solid tune that sounds consistent with the rest of the record. There was some pushback from fans about the cover art as well.

"Originally, we were going to bring medical technicians into the studio and take the brainwave readings of Geddy, Alex, and Neil at a certain measure of the music," album cover artist Hugh Syme said. He added that the title *Signals* also made the band consider "signal"-centric visual allusions to Marconi, Morse code, and the RKO Pictures radio tower. Still, none of those ideas hit the mark. Then, one lucky day, Syme saw a dalmatian on the sidewalk by a fire hydrant, and a figurative light bulb went off above his head.

"It struck me that dogs sniff hydrants and leave their own signals," he said. He proposed the idea, but the trio didn't embrace it initially. After a while, they came around.

Generally, it's hard to understand what anyone's beef with *Signals* was. Is it possible that it was an overreaction to the changing balance between the guitar and keyboards at the time, and its status as one of the band's lesser efforts is just inherited wisdom?

Whatever the case, some fans moved on after this record came out, saying it was where the band "lost" them. It's a shame, since *Signals* is among their most essential releases and the band had plenty to offer afterward. Hopefully, someday, the people who have given it short shrift over the years will warm up to it and give it the accolades it deserves.

Alex Lifeson and Geddy Lee during the *Signals* tour in November 1982 at Joe Louis Arena in Detroit, whose dress code apparently required a red tie for entry.

Alex Lifeson and Neil Peart under the mood lighting at Detroit's Joe Louis Arena in November 1982 during the *Signals* tour.

19

IT'S NOT YOU, IT'S ME
Rush break up with their fourth man

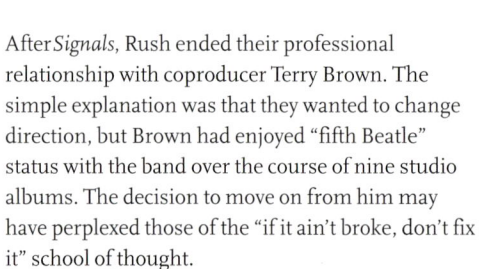

After *Signals*, Rush ended their professional relationship with coproducer Terry Brown. The simple explanation was that they wanted to change direction, but Brown had enjoyed "fifth Beatle" status with the band over the course of nine studio albums. The decision to move on from him may have perplexed those of the "if it ain't broke, don't fix it" school of thought.

Brown didn't characterize the split as an angry one. He wasn't happy about it but wasn't bitter either. He told *Canadian Music Scene* in 2011 that the group's sound was moving away from hard guitar rock and "becoming very heavily keyboard-oriented," and he wasn't feeling it.

He also told *Prog* magazine that he hadn't bargained on the trio incorporating certain influences into their music. However, ultimately, he didn't believe it compromised the overall quality of *Signals*.

"I was a little taken aback by the reggae [and] ska influence, but juxtaposed to 'Subdivisions,' 'Countdown,' and 'The Weapon,' I felt we had a really strong record," he said.

All parties involved have said that it was Lee, Lifeson, and Peart who relieved Brown of his production duties, so despite Brown's misgivings about the band's new direction, it wasn't necessarily a mutual split. The trio never aired their dirty laundry publicly, so there were no angry recriminations or accusations of wrongdoing. All Lee would say about it to the *Los Angeles Times* in 1986 was that the decision was only about one thing.

"We wanted to change our music," Lee said. "We were just bored with our sound."

The band had taken a considerable risk. Rush and their longtime coproducer had made a long run of successful, popular albums together, and now the trio were changing the recipe with no guarantee of success. Album cover artist Hugh Syme said that when news of the split reached the fan community, quite a few were displeased and said so.

"That's part of the nature of fans as well informed as Rush fans," he said. "They know Howard Ungerleider does the lighting. They know the family, so to speak. So there was a bit of an uproar when they looked beyond Terry for production."

Despite the professional association coming to an end, Brown told *Sonic Perspectives* in 2022 that his personal relationship with the band had always remained amicable. He even found himself back at the console when it came time to mix the two hours of bonus live material included in the fortieth-anniversary reissue of *Moving Pictures*, an effort that received the full approval of Lee and Lifeson.

Looking back, Brown said there had been far more good times than bad when they worked together. Their unusually long association spoke for itself.

"It's a rare thing for a producer to be able to make nine albums with any given band," he said. "I think we grew together. The boys were always pushing themselves to exceed their previous release, and I had to keep up."

The band agreed. Lifeson told *Prog* magazine in 2023 that the trio always held Brown in high regard, professionally and emotionally.

"He understood our music, he was a great producer, a great engineer," the guitarist said. "He was a brother."

To any fan of Rush's output from the 1970s and early 1980s, none of this is news, and even fans of their later material will freely acknowledge that Brown was the right man for the job. But Brown's simple statement to *Canadian Music Scene* in 2011 perhaps sums it up best: "We had a really good run together."

Alex Lifeson, Neil Peart, coproducer Terry Brown, and Geddy Lee in 1978. Brown collaborated with the band on nine consecutive albums, all of them bangers.

20
IN A BIG COUNTRY
"Mr. So-and-so" hates odd time signatures

If parting ways with longtime coproducer Terry Brown was hard for the members of Rush, finding somebody to step into his shoes was harder. In the program for the *Grace Under Pressure* tour, Peart referred to the effort as "The Great Producer Hunt," which meant looking over the liner notes of albums they liked and saying, "How about this person?"

The trio approached it like a fantasy football draft and eventually came up with a few names. Peart said that finally, one contender broke away from the pack and agreed to take the job, but the drummer would only refer to him as "Mr. So-and-so."

Two weeks before they were supposed to start working on the album, the producer in question bailed to work with Simple Minds. In a 2016 interview with *Classic Rock*, Lifeson revealed that "Mr. So-and-so" was Steve Lillywhite. Lee said he had been impressed with the producer's work and thought he was the right man to point them in a new direction.

"I remember the Big Country record he'd just done, *The Crossing*," Lee said. "I loved the way the guitars sounded on that record—they had an attitude. We were thinking of doing a more guitar-driven record at that time, and we thought that Steve would give us a fresh approach."

In addition to working with Big Country, Lillywhite had also worked with XTC, Siouxsie and the Banshees, and U2. None of them had ever written a twenty-minute suite about futuristic totalitarian dystopias, and the major stylistic left turn was exactly what Rush were looking for.

Unfortunately, Lillywhite changed his mind at the eleventh hour, putting the band in a tough position. He told *Sounds* magazine in 1984 that his reason for backing out was the group's songwriting, specifically their use of odd time signatures.

"Someone should explain to Geddy Lee that you must be a good songwriter to get an 'odd-time-signatures' tune across pop radio," he said. He cited The Beatles' "All You Need Is Love" and Pink Floyd's "Money" as songs that had gotten airplay despite their odd-time handicap. Almost thirty years later, on the July 5, 2013, episode of the *Mohr Talk* podcast, the producer reflected on the dustup.

"Rush hate me," he said. "I said I'd produce them, and then I didn't."

He said their manager Ray Danniels "almost" threatened to break his legs for backing out. Still, Lillywhite said somewhat unartfully that since he didn't care for the music, backing out was in everybody's best interest.

"You don't want to shag someone if they don't want to shag you," he said. Eventually, the job went to Peter Henderson, who had coproduced *Breakfast in America* with Supertramp.

It had been relatively excruciating, but the band felt that a new perspective in the studio was worth the agony. Despite the pain and suffering that "The Great Producer Hunt" had caused, a small dedication in their next album's liner notes showed their affection for their longtime coproducer had never waned.

"*Et toujours notre bon vielle ami*—Broon," the dedication read.

Left: Alex Lifeson and Geddy Lee at Joe Louis Arena in Detroit. The smart money says this was the 1980s, as do the red leather pants.

THREE: IN CONSTANT MOTION / 67

21

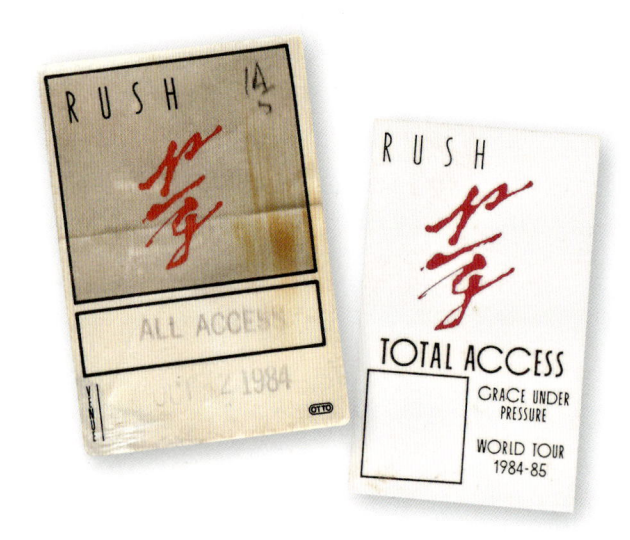

"A LUMBERING METAL ANACHRONISM"
Rush make a dark and stormy record

Grace Under Pressure (1984) was a stress test for Rush. It found them working without their longtime coproducer, Terry Brown, and they had done all the preproduction themselves. That's not a small task, and it can sometimes prove too much for the foolhardy musician who has never tried their hand at it and asks, "How hard can it be?"

Peart said in the *Grace Under Pressure* tour book that, to the contrary, the experience of being thrown in at the deep end had united the three of them. Like in any good marriage, the adversity had made them pull together rather than give up.

"We were suddenly totally on our own, responsible to make the decisions and set the wheels in motion," he wrote. "This really drew us together and gave us a strong resolve and a mutual determination to make a really great record."

They succeeded on that score. *Grace Under Pressure* turned out to be a really great record. Furthermore, it brought newer and younger fans to the table. Brent Carpenter, Rush's monitor engineer from 2002 to 2015, said that while some hard-core fans had complained about the keyboards and shorter songs, those elements drew him in. Older brothers might have jumped ship when *Signals* came out, but younger brothers were all over it.

"I loved the 1980s records," he said. "I thought *Grace Under Pressure* was amazing."

Grace Under Pressure expanded upon the band's love of reggae and saw them experiment further with New Wave. It starts with "Distant Early Warning," whose rhythm owes a debt to the recently disbanded Police and communicates anxiety very clearly. Lifeson goes for the jugular on his solo, choosing melodic lines instead of going into pentatonic scale autopilot.

The anxiety is also prominent on "Afterimage," a song about Le Studio tape operator Paul Whelan, who died in a car accident before the album sessions. "The Enemy Within (Part I of Fear)" closes out the first side, and it's among their most underrated songs, bolstered by brilliant drumming from Peart. "The Body Electric" also features an excellent drum performance and the catchiest chorus ever written in binary code.

The record ends brilliantly with "Between the Wheels," a morose conclusion to a hopeless album. The guitar solo is excellent, and it's worth noting that Lifeson truly distinguished himself during this era of the band. He rose to the occasion and capably met the challenge of recontextualizing his playing.

"Alex's guitar sound had moved from being pretty heavy to being almost another keyboard to some degree," said Robert Scovill, Rush's live sound engineer from 1989 to 1997. "It was much cleaner sounds, all this sparkling delay, and he really embraced it."

He rightly declared Lifeson the most underrated guitarist in the history of rock music. He said external trends during the 1980s should shoulder much of the blame for that.

"He got lost in the shuffle a little bit during the Eddie Van Halen era," he said. "If you weren't that type of guitarist, you wouldn't even get considered in any of those stupid guitar polls. He really has gone unnoticed, and it's criminal."

While much is made of him getting short shrift on the band's 1980s records, he told *Classic Rock* in 2016 that he was delighted with *Grace Under Pressure*.

"There's something about the sound and the power and the quality of the songwriting that really strikes me," he said. "I really love that record."

By this point, the critics were starting to understand that their services were surplus to requirements when it came to reviewing Rush albums. Kurt Loder said as much in his review in *Rolling Stone*.

"This album needs no critical assistance," he wrote. "If you like Rush, you'll love it; if not, then *Grace Under Pressure* is unlikely to alter your assessment of the band as a lumbering metal anachronism."

Fans didn't get a stand-alone souvenir of the *Grace Under Pressure* tour for twenty-five years. The three-night stint at Toronto's Maple Leaf Gardens in September 1984 was filmed and released on VHS (and Betamax!) in 1986. It was reissued on DVD in 2006 as part of the *Rush Replay 3X* box set, alongside the DVD versions of *Exit . . . Stage Left* and *A Show of Hands*. The audio from 1984 was included on CD as part of that package, but in 2009, it received a stand-alone release with the creative title of *Grace Under Pressure: 1984 Tour*.

The name may leave something to be desired, but don't let that fool you. Lee is in magnificent voice, and the band perform with relish. You never get the sense that they're on day one million of some intercontinental slog and just cycling through the hits. They seem very aware that these people paid for a ticket, and it should be worth their while.

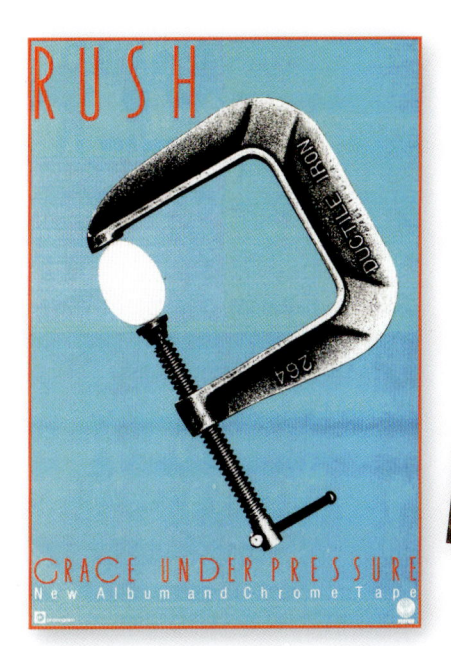

It's the 1980s, and accordingly, Alex Lifeson and Geddy Lee are dressed like drug dealers on *Miami Vice*.

Geddy Lee, most likely somewhere in North America on the 1983–1984 *Grace Under Pressure* tour

Longtime friends Alex Lifeson and Geddy Lee during the *Grace Under Pressure* tour. Rush had been recording and touring for almost a decade, and this friendship was part of what kept them grounded through the ups and downs.

70 / RUSH AT 50

Alex Lifeson bends that note all the way up there on the *Grace Under Pressure* tour, or the *P/G* tour as it has come to be known by some.

THREE: IN CONSTANT MOTION / 71

22

YES + THE SEX PISTOLS = *POWER WINDOWS*

We really hope you like keyboards

Power Windows marked more changes for Rush. For the first time, they hired an outside musician, Andy Richards, to augment their sound. The British keyboard player and composer had worked with Frankie Goes to Hollywood, George Michael, and Pet Shop Boys, names that would make most 1980s hard rockers recoil in horror.

They enlisted a new coproducer, Peter Collins. Unlike the trio's experience during "The Great Producer Hunt," securing Collins's services was a breeze. He was their first choice, and he said yes. Furthermore, if it was a big, glistening 1980s production that Rush wanted from him, they got it. From the moment the leadoff track "The Big Money" starts, it's clear the band believed in this direction and had resolved to go there as hard as possible.

Structurally, the song has some of the same DNA as "The Real Me" by The Who, demonstrating again that Keith Moon and company had a more considerable influence on this band than many people realize. Lee and his arsenal of gadgets dominate the proceedings, and though they don't hopelessly overwhelm the songs, they're hard to ignore.

"Manhattan Project" is one of the best songs on the album. It feels natural and is the best and most fully realized example of the sound they were going for. It's compositionally solid, and the string section in the middle gives it an epic feeling that feels earned and deserved.

Carried by a ska-inspired bassline, rousing lyrics, and propulsive drumming, "Marathon" almost achieves the same high quality as "Manhattan Project." However, Lifeson is definitely not given enough to do here. When you can hear it clearly, his playing is uniformly excellent, with the guitar solo on "Marathon" standing out as truly exceptional. Still, the decision to submerge everything under a wash of keyboards obscures not only his playing but some of the album's other strengths as well. Plenty is going on in the arrangement without the liberal sprinkling of Howard Jones–style keyboard stabs, thank you very much.

72 / RUSH AT 50

"Middletown Dreams" expresses a yearning that anyone of any age can relate to if they want something more than their lives offer them. It's almost a companion song to "Subdivisions" in that sense and features a very emotional vocal from Lee. The same goes for "Emotion Detector," which projects the same thoughtful melancholy that dominates much of the record.

"Mystic Rhythms" closes out the album on a solid note, emerging from under the shadow of the overproduction because it's just so damn good. The brooding atmosphere comes through, even with all the abrupt Debbie Gibson noises intruding on the proceedings.

Generally, *Power Windows* survives its overproduction because the writing is top-notch, and you can feel a unity of purpose coming from the band. You don't get the sense that it was Lee alone dragging the other guys into it unwillingly, like Dennis DeYoung dragging Styx through *Kilroy Was Here*, a crime for which they have never forgiven him and never will.

To their credit, the critics were starting to understand that this band was not only not going away but evolving and going from strength to strength. Look no further than David Fricke's review of the album for *Rolling Stone*.

"*Power Windows* may well be the missing link between Yes and the Sex Pistols," he wrote.

Rush in 1985, apparently using the same stylist that coordinated looks for the members of Orchestral Manoeuvres in the Dark.

23
WHAT'S THAT SMELL?
Rush eat themselves

Hold Your Fire is one of the weakest albums in the entire Rush catalog, if not the weakest. It's not a full-on stinker, as it features typically excellent performances and Peart turns in some truly inspired lyrics, but its fifty minutes seem to pass very slowly, and you often wonder what they intended for this album because surely, this can't be it.

Anyone who hoped that Rush had reached peak gadget saturation on *Power Windows* would have been immediately disappointed by "Force Ten," which starts with samples and electronic sound effects, so if you were hoping for a "back to basics" approach, too bad. The guitar is a little brighter and more prominent, but otherwise, the arrangements and production are where they left off in 1985.

Honestly, it's hard to understand what they were going for here. Rush had already proven many albums prior that they were beyond doing weird things in crazy time signatures, so anyone keeping up with them at this point in their career wouldn't have expected "Cygnus X-1 Book III." It's just that *Hold Your Fire* is so . . . average. And *average* is not a word generally associated with this band.

The trio fare no better on the unremarkable "Second Nature," which is briefly redeemed by the instrumental middle section but otherwise feels half-formed. The same goes for "Prime Mover." Really, almost anybody could have written this music, and it's baffling that a band that have taken so many artistic risks and critical tongue lashings would turn in something this bland.

Alex Lifeson on the *Hold Your Fire* tour, which featured performances of half the songs on the 1987 album. But where was "Tai Shan"?

74 / RUSH AT 50

"Mission," "Turn the Page," and "High Water" fare no better, and again, it's not because nothing is in 11/8 time. Many other Rush songs are straightforward and don't take huge stylistic leaps, but these sound—God help us—like the trio are playing it safe and trying not to offend the eardrums of any defenseless babies who might be nearby.

"Lock and Key" is a slight improvement, since it has a more engaging melody and Peart cuts loose a bit at the end, but overall, the boys sound like they've been neutered. Worse yet, they did it to themselves, so you can't even blame the coproducer or the record label.

Fortunately, it's not all bad news. "Open Secrets" rewards repeat listens, especially if you're listening on headphones, so you can hear what the drums are doing. Even though band and fan alike have said loudly and frequently that "Tai Shan" is a terrible song, it's served well by the simplicity of the arrangement. Instead of laboring over it for weeks in the studio, it feels like they got out of the song's way and let it happen.

The best song on *Hold Your Fire* is the uncharacteristically poppy "Time Stand Still." The lyric is heartfelt and perfectly captures those brief moments of perspective you occasionally get in life if you live long enough, those moments of "I'm lucky to have these people around me" or "I'm lucky to be doing what I'm doing right now."

While *Hold Your Fire* is probably one of the weakest albums Rush ever made, it's important to note that none of it is phoned in. Whatever flaws it has are not a by-product of laziness or complacency. This is the album they set out to make, and they made it, while putting a lot of thought and creativity into it. If you believe it was the product of less effort on the band's part, you are mistaken. So, even if it falls short or isn't a favorite, it's what they intended, and they should make no apologies for it. And they didn't!

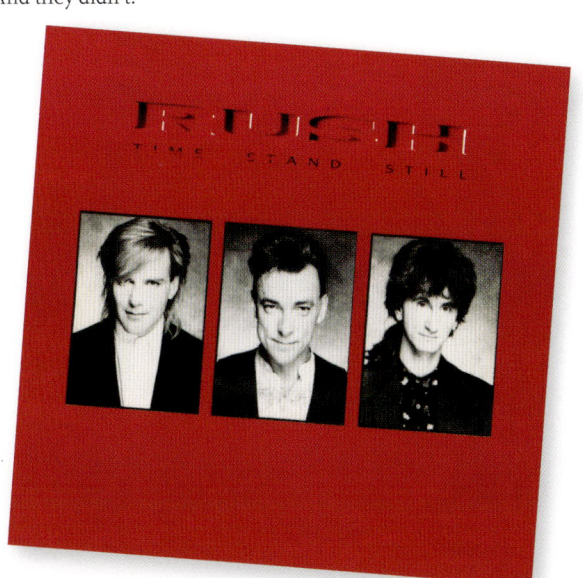

Geddy Lee looking downright billowy at the RPI Fieldhouse in Troy, New York, on November 12, 1987.

A smiling and cooperative Alex Lifeson in 1987, treating photo shoots as the necessary evil that they are for people who would much rather be playing music.

76 / RUSH AT 50

Alex Lifeson wears a nice dinner jacket at the RPI Fieldhouse in Troy, New York, on November 12, 1987.

THREE: IN CONSTANT MOTION / 77

Alex Lifeson and Geddy Lee at Los Angeles' Great Western Forum in February 1988 during the *Hold Your Fire* tour.

24

"THE EMOTIONAL EMPTINESS OF BAD JAZZ FUSION"
I can't believe it's a live album!

By the late 1980s, Rush had established a schedule for album releases. There would be four studio albums, then one live album, a blueprint they had followed up to *All the World's a Stage* and repeated with *Exit . . . Stage Left*. The time had come again after 1987's *Hold Your Fire*, and the trio obliged with *A Show of Hands*.

On previous live albums, they had always turned in faithful renditions of the studio songs, but there was always something a little "extra" about them. They would never embark on a forty-five-minute Grateful Dead feedback exploration, but there was always some *oomph* that made the live stuff more exciting. Having said that, it's hard to see why anyone would prefer these versions to the originals. If you don't like the studio versions of these songs, the interpretations on *A Show of Hands* won't change your mind.

One gets the sense that the band are limited by having to trigger samples and deal with all the other technology that was part of their live show. It's hard to imagine Rush came up the hard way in Toronto bars and endured the "Down the Tubes Tour" so they could one day trigger samples of Aimee Mann's voice onstage. It feels like a waste of their talent and something almost anybody could do.

A Show of Hands has its strengths. "Marathon" has a bit more interplay, and between that and Lee's soaring vocal, it amounts to an energetic version. Lifeson's guitar is a little more up-front on "Turn the Page" and "Manhattan Project," which is nice to hear if you feel like the band did him dirty over the past few albums and made his fader too low.

"Witch Hunt (Part III of Fear)" is the best thing on the record. Lifeson and Peart get to change it up a bit, possibly because the song had been in their set for a few years, and they probably felt they could take a few liberties with it. There are no significant departures, but the little differences are fun to hear.

"Mystic Rhythms" also fares well, but if you want to hear the band interpret these songs differently, you're out of luck. It's honestly weird to hear Peart avoid any deviation from the studio stuff. He was never a Bill Bruford type of drummer who radically changed up his performance every night, but it's still a bummer to hear him chained to verbatim replicas of what he did in the studio. That had to be a little not fun. He turns in an excellent solo on "The Rhythm Method," though, and he deserves all the kudos in the world for playing a drum solo that isn't boring, something rarer than the Chupacabra.

Guy Charbonneau, who had recorded the band on 1981's *Exit . . . Stage Left* with his Le Mobile studio, came back to the fold to record and co-engineer this newest live album. He had enjoyed working with the unusually welcoming band before, and little had changed in the intervening years.

"Rush was a family," he said. "You don't see that anymore."

As always, the critics had little use for the album. That included Michael Azerrad, who gave it a two-star review in *Rolling Stone* and said it had "the emotional emptiness of bad jazz fusion."

Sadly, Azerrad was right on the money. *A Show of Hands* is essentially a greatest-hits album of Rush's 1980s material with applause piped in. It's not a total bore, but you won't hear anything revelatory, and only completists will want it.

25
OUT WITH THE OLD
Where's the synthesizer off-ramp?

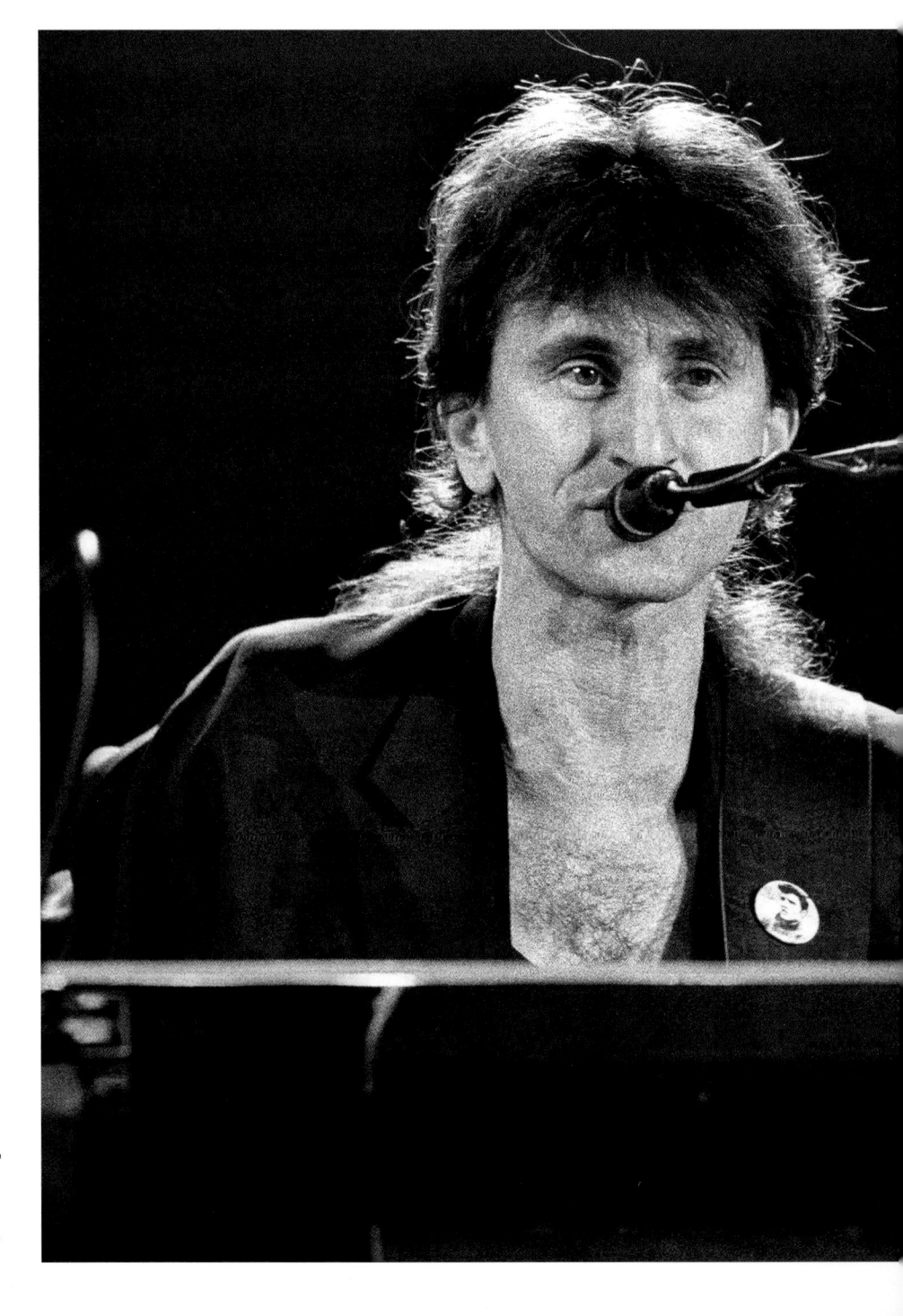

Geddy Lee at Ahoy Sportpaleis in Rotterdam, Holland, on May 2, 1988. Why wasn't the fragrance of Amsterdam mentioned in "A Passage to Bangkok"?

As the 1980s waned, Rush found themselves right where they were a decade earlier. They had taken their current approach as far as they could, which Lee alluded to in the liner notes of their 1990 *Chronicles* compilation.

"*Hold Your Fire* is an arrival record," he said. "We climbed up a hill and now we've gotten to the top and we have to decide where we go from here."

Lee's observation made *Hold Your Fire* sound like a triumph, but all three members said things around then that suggested all was not right within the band. In 1989, Lifeson told *Kerrang!* that live performance—something the band had staked their entire reputation on—was becoming a grind.

"Because of all the pedals, it means that we're stuck in one place all night," he said. "It really became a chore; we missed the fun of it."

Peart echoed Lifeson's sentiment in a 1990 interview with the *Toronto Star*.

"I always came back from a tour feeling that I'd developed a lot of drumming ideas and skills," he said. "Within the last couple of years, that reward has kind of slipped away and we got the sense that we were spending six months just doing the same thing. It was difficult for me because I thought there were ways I could better spend that time."

He ultimately decided that the band should keep touring. If they weren't out there playing live, they were an abstract idea, not a band, and he didn't want that.

"I wanted Rush to be a living and breathing thing, and to me, a band that isn't working live isn't living," he said. "I realized that the only thing worse than going on tour would be not going on tour."

Anyone shocked that there was a desire to throw in the towel on touring underestimates its relentless brutality. The travel alone will take a toll on you, and you don't even have to be a musician to see that.

"I'm not shocked that they got to a point where they were really worn down," former WMMS radio music director Donna Halper said. "I was a consultant. I was on the road three hundred days a year. I loved my work, and I loved going from city to city, but at a certain point, you just can't take another day of running for planes. . . . They were going through a period of feeling creatively stale and worn down."

There was also the issue of keyboards, synthesizers, and other beeping electronic doodads. Lee told *Classic Rock* in 2016 that he felt the band had reached peak keyboard on *Power Windows*, but on *Hold Your Fire*, a line had been crossed. This caused the band to reevaluate their sound, just as they had after *Hemispheres*.

"Overall, I thought *Power Windows* was a great accomplishment for us," he said. "After that . . . the keyboards were still present, but not in so positive a way. That was making the case, once again, for realigning the sound."

WHY DO PEOPLE HATE GEDDY LEE'S VOICE?
A technical analysis

If you listen to Rush, one thing is probably noticeable to you instantly. Specifically, many people out there hate Geddy Lee's singing voice. They hate it. Or, as the late, great Roger Ebert once put it in his review of the 1994 movie *North*, they "hated hated hated hated hated" it.

The critics never held back when expressing their hostility toward Lee's vocals. In Gary Tannyan's *Saskatoon Star-Phoenix* review of the band's 1974 debut, he lambasted the vocalist excessively, cruelly, and personally.

"The band would not be quite as bad if it were not for Lee's incredibly awful singing," he wrote. "He tries to scream and wail his way through every number as if trying to emulate Led Zeppelin's Robert Plant but sounds more like a prepuberty choir boy singing rock and roll after having his tonsils removed."

With every new album, critics would line up to pillory Lee for the crime of singing. That included 1975's *Fly by Night*.

"Lee's voice, a blatant copy of the uncontrolled hysteria of Robert Plant, is unpleasant in the extreme," Pam Simon wrote in the *Statesville (North Carolina) Record & Landmark* in March 1975. Stan Tepner's review of *Caress of Steel* in the *Kingston (Ontario) Whig-Standard* in 1975 was just as venomous.

"Obliterated by Geddy Lee's obnoxious vocals, the album is an earful of torture," he wrote. "His voice is downright disgusting. . . . Pass the Excedrin."

In 1979, Alan Niester said in the *Rolling Stone Record Guide* that Lee "sounds like a cross between Donald Duck and Robert Plant." Reviewing a 1980 Los Angeles concert for *Rolling Stone*, Steve Pond said Lee's "amazingly high-pitched wailing often sounds like [*Saturday Night Live*'s] Mr. Bill singing heavy metal."

The *New York Times* did no better. In its 1994 review of the band's appearance at New York City's Madison Square Garden, writer Jon Pareles said Lee's singing "suggests a munchkin giving a sermon."

Not all the lambasting came from professional critics—many people have been happy to do it for free. An undated article on *Rate Your Music* written by someone using the screen name "finulanu" lists "Twelve Things I'd Rather Hear Than Geddy Lee's Voice." These include "a fifty-six thousand year Keith Emerson polymoog solo [*sic*]" and the voice of the late comedian Gilbert Gottfried.

So, why do some people hate his voice so much? Is there a technical explanation?

Mardie Millit, a multi-award-winning professional singer with a degree in vocal performance and more than forty years of training in classical, pop, jazz, rock, and theater music, watched the 1981 video for "Tom Sawyer" and analyzed Lee's delivery to shed light on this long-standing issue. She said he doesn't shriek indiscriminately, contrary to some people's beliefs. He practices proper vocal technique.

"His vocal production seems quite natural, even when it sounds like he's screaming," Millit explained. "There's no hyperextension of the jaw, no popping neck tendons. But he does have a naturally very, *very* high-pitched voice, and he sings with a forward-placed, nasal sound."

She added that from what she could observe, he handled his vocal cords with care.

"The use of the nasal cavity for resonance is very healthy," she said. "It means he transitions easily from chest to head voice, and this placement is probably one of the reasons he still has use of his voice today. But it doesn't make for a very mellifluous sound without a raised soft palate behind it—that's the 'about to yawn' feeling in the back of the throat that gives color and depth to the voice."

Millit said that if there's anything Lee does consistently to trigger the haters, it's most likely his approach to gliding vowels, known to professional singers, speech therapists, and literacy specialists as "diphthongs."

"When holding a long note, he tends to go right to the diphthong or voiced consonant rather than holding the main vowel, which makes him sound even more nasal," she explained. "So, if the word is 'way,' you get 'wayeeeeeeee' rather than 'waaaaaaaaaaaay,' and not "time" but 'ty-eeeeeeeeeem.' The combined effect of nasal placement and bitten-off vowel sounds makes for a fairly goat-like overall impression."

She added that Lee's tendency to stay at a consistent volume might also alienate some.

"There's no dynamic variation between loud and soft in his singing," she said. "It's pretty monochromatic. A little breath support—manufactured tension in certain muscles in the thorax to squeeze the lungs strategically—would make the sound more energized."

So, how does the man himself feel about it? In 2023, he told *Louder* magazine that he had taken some of the more constructive and less hysterical criticism over the years and worked to expand his vocal range to be "more melodious." But he has no regrets about his original 1974 banshee shriek and said that the band's most hard-core devotees don't either.

"The real fans like it when I go all the way up there," he said.

Geddy Lee practices good vocal hygiene as he mellifluously emotes at Toronto's Maple Leaf Gardens on December 28, 1978.

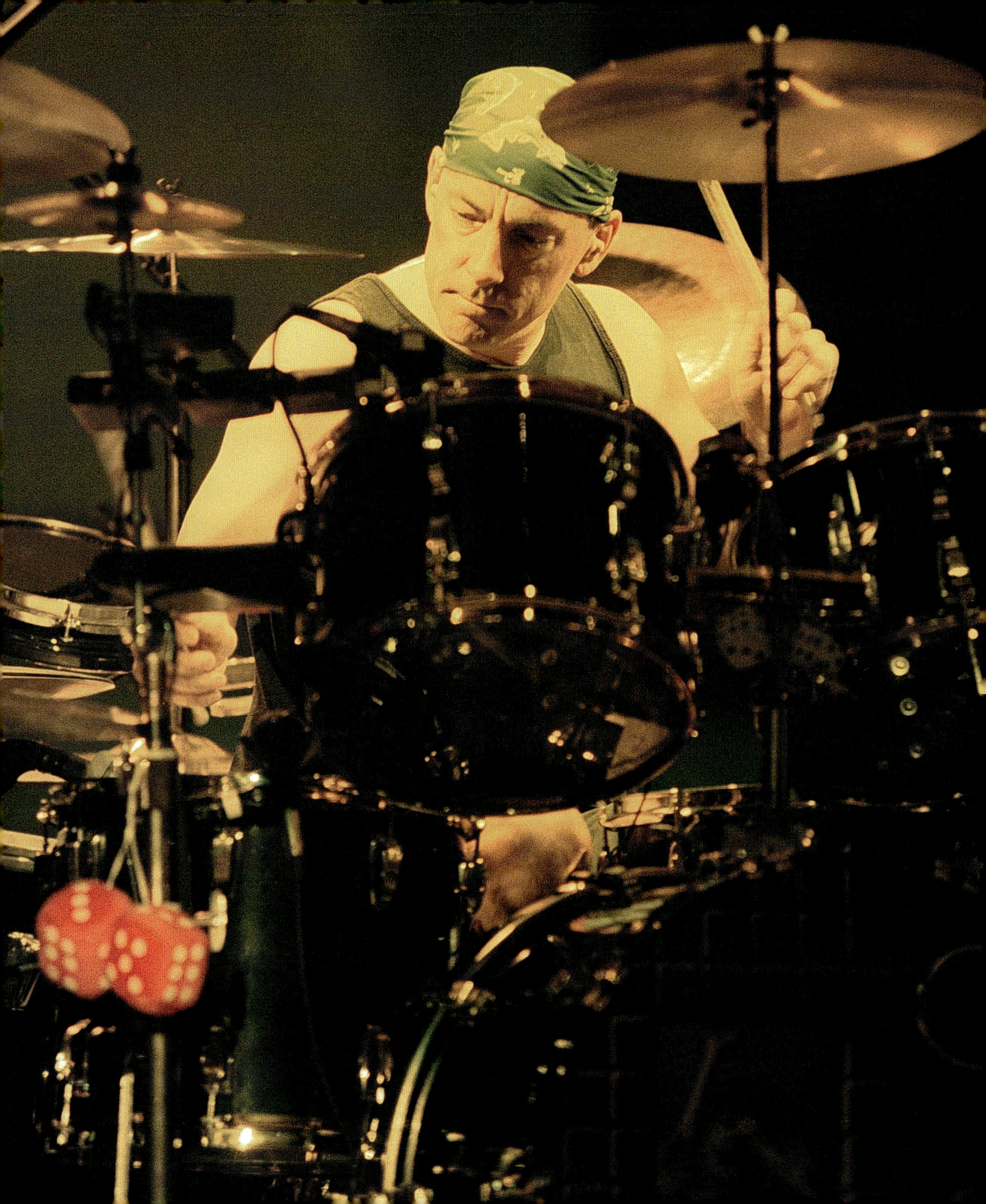

FOUR
A LIMITED TIME

Neil Peart bids farewell to the 1980s during the *Roll the Bones* tour at the Shoreline Amphitheater in Mountain View, California, on May 31, 1992.

26

SCISSORS, PAPER, STONE

A tight three-piece band and a tight two-piece production team

Breaking bread at Le Studio during the *Presto* sessions (left to right): recording and mixing engineer Stephen W Tayler, drum tech Larry Allen, guitar tech Jimmy JJ Johnson, keyboard tech Tony Geranios (aka "Jack Secret"), Neil Peart, Alex Lifeson, and Geddy Lee.

Presto was Rush's first album for Atlantic Records. It was coproduced by Rupert Hine, who had worked with The Fixx and Howard Jones. His résumé may not have suggested that he was the right coproducer for Rush, but Robert Scovill said he was what the band wanted.

"Who would listen to those Fixx records and say, 'That's a producer for Rush right there?' he asked. "Yet Neil was really taken with him and wanted to work with him."

Hine coproduced *Presto* alongside recording and mixing engineer Stephen W Tayler, his production partner since 1980. While the artists that the pair had worked with in the past didn't sound remotely like Rush, Tayler said there were other reasons why everyone hit it off.

"It was quite special to bring together a tight three-piece band with a tight two-piece production team," he said.

He recalled that while the entire band always did their homework and always came prepared, Peart took it to the next level.

"He was probably one of the most intensely well-rehearsed drummers I have ever recorded," he said. "He would record a complete take, always played perfectly. He might suggest a couple of sound adjustments and then go and refine his performance, but they were almost always complete takes from start to finish."

From the first song, "Show Don't Tell," it's clear that *Presto* is more direct than its immediate predecessors. The song is more "rock" and features a more prominent guitar than anything on *Hold Your Fire*. That goes for the entire record, although one must stress that Lifeson traffics in neither Pantera-esque crunch nor Malmsteen-esque 64th notes. Still, it's nice to hear his fader get goosed a bit.

The album also contains "The Pass," a song about teenage suicide that became a favorite of both the band and their fans. Like everything on *Presto*, its lead vocal is prioritized in the mix so the listener can better appreciate both the lyrics and Lee's performance. Not coincidentally, the record features some of the bassist's best vocals, particularly on "Available Light."

While Lifeson did not say, "It's about time," he told *Guitar World* that he was happy to hear his guitar get more love again. "You can do some interesting things with keyboards in terms of effects and textures, but they don't really hold the energy of the song like a guitar can," he said.

Robert Scovill began his tenure as the band's live sound engineer on the *Presto* tour. As a longtime fan, he understood what the group needed from him. "I had already studied the music for fourteen years, so I knew it like the back of my hand," he said. He noted that he was immediately taken with the high level of organization within the band, their inner circle, and their crew. But as organized as everyone was, Peart was insanely organized.

"He would come into rehearsal weeks early," Scovill said. "He was there before anybody."

He recalled that early in his tenure, he overheard a discussion between Peart and drum tech Larry Allen. Peart had walked in and asked if his kit was set up, to which Allen responded, "Well, I think so." The drummer gave a classic response: "Well, if it's perfect, it's right," he said.

Geddy Lee interacts with "Rocky Raccoon," a frequent visitor at Quebec's Le Studio during the *Presto* recording sessions in the summer of 1989.

Alex Lifeson and Geddy Lee engage in some good-natured screwing around during the *Presto* sessions.

FOUR: A LIMITED TIME / 87

27
WHY ARE WE HERE?
Rush rap, chaos ensues

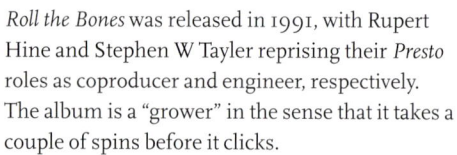

Roll the Bones was released in 1991, with Rupert Hine and Stephen W Tayler reprising their *Presto* roles as coproducer and engineer, respectively. The album is a "grower" in the sense that it takes a couple of spins before it clicks.

The weather conspired to stop the album from getting made. Ten days had been set aside to record drums, but the electrical feed to Le Studio had an outage when a truck hit a power line during a snowstorm. This meant they couldn't use the Mitsubishi thirty-two-track digital tape machine. And no digital tape machine, no album.

"The weather was appalling, and the tape machine could not be repaired for a whole week," Tayler said. "Neil was so upset, he came in every day to run through his drum parts along with a stereo rough mix, but he was so ready to record the parts, he became more and more angry and frustrated every day."

Repairs were finally made, and recording could resume. If Peart was in any way flustered or thrown off by the unexpected bout of inactivity, his performance didn't reflect it. Tayler said that Peart recorded all his drum parts in a day and a half.

"Shockingly, even after all that delay, we were now ahead of the schedule, and Geddy wasn't quite ready to start with his bass parts," the engineer said.

"Dreamline" opens the record on a very immediate note, and even though they weren't trying to compete with the era's thrash metal bands, it's nice to hear Lifeson's guitar clearly without scouring the mix for him with a flashlight. "Ghost of a Chance" has a grinding main riff that anchors the entire song, something you couldn't say about much of the material Rush made in the previous decade.

The title track, infamously, contains a single incident of rapping, one too many for some fans. However, in terms of pacing and the listening experience, *Roll the Bones* is a much less effective album if you skip that song, which many people likely did. Whatever its flaws, it makes the album flow well.

Roll the Bones came out between the collapse of hair metal and the rise of grunge, and it sounds like neither one of those things. It continues in the vein of *Presto*, blissfully and gloriously oblivious to the momentary trends in that year's popular culture.

The paths of the three-piece band and the two-piece production team diverged after *Roll the Bones*. Hine and Tayler went to work on other projects, and sadly, Hine passed away in 2020 at seventy-two.

Tayler has continued working as an engineer, producer, composer, and musician and has also created surround-sound mixes for such bands as Van der Graaf Generator, which you should run outside and buy right now without asking any questions. He said he'd love to perform the same service for the Rush albums he worked on.

"I fell in love with this music and adored being a part of the process," he said.

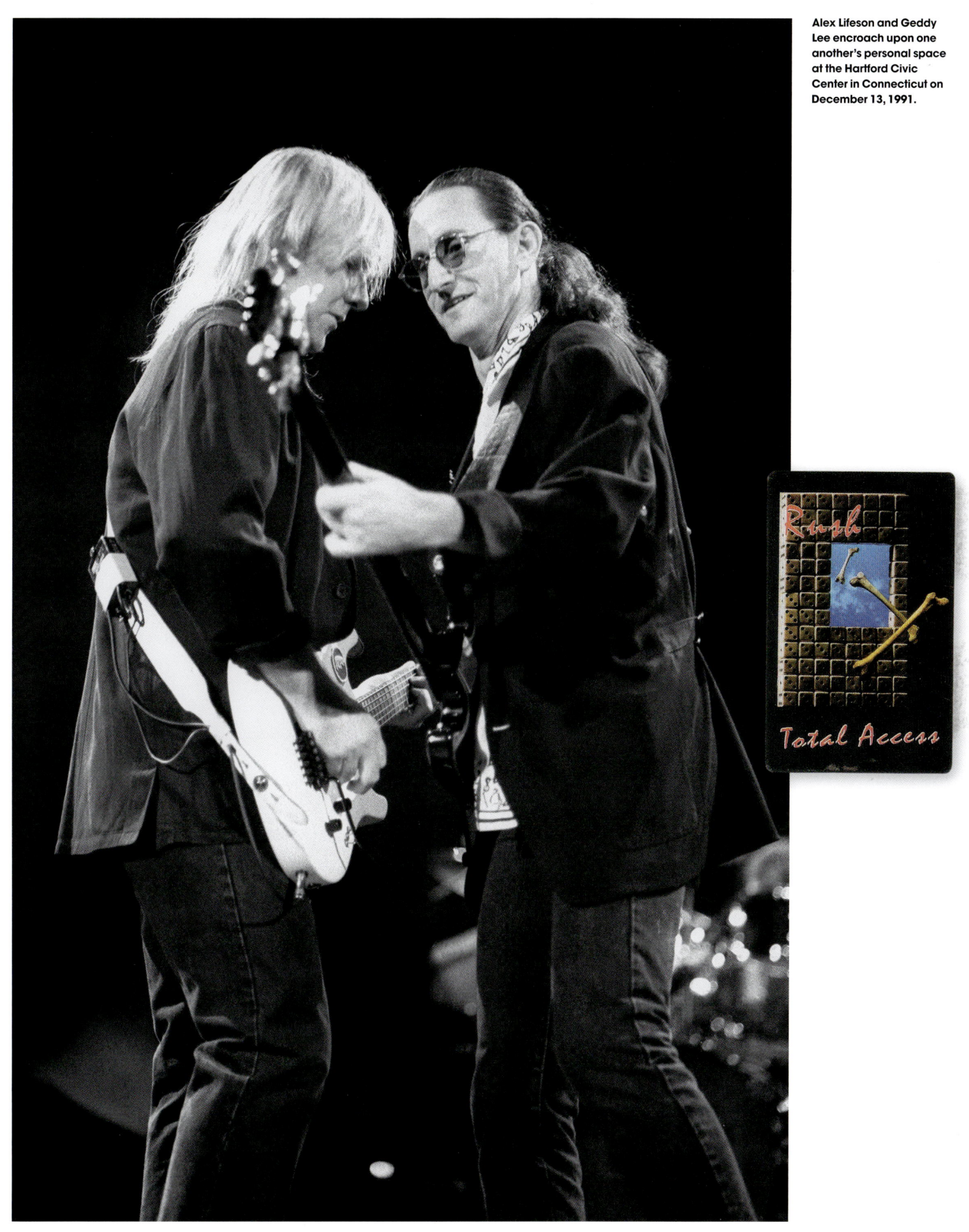

Alex Lifeson and Geddy Lee encroach upon one another's personal space at the Hartford Civic Center in Connecticut on December 13, 1991.

FOUR: A LIMITED TIME / 89

28
R-E-S-P-E-C-T
Unlikely Rush fans come out of the closet

In the 1990s, a weird thing started happening. People began expressing their love for Rush publicly, and not just at the civilian level. Musicians they had influenced started speaking up, and, stranger still, some members of the notably hostile press got into the act, too.

SPIN, the hipster publication of choice, ran an article by journalist Bob Mack called "Confessions of a Rush Fan." He wrote paragraph upon rhapsodic paragraph about how much he loved the trio, calling them "the ultimate punk band for people who thought punk was bogus."

He went on to name-check a long list of artists who had claimed the trio as an influence. It was a who's-who of bands that had emerged in the 1980s with a unique sound, many of whom were as committed to evolution as the Canadian trio.

One was Metallica, the only band in the world as frequently accused of selling out as Rush. During the 1991 release of their massive-selling self-titled album, Lars Ulrich told SPIN that they had learned to risk alienating their hard-core fans from the masters.

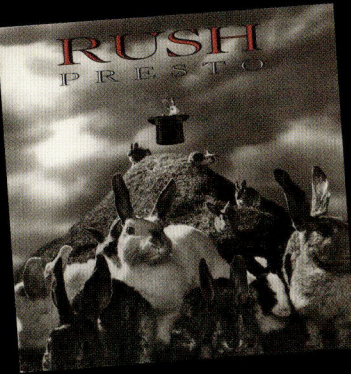

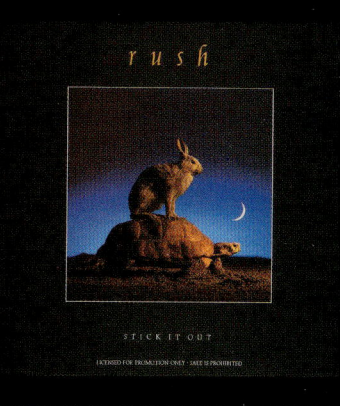

1989
Where's the synthesizer off-ramp?
June–August

1989
A tight three-piece band and a tight two-piece production team
November 21

1991
Rush rap, chaos ensues
September 3

1993
Unlikely Rush fans come out of the closet
October 19

1998
The walking wounded try to press on
November 10

2000
A wounded trio ponders their return
October 20

2002
The hiatus ends
May 14

2002
A performing entity comes roaring back to life
June 28

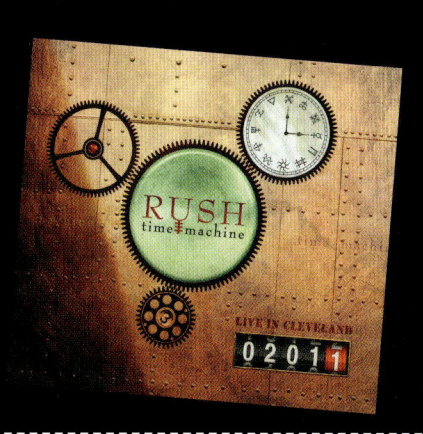

2008
Pop acceptance on the thirty-five-year plan
April

2008
Another live album, yet again
April 15

2009
Peart becomes a father again
August 12

2011
Rush take a glorious look backward
November 8

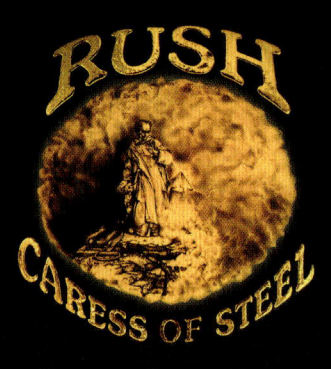

1975
Rush avoid the sophomore slump
February 15

1975
The band get the cold shoulder
September 24

1976
The heartbreaking tale of the "Down the Tubes Tour"
January 10

1976
No single, no Top 40, no problem
April 1

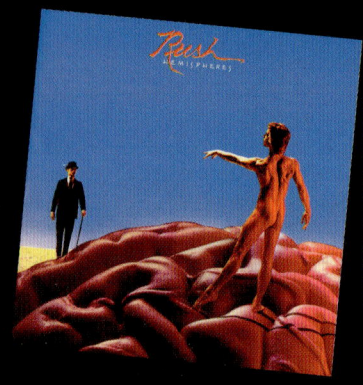

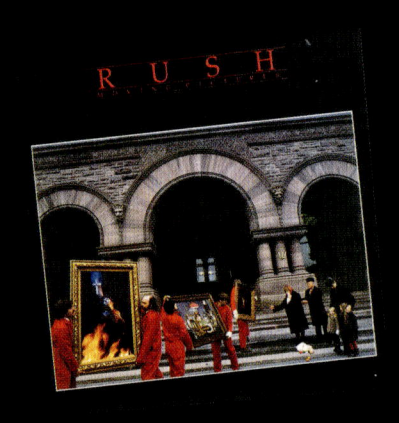

1978
Lee, Lifeson, and Peart lose their minds
October 24

1979
Leaving the formula behind
June 4

1980
Rush step into the 1980s
January 14

1981
The band deviate from the norm
February 12

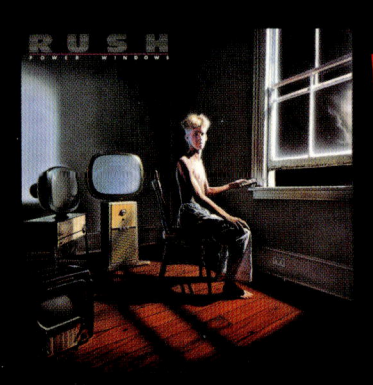

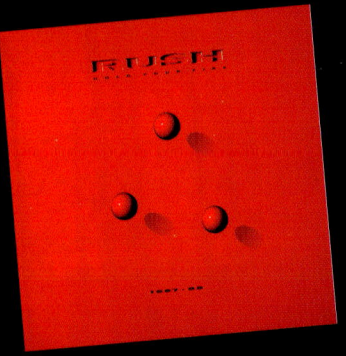

1984
Rush make a dark and stormy record
April 12

1985
We really hope you like keyboards
October 21

1987
Rush eat themselves
September 8

1989
I can't believe it's a live album!
January 10

1973
A young power trio goes 45 rpm
September

1974
"Terry really fixed that record"
March 18

1974
A seven-minute song blows up on WMMS
April

1974
Toronto power trio ISO drummer, lyrics a plus
July 29

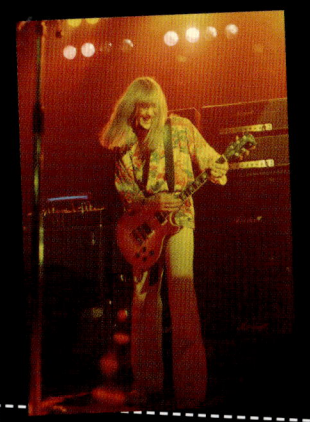

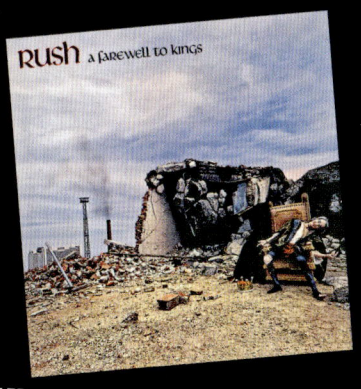

1976
Rush record their *Double Live Gonzo*
September 29

1977
A band takes their artistic freedom out for a spin
June–July

1977
Heading for the heart of Cygnus
August 29

1978
Geddy Lee has the worst two weeks of his life
June–July

1981
Rush close out 1981 with a stellar live set
October 29

1982
Rush get the seven-year itch
September 9

1983
Rush break up with their fourth man
July 23

1984
"Mr. So-and-so" hates odd time signatures
March

1994
Neil Peart learns all about traditional grip
May 7

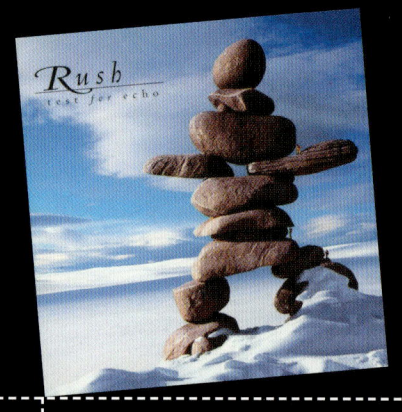

1996
Let's get mediocre
September 10

1996
News flash: no one wants to see Rush's opening acts
October 19

1997
A drummer enters limbo
August 10

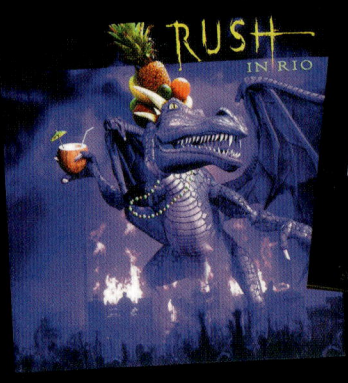

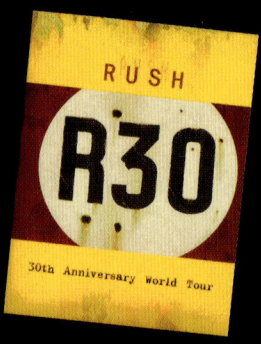

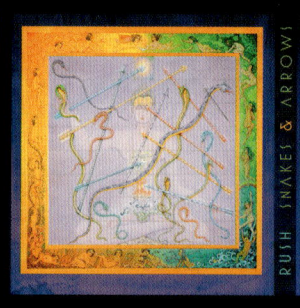

2002
Rush endure a grade-A Charlie Foxtrot
November 23

2003
The Rio crowd sings all the lyrics to "YYZ"
October 21

2004
The band's first EP and least essential release
June 29

2005
What do you get for the band that have everything?
November 22

2007
Another unique entry in the Rush catalog
May 1

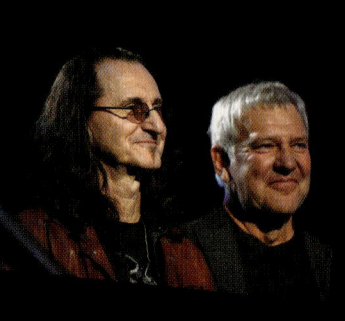

2012
Rush make their favorite album
June 12

2013
Why add one member when you can add nine?
November 19

2015
10-4, good buddy, over and out
August 1

2020
"I miss him even to this day"
January 7

2023
"It's what we do"
November 19

"More than any other band, we are like Rush," the drummer said.

When he learned the band wanted to call their next album *Counterparts*, album cover designer Hugh Syme said he embraced a more minimalist approach than he had previously used with the trio. "I proposed a mechanical drawing of a nut and a bolt," he said. "The band was a little uncertain about having that amount of minimalism on one of their covers, but in the end, it became one of their best-selling T-shirts."

Rush released *Counterparts* in 1993, and many fans rejoiced. The distorted guitars are at the front of the mix, tempting some to believe it was a conscious choice meant to court the "Smells like Teen Spirit" set. Some even called it Rush's "grunge album."

Peter Collins, the man who had helmed their two most synthesizer-centric albums, may have seemed a strange choice for the trio's return to heavy guitar rock, but he understood what they wanted and embraced their vision. While the resulting album is not side 3 of *2112*, the overdriven guitars are welcome. The stomper "Stick It Out" is probably the heaviest thing the band had done in years.

Naturally, the record is not perfect. "Alien Shore" has jarringly awkward lyrics like, "Sex is not a job description," which has been known to cause some cringing in some listeners, such as this author. Luckily, it's offset by things like the grinding and dissonant "Double Agent," so you can't really complain.

Counterparts is a strong record, and between that and the growing acceptance they were experiencing, 1993 was an excellent year to be in Rush. In 2015, Peart told *Rolling Stone* that it had been hard to weather the hatred they suffered at the hands of critics and hipsters during the first two decades of their career, and it was nice of the laggards in the press and elsewhere to get a clue finally.

"I feel like we waited it out and the respect came around," Peart said. "It astonished me in the early nineties to suddenly have musicians admit that they had been inspired and influenced by us."

It's March 31, 1992, at the Shoreline Amphitheater in Mountain View, California, and Alex Lifeson and Geddy Lee appear blissfully indifferent to grunge and every other musical fad of the day.

Neil Peart demonstrates his mastery of flams, ruffs, and ratamacues on the *Roll the Bones* tour, December 1991.

29
FEELS LIKE THE FIRST TIME
Neil Peart learns all about traditional grip

While some find the music of Rush insufferable, one thing even the most devoted hater will grudgingly concede is that Neil Peart knew his way around a drum kit.

As lovely as that was, it wasn't enough for him. He wanted his playing to improve continuously, so in the 1990s, he started taking lessons, much to the surprise of almost everyone who had ever heard him play.

The decision had its genesis in 1991. Peart played a concert with the Buddy Rich Big Band at the invitation of Rich's daughter Cathy. Technical problems affected the performance, and they nagged at him long after he got offstage.

"Given that it was a live concert with six drummers, the rehearsal time was limited to none, sound check was chaotic, the monitors were chaos and I couldn't hear the horns at all," he told *Canadian Musician* in 1994.

This led to a performance that he felt was well beneath his standards. Luckily, when the *Counterparts* tour ended, the band took two months off, allowing Peart time to produce *Burning for Buddy: A Tribute to the Music of Buddy Rich*. It included performances by such percussion masters as Max Roach, King Crimson's Bill Bruford, and Journey's Steve Smith.

In 1995, he told *Modern Drummer* that he was especially impressed by Smith's contribution and asked what the secret to his improved approach was. The Journey drummer answered with one word: "Freddie."

"Freddie" was jazz drummer Freddie Gruber. A veteran of New York City's bebop scene, Gruber had played with Charlie Parker and given lessons to drummers you wouldn't think needed them, such as Vinnie Colaiuta and Dave Weckl.

"I spent a week in New York with Freddie and completely rebuilt my drumming from the ground up," Peart told *Canadian Musician*, adding that the lessons gave him what no amount of practice could: a deep understanding of big band music.

"When I first came into this music, I bluffed my way through it," he said. "Now I'm calling my own bluff."

Learning everything again from scratch was a rewarding experience, even for the greatest drummer who ever lived. He relished the opportunity and was fascinated by what he had learned.

"When you're working with two bass drums in a rock band, you learn not to be a slave to the hi-hat," he said. "Now I *am* a slave to the hi-hat on two and four. It changes the structure of time, which is a real interesting discovery for me."

Peart started playing in his new style on the *Test for Echo* album and tour and stuck to that technique for the rest of his career. When Gruber passed away in 2011, Peart wrote an obituary for him in *Hudson Music*. It described the effect he'd had on all of his students, and while Peart was not a man who believed in the afterlife, he said there would be one for Gruber.

"All of those musicians will continue to pass along that fundamental and immortal language of human life, to listeners and to younger drummers, and thus Freddie's place in that divine continuum will continue to resonate forever," he wrote. "He will be missed, but he is not gone."

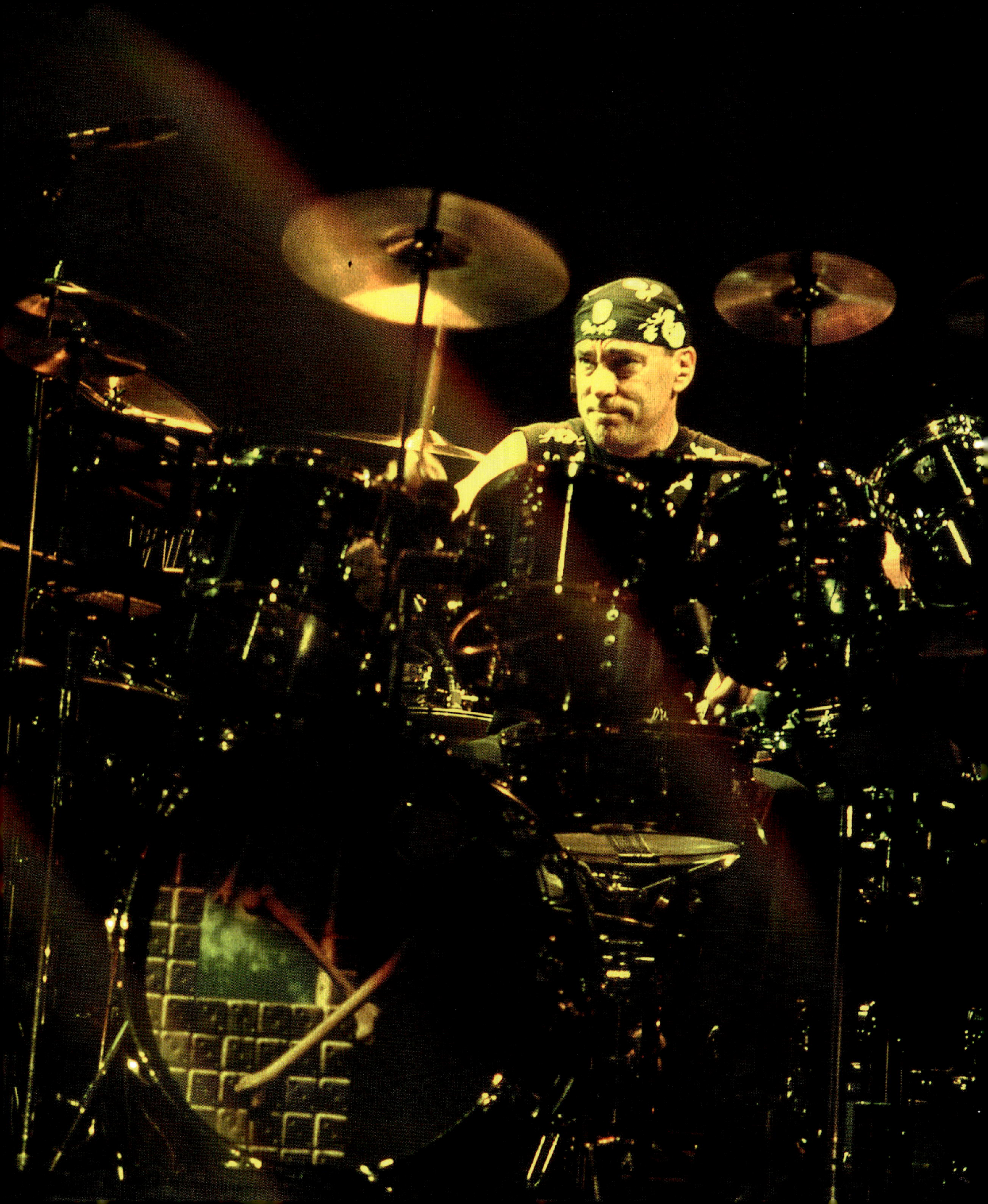

30
IS THAT A BONG?
Let's get mediocre

Test for Echo (1996) is Rush's most mediocre album. Of course, a mediocre Rush album still beats the best ones ever made by many other bands, so it still has much to recommend it. The issue is more that it's a mixed bag as opposed to being an out-and-out stinker. Somehow, Rush releasing an unexceptional album is more upsetting than if they had released a truly god-awful one.

Test for Echo has some solid ideas and others that fall flat. Both often appear in the same song, the title track being the perfect example. It starts well enough and sounds like it's really going to go somewhere, but at six minutes in length, it just goes on for way too long. It sounds like it never emerged from the rough-draft stage.

"Driven," meanwhile, is excellent. It seamlessly transitions from a dissonant main section to a rocking and swaying 6/8 chorus. If you've ever wondered what it's like to be at sea on a ship's deck in very violent weather, this lumbering and unwieldy section will give you a close approximation.

"Time and Motion" has a slow, dissonant grind, and Lifeson's noise solo over its inharmonious riffs is glorious. The sudden dynamic changes are effective, and even the dreaded keyboards work well here. More material like this would have been very welcome and strengthened the record.

"Resist" is a simple ballad that also fares well. Because they left the idea alone and didn't overwork it, it feels natural and less like the band are fighting themselves. It would have been an excellent approach to the whole record to go for more straightforward ideas and let them play out, as they did on the instrumental "Limbo." Also, is that a bong?

"Half the World" and "The Color of Right" are so-so and weigh the record down. We know that this trio worked very hard on every song they ever recorded and never half-assed anything, but is it better that they worked hard on something that came out sounding half-assed?

Beyond the run-of-the-mill stuff, *Test for Echo* has two very low points. "Dog Years" opens at a fast, almost punk rock tempo; but the trio don't know what to do with it. It's only five minutes long but feels significantly longer, so maybe its length should be tabulated in dog minutes?

The other lowest point on *Test for Echo* is "Virtuality." It has an excellent opening riff that's very promising, and if they had just stuck with it, you'd have something. Instead, the songwriting suffers from overthinking. That's not the worst part, though. The "net boy, net girl" lyric is physically painful and could well constitute the worst Peart ever wrote. Overall. If they had stuck to the main riff and chopped the six-minute running time in half, it might have fared better, but they didn't.

Much like *Hold Your Fire*, another Peter Collins co-production job, *Test for Echo* buckles under the weight of its own ideas and ambition. It's not terrible, but only the most loyal, die-hard fans will return for repeat listens.

Geddy Lee at Nassau Veterans Memorial Coliseum on December 14, 1996. The venue is located in Uniondale, New York, in what is known to its residents as "Lawn Guyland."

Rush
test for echo

Front Row at Rush

FOUR: A LIMITED TIME / 95

31

AN EVENING WITH RUSH

News flash: No one wants to see Rush's opening acts

There may be a few exceptions, but for the most part, you don't want to be Rush's opening act. The band's quite vocal fans are more than happy to let you know you suck for the duration of your sparsely attended set. Those fans are generally nonviolent, so you likely won't have to dodge projectiles, but it's apparent from the opening note whom everyone is there to see, and it isn't you.

The *Test for Echo* tour showed that the band may have been aware of the situation. Dubbed "An Evening with Rush," it marked a significant change from the band's previous tours. For the first time, there would be no opening act. Stage time that would otherwise have been given to support bands was now given to the one everyone had actually paid to see. The extra time turned each concert into a sprawling event containing two separate sets and an encore, and the whole evening regularly stretched to approximately three hours.

This was not only fortuitous for Rush and their fans. It was also a godsend to bands who didn't want to get booed every night for forty-five minutes in different cities for six months. While some opening bands were well received by fans (Primus is probably the best example), nobody went to see Rush so that they could also see Candlebox. No one was there to see The Joe Perry Project.

"An Evening with Rush" also afforded the band an opportunity to stop truncating its epic suites, a welcome change. Those who went to see them on the *Power Windows* tour got to hear only the "Overture" and "The Temples of Syrinx" sections from "2112." They didn't want three-quarters of it excised so The Fabulous Thunderbirds could have more stage time. "An Evening with Rush," meanwhile, allowed the trio to play the "2112" suite in its entirety, right down to the waterfall sounds.

This is not to say that 100 percent of the fans hated The Fabulous Thunderbirds. But when those fans were parting with their hard-earned dollars to buy a concert ticket—a *Rush* concert ticket—they simply didn't give a single, solitary crap about the opening band. The trio's most hard-core fans thought nothing of forgoing sleep for five straight nights or enduring extreme financial hardship to see the band perform whenever they could, and the decision to forgo opening acts was one thing that probably made their lives a bit easier.

From 1996 on, Rush never had another opening band, and the fan base was unanimous in their assessment that this was a good thing. While we'll never know if this route was taken for the fans' sake or for their own, one thing is for sure: Nobody was sorry when they took it.

Alex Lifeson shows off his sleek, panther-like wardrobe at Nassau Veterans Memorial Coliseum in Uniondale, New York, on December 14, 1996.

32
AFTERIMAGE
A drummer enters limbo

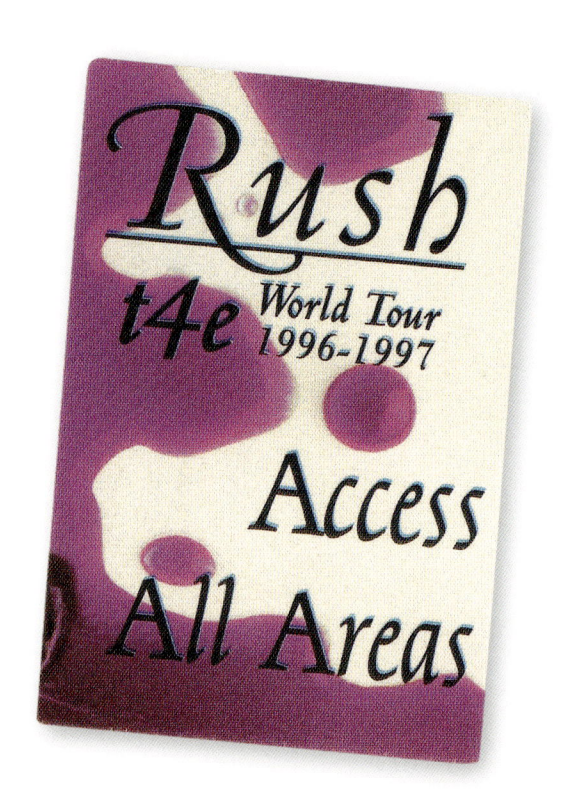

The *Test for Echo* tour ended on July 4, 1997, and by all accounts, it had been a triumph. Just one month later, all of that was swept away. Peart was dealt a crippling blow when Selena Peart, his nineteen-year-old daughter with common-law wife Jackie Taylor, was killed in a car accident as she drove to college.

The couple barely had time to come to grips with the tragedy before they were rocked by another. On June 20, 1998, Taylor died of breast cancer. It was less than a year after their daughter's passing, and Peart would later say that what really killed his wife was the overwhelming grief that came in the wake of the accident.

"She just wanted to die," Peart said. "She had to be coaxed into eating anything at all and talked of suicide constantly."

While these two tragedies directly harmed the drummer, his bandmates were also profoundly affected, and staying busy didn't guarantee them a distraction from what had happened. Rush released a live album in October 1998, and Lee conducted interviews to promote it. Every time he did, he was asked about the band's long-term plans after what had happened to the drummer's wife and daughter. He told *Long Island Entertainment* that there weren't any.

"No plans to record the next album right now, no plans to tour," he said.

The bassist was being diplomatic. The band had always been a tight-knit unit, and while some musicians might have seen an open-ended time with no obligations as an opportunity, Lee and Lifeson weren't thinking that way. They were thinking about the man who had been their brother over the previous twenty-plus years, a man going through an unimaginably painful time.

People around the band were also profoundly affected. Donna Halper, former music director for WMMS radio in Cleveland, remembered receiving the phone call in which she learned about Selena's accident. As unbearable as that news was, Jackie's passing the following year was a compound tragedy.

"How much can one person take?" she asked. "It was such a heartbreaking period of time. To lose two people that helped anchor him, that helped ground him. . . . He loved the band, he loved Geddy and Alex, he loved drumming, but he also loved being home with his family."

Peart had spent a lot of years on the road as a musician, so he hadn't gotten as much time with his family as he wanted. Now, he would never have the chance to address that. He could never make it up to them.

"By his own admission, he wasn't there a lot for them, but he really did love them," Halper said. "Selena was going to college, and he really was proud of her, and he wanted to let her know that. I think that probably one of the biggest regrets is that he never was able to see her graduate from college. . . . She was young, she was vibrant, and she had her whole life ahead of her."

Lifeson told *Classic Rock* in 2016 that, at the time, it was difficult to see any future for the band. He just couldn't see the point. "After the tragedies in Neil's life, the band just didn't seem at all important," the guitarist said.

Their very loving fans extended the group some much-needed grace. While the term *fan* can summon images of Beatlemania and screaming teenagers chasing musicians down the street, Rush fans were themselves affected by the tragedies. They didn't know Peart, but they wanted to help, and they ultimately did so by leaving the band alone.

"No one was pushy or prodding or anything like that," Lifeson told CNN. "We were given some space, and we really appreciated that."

Peart dealt with the tragedy the same way he had dealt with other major changes in his life: by leaving everything behind and taking a solo journey to parts unknown. He got on his motorcycle and rode off, and nobody knew if they would ever see him again. Ultimately, he would be gone for a year.

"There was a period of time where nobody knew where he was," Halper said. "He just had to be off coping with it."

Peart eventually wrote a memoir about his long journey, *Ghost Rider: Travels on the Healing Road*. It detailed his entire trek through North America and Central America and offered a more vulnerable look at the drummer than most Rush fans were accustomed to.

To fans, Peart was nothing less than an invincible superhero, and no kryptonite could stop him. The memoir showed him in a completely different light and presented him to readers as a very real, heartbroken, mortal man brought low by unthinkable tragedy. For those who only knew him as the greatest drummer who ever lived, the memoir humanized him.

Howdy, pardner! Geddy Lee hits the vocal upper stratosphere at the Woodlands Pavilion in Texas on May 25, 1997.

This page: A leather-clad Alex Lifeson channels the Lizard King at the Shoreline Amphitheater in Mountain View, California, on May 11, 1997.

Opposite: On June 22, 1997, at the Blockbuster-Sony E-Center in Camden, New Jersey, Neil Peart demonstrates his revamped playing style, courtesy of instructor Freddie Hubbard.

FOUR: A LIMITED TIME / 101

33
FOUR STUDIO, ONE LIVE
The walking wounded try to press on

Alex Lifeson, Geddy Lee, and Neil Peart at London's Hammersmith Odeon on February 20, 1978. The recording is among their best and was released in full on the fortieth-anniversary edition of *A Farewell to Kings*.

Rush always had a set way of releasing live albums that they stuck to very closely. It was four studio albums, then one live album. Four studio, one live. Four studio, one live—et cetera.

This kept them in good stead when the late 1990s rolled around and the band's entire future was in doubt. They had recorded the *Counterparts* and *Test for Echo* tours so they could use the audio for whatever live album they would make next, but after the deaths of Peart's daughter and wife, the recordings stood a good chance of being the last thing the band ever released.

Peart had left the band behind and hopped on his motorcycle, so he had no involvement in the album's production. Lifeson told the *Calgary Sun* that he and Lee were not about to pressure him and ask about his plans. He acknowledged that he and the bassist had discussed the band's uncertain future—maybe the two of them would still play together in some capacity, but the one thing they knew for sure was that if Peart didn't come back, Rush were over.

In the meantime, there were hours and hours of tapes to sift through. The band had recorded every date on the *Test for Echo* tour, so if anyone wanted to distract themselves from the heartbreak with work, this was a grand opportunity.

Lee told the *Toronto Globe and Mail* that Lifeson wasn't involved in putting the album together. He and coproducer Paul Northfield took on the Herculean task of going through all the recordings and choosing the right ones for the album. Despite the circumstances surrounding the group, the album that emerged, *Different Stages*, was one of their best live packages ever.

The sound quality is top-notch, the performances are excellent, and the set list features a comprehensive cross section of the band's catalog. They even included a third disc containing highlights from the band's 1978 performance at London's Hammersmith Odeon to sweeten the pot.

Most of the performances on the first two discs come from a single date at the World Music Theater in Tinley Park, Illinois, on June 4, 1997. The opening track, "Dreamline," is a good representation of what to expect from the remainder of the album. It's performed with high energy and more discernable interplay between the musicians.

It was a very good night from which to cull performances, even regarding the audience levels in the mix. The applause and fan commentary are never intrusive, although on "Driven," one dude is very aggressively in the left speaker, so he got his money's worth.

Neil Peart at London's Hammersmith Odeon on February 20, 1978, where a discussion with *New Music Express* writer Barry Miles snowballed into accusations that the band members were fascists.

Geddy Lee, Alex Lifeson, and Neil Peart at New York City's Madison Square Garden. Fashions change, but a double-neck SG never goes out of style.

If the band were getting tired of playing the oldies, it doesn't show. They had played "Limelight," "The Trees," "Closer to the Heart," you name it, a kajillion times for international audiences over twenty-plus years, and if any band had earned the right to get bored by their back catalog, it was this one. But remarkably, they never sound like they've played the music to death or like they're going through the motions. It sounds like they instinctively know how to play the songs well and enjoy doing so.

Also, kudos to whoever decided to index "2112" into seven different tracks instead of one long one. People of a certain age who want to replicate the Walkman days and make Rush mixes that last no longer than ninety minutes are very grateful to have the suite in bite-size morsels as opposed to an entire unprocessed side of beef.

Different Stages is not quite the excellent value it was when it was released because of the third disc. In 1998, the band were aware of what a multidisc set would cost fans, and three CDs kept the retail price low. The problem was that a good chunk of the Hammersmith performance had to be excised to keep it under eighty minutes.

In 2017, the band released a fortieth-anniversary edition of *A Farewell to Kings*, including the entire concert spread over two discs. It works even in truncated form because the performance is so good, so it remains a nice companion to the first two discs. But if you want the whole thing, you must splash out for the fortieth-anniversary edition of *A Farewell to Kings*.

It's hard to say what the members of Rush intended as *Different Stages* came together. Was it a project that Lee could immerse himself in while Peart recovered? Was it the last thing they would ever put out? It's hard to say what they were thinking, since the band were in a holding pattern with an uncertain future. But if it were the final thing Rush ever released, it would have been a great note to go out on.

Geddy Lee treats the Shoreline Amphitheater in Mountain View, California, to "An Evening with Rush" on May 11, 1997.

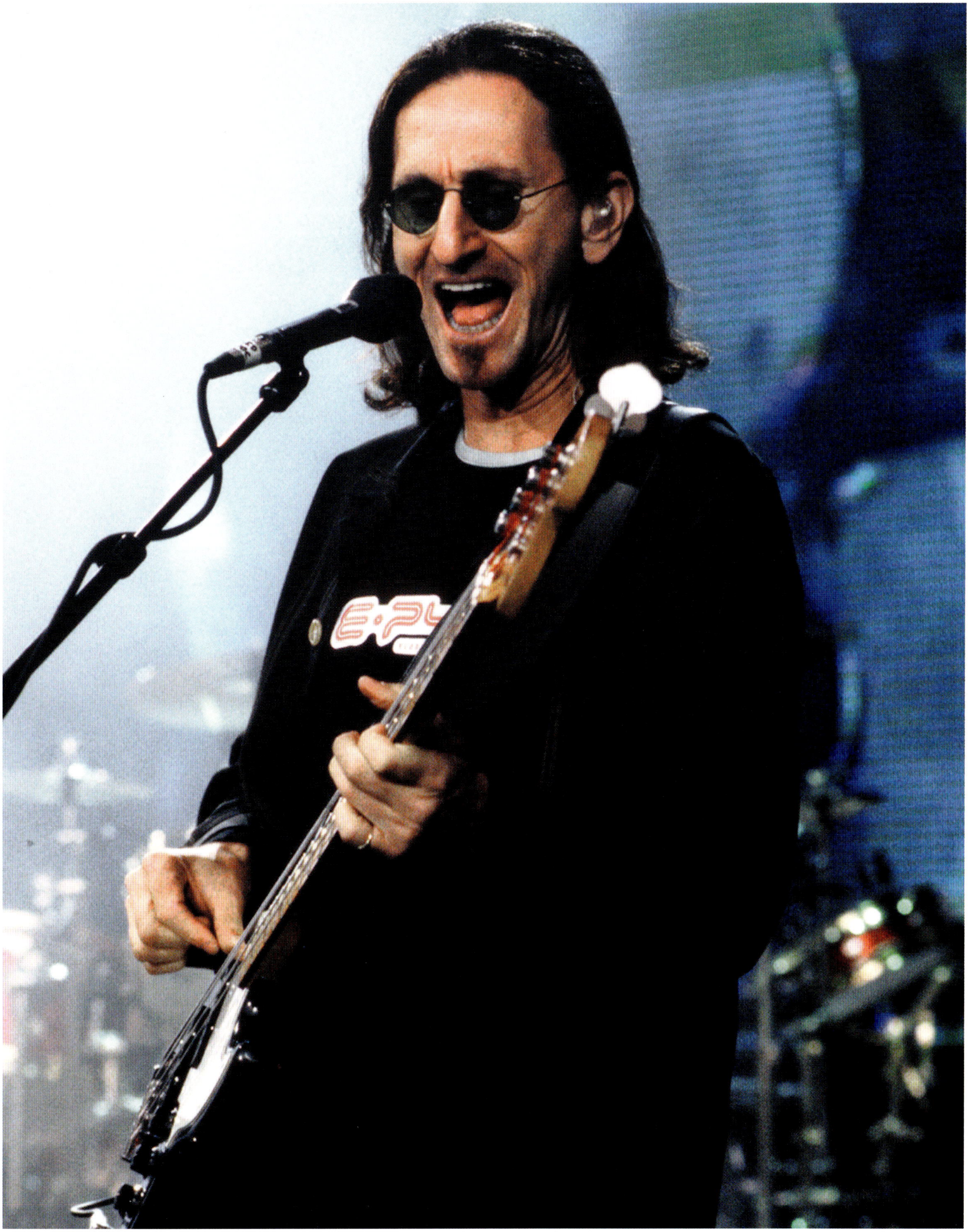

SYNTHESIZER HATRED
The quite thorny issue of Rush and keyboards

It's been an article of faith for many people that Rush were great in the 1970s and then sucked in the 1980s when they went all New Wave with the damn synthesizers. The truth, of course, is more complicated.

The prevailing view would have you believe that during the 1970s, Rush were a progressive hard rock power trio, and when the decade ended, Geddy Lee showed up at the studio with a keytar under his arm and a whip in his hand, the better to forcefully consign his group to techno-pop oblivion until 1993's *Counterparts*. The truth is that keyboards and synthesizers had been a part of the band's arsenal since the *2112* album.

From there, the presence of keyboards grew, and you hear plenty of them on the albums leading up to *Signals*, where many fans of Rush's earlier work will say the band lost the plot. Yes, the band used the instrument quite a lot in the 1980s, but Lifeson told *Prog* magazine in 2023 that all three members were excited to use them, and it wasn't just Lee grabbing the reins and going all Roger Waters on everybody.

"It was a group effort," he said. "We wanted to expand our sound, but we didn't want to add any more members. I was happy to use them. I thought they did a great thing for our sound."

He went on to say that it was only when the keyboards became the dominant instrument that the grumbling started. However, on the *Make Weird Music* podcast in 2021, he denied that the much-ballyhooed "guitars vs. keyboards" dustup caused him to lose any sleep.

"I don't have a problem really with keyboards," he said, explaining that their introduction into the band's arsenal came from a musical desire to evolve. "We always wanted to go somewhere else—to explore something else."

Lifeson said he and Lee wanted to see what possibilities these new instruments would open for them. Working with coproducer Peter Collins in the 1980s was intended to do that. "He came from that sort of background, so the whole exploration of really developed keyboards happened," he said.

Then it got excessive. Keyboards were recorded before the guitars, and it was then that Lifeson said his job changed. Previously, he had led the music with power chords, and now he had to figure out how to be heard above the wash of whole-note synthesizer padding.

"I was competing for space sonically amongst the keyboards," he said. "It was a real challenge to fit the guitar in."

Looking back, he said he still liked the results and was proud of the "keyboard-era" records. Those albums have a distinct character, after all, and taken as part of the entire Rush catalog, it's easy to see them as representing an era unto itself, similar to the period in which the band recorded twenty-minute songs. Eventually, though, the keyboards fell victim to the same fate as the 1970s epics—Rush had been there, done that, and it was time to move on to the next thing.

Many fans were delighted when the guitar returned to its role as a forefront instrument on Rush albums. At the same time, those keyboard-era albums have always been popular, and to fans who came on board around the time of *Moving Pictures*, the "classic Rush sound" involves a lot of keyboards.

Although former WMMS radio music director Donna Halper had championed the band when they were a very guitar-centric hard rock trio, she said she also enjoyed those albums from the 1980s. She said that fans who abandoned Rush when the synthesizers started creeping in were reminiscent of the 1965 audiences who booed Bob Dylan and called him "Judas" for playing with an electric backing band. She also mentioned The Beatles as an example of a band who changed their sound from album to album, sometimes radically, to magnificent effect. To her, the Canadian trio was following the Fab Four template and embracing progress.

"I like that they never mailed it in," she said of Rush.

Geddy Lee, the man who gets most of the credit (or blame) for Rush's synthesizer era, told *Rolling Stone* in 2023 that in the 1980s, he was so infatuated with the new toys and gadgets that he lost sight of the band's essential power trio sound. However, he explained that his enthusiasm for the latest technology was what drove him, not a desire to control the band. Still, he admitted that something was lost during that period.

"I used to say, 'When we make a record, it doesn't matter how much stuff we have on it. You got to hear the trio,'" Lee said. "I had obscured that without realizing it by being so synthesizer-centric."

Geddy Lee plays the much-maligned synthesizer during the *Grace Under Pressure* tour. For some fans of the band's early guitar-driven music, the ever-increasing presence of this instrument was a bridge too far.

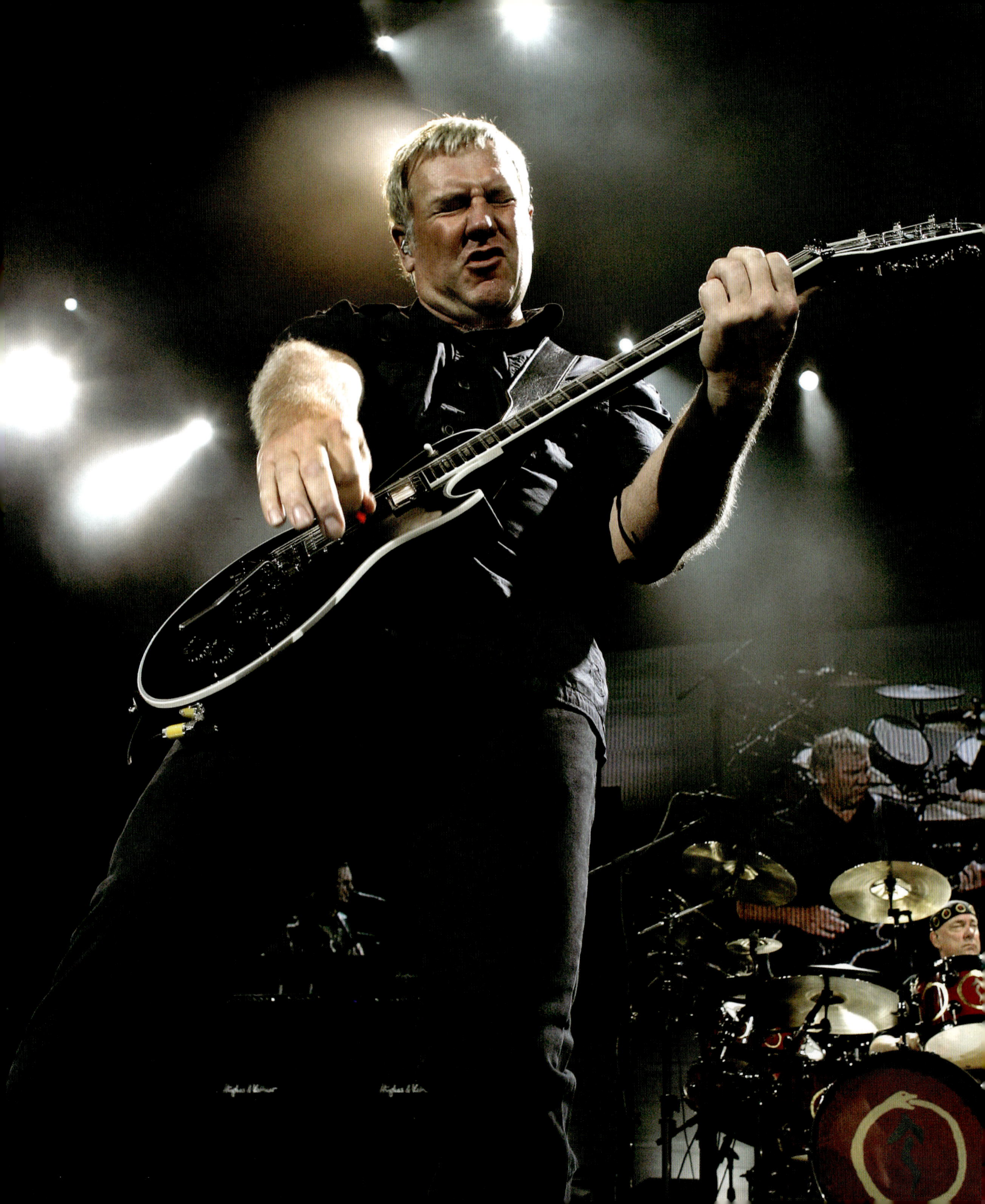

FIVE
THE TIME IS NOW AGAIN

Alex Lifeson strikes an E major chord on the *Snakes & Arrows* tour at the Sound Advice Amphitheater in West Palm Beach, Florida, on June 15, 2007.

34
OUT OF THE CRADLE
A wounded trio ponders their return

As the new millennium approached, it was hard to say if Rush would ever be a band again. Even the group's most rabid fans knew there was a very strong possibility that they might never hear another note of music from the drummer. They also knew that even if Lee and Lifeson came back to the music world at some point, either as solo artists or together, it wouldn't be called "Rush" unless their friend, brother, and bandmate was involved. Other than that, everything was still up in the air.

Lee told *Loudwire* that a 1998 phone call from former Led Zeppelin singer Robert Plant went a long way toward helping him and Lifeson figure out their next move. The singer had lost his five-year-old son Karac in 1977 to a stomach illness, so he understood the nature of what Peart had endured. He also understood what the drummer's devastated bandmates were feeling.

He wanted the pair to see him and Jimmy Page perform together on their 1998 *Walking into Clarksdale* tour. He characterized it as a crucial step that would help the dejected bassist and guitarist find their footing again.

"I remember him saying: 'You've got to rejoin life, and sooner is better than later,'" Lee said. "So I called Alex up and said we're going to see Page & Plant."

Lee said Plant's gesture helped shift their perspective to the point where they could start thinking a bit about what their future might look like. It didn't hurt that the gesture came from a member of Led Zeppelin, a primary influence on Rush since their earliest days.

The meeting gave Lee and Lifeson cause for optimism, but they had no guarantee that Peart would feel the same way. Lifeson told CNN that he and the bassist, at one point, reached a place of acceptance if their drummer never came back.

Eventually, Lee picked up his bass again and made a solo album, 2000's *My Favorite Headache*. It was a mixed blessing for fans because, on the one hand, they could close their eyes when they listened to it and pretend it was a new Rush album, with Geddy's vocals and everything. On the other hand, it might prove to be the first of many solo albums from former Rush members, since the end of the band was a real possibility.

Just as *My Favorite Headache* was being released, some good news trickled out of the Rush camp. Whispers that the band might regroup started to get louder. Happier still was the news that Peart had gotten married again.

The lucky bride was photographer Carrie Nuttall, and the union represented a big step toward rejoining life. Peart had met her through the band's photographer, Andrew MacNaughton. The drummer said on his official website that MacNaughtan "was determined to find a 'match' for this crusty old widower." Nuttall, whom Peart described as "a pretty dark-haired girl," was MacNaughtan's photo assistant, and initially the drummer said he wasn't interested.

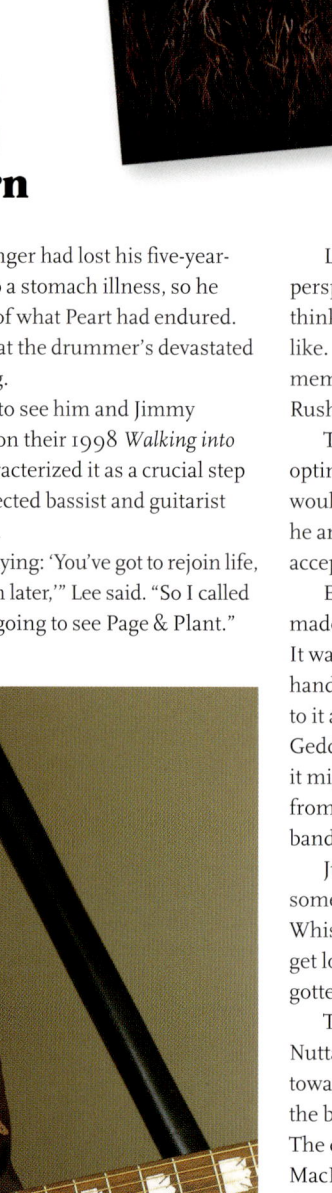

Alex Lifeson, Neil Peart, and Geddy Lee in 1996 during the *Test for Echo* era. One year later, everything would change.

Undeterred, MacNaughtan arranged a double date with her. This eventually led to a hike together, during which Nuttall and the drummer "talked easily." A few days later, he rode off on his motorcycle.

Before long, he came back.

"I met Carrie in Laguna Beach for our first date alone," he said. "It was there I saw her across the proverbial crowded room and fell. That was in late 1999, and the following September, Andrew was an usher at our wedding in Santa Barbara and gave a sweet speech as our 'benefactor.'"

When word got out that they had married, it was a relief and a joy. Anyone with a shred of decency was overjoyed to hear the news, given how life had dealt the drummer such a sustained beating. Really, it was just nice to see something good happen to him for a change, particularly something that suggested he was in a different place in his life.

A month after Peart and Nuttall were wed, more good news emerged. Lee told *Yahoo!Entertainment* that the topic of moving Rush back to the front burner had been broached by the only people that mattered: Lee, Lifeson, and Peart.

"[We've] talked about getting together in the new year to begin a kind of writing session and see how that goes, kind of like the first step," he said. "If all goes well when we sit down to write, before too long there'll be another Rush record. Truthfully, I can't imagine it not happening."

Album cover illustrator Hugh Syme said he wasn't surprised to hear that the drummer was taking steps to return to the band, however tentative.

"Musicians can't stop being musicians, and I think eventually Neil genuinely missed his bandmates," the illustrator said. "It just brought everything full circle, and it was time to get back to it."

Opposite: Alex Lifeson with an acoustic guitar, which he said helped him isolate ideas worth pursuing during the songwriting process.

FIVE: THE TIME IS NOW AGAIN

35

"A VERY FRAGILE REPRESENTATION OF THE BAND"
The hiatus ends

When *Counterparts* was released in 1993, many people responded to its heavy guitars by calling it "Rush's grunge album." They were all wrong. If any record deserves to be called "Rush's grunge album," it's 2002's *Vapor Trails*, with its overdriven sound, morose mood, and darkly autobiographical lyrics. It lacks the heroin vibe of the 1990s Seattle bands, but the genuine anguish more than makes up for it.

The fact that it even got made is remarkable. It wasn't simply that the band had gone on an indefinite hiatus while their drummer wrestled with his grief. The fact was that this wasn't the same band anymore, and expecting things to happen quickly and efficiently was not realistic. They needed time to get their chops back and relearn how to play together all over again. It wasn't easy. "This project is about so much more than us making a record," Lee told *Jam!Showbiz* in January 2001. "It is about us coming back together. It is about the psychological health and welfare of all the people who have gone through a very difficult time."

They decided there should be no deadline for finishing the record and making it would take as long as it took. Ultimately, it took fourteen months, a far cry from the years when *Fly by Night* could be recorded in just days.

The record that emerged was worth the wait. While it had fallen victim to the 2000s trend known as the "loudness wars," the redlined sound of *Vapor Trails* in its original form was appropriate. It was a dark, raw mix of noise, anxiety, and grief, and a highly polished mix wouldn't necessarily have made sense. This mix was a mess, but it was an honest mess, reflecting how the band were coping after five years of darkness and uncertainty.

The album starts with a drum pattern from Peart, which is fitting. He was the person who had sustained the most emotional damage, and if anyone bought the record hoping to glean what his emotional state was, he got that right out of the way at the beginning. His photograph in the CD booklet shows him serious and unsmiling, and while that was his default setting for many photos, here it communicated that the transition back to life was still a work in progress.

The lyrics show that the drummer was actively grappling with the fallout of the previous few years. "Ghost Rider" and "Vapor Trail" are as gloomy lyrically as they are musically, but even the songs that don't necessarily touch on Peart's personal life have a darkness that can't be ignored. This even holds true for more celebratory songs like "The Stars Look Down" and "Earthshine," which

"The time is now again." Neil Peart at the MGM Grand Garden Arena in Las Vegas on September 21, 2002, after a five-year hiatus.

114 / RUSH AT 50

This page: Geddy Lee during the *Vapor Trails* tour at Atlanta's Philips Arena on October 13, 2002. Whatever he's singing here, he's *feelin'* it.

Opposite: Alex Lifeson at the MGM Grand Garden Arena in Las Vegas in 2002. Hopefully, he had some time to try his luck at the slot machines.

both lighten up the proceedings musically but can't make us forget what happened.

The song that seems to get the point across most effectively is "Secret Touch." The immediately engaging music aside, it distinguishes itself through its lyrics, which embrace the fact that love equals risk. The more you love, the more pain you'll feel when something bad happens to the people you care about. But without risking that pain, you'll never experience love—and the song suggests it's worth the risk.

Vapor Trails is the first Rush album since *Caress of Steel* to feature zero keyboards. It was the best album the band had made since *Grace Under Pressure*, and there's not a weak track on the whole thing. Unfortunately, the band members weren't happy with the sound quality, as Lifeson explained to *Modern Guitars* in 2009.

"We've never been pleased with the mix, and particularly the mastering on it," Lifeson said. "We're to blame for a lot of that . . . we used a lot of the stuff that we did in the writing phase, rather than rerecording things. So, to maintain the pure energy of what those ideas were, we gave up a bit on the sonic end."

The guitarist said that all three band members were in rough shape at the time of the recording, and while the overdriven mix and overloaded mastering were disappointments to the band, it was true to what they were living at the time. "That record was a very emotional record for us," Lifeson said. "It was a very fragile representation of the band."

At first, the trio weren't sure they wanted to go back and revisit it, but recording engineer Richard Chycki had remixed "One Little Victory" and "Earthshine" for the 2009 *Retrospective III* compilation. The band and their fans were impressed enough that the whole album got a mulligan. *Vapor Trails Remixed*, which David Bottrill helmed, was released in 2013 and is now the default version of the album.

While people with more audiophile tastes were happy with the remix, something was lost in the process. By removing its flaws, the emotional impact of the final product was compromised. Still, it's an excellent album, one of the best things the band ever did, and it marked Neil Peart's return to the group, so fixating on the mix is kind of silly.

Opposite: Geddy Lee puts his whole thumb into it at Atlanta's Philips Arena during the *Vapor Trails* tour.

Below: Neil Peart, back with his band and doing what he loved on the *Vapor Trails* tour. It was wonderful to have him back.

Above: Alex Lifeson not wearing white after Labor Day at Atlanta's Philips Arena on October 13, 2002.

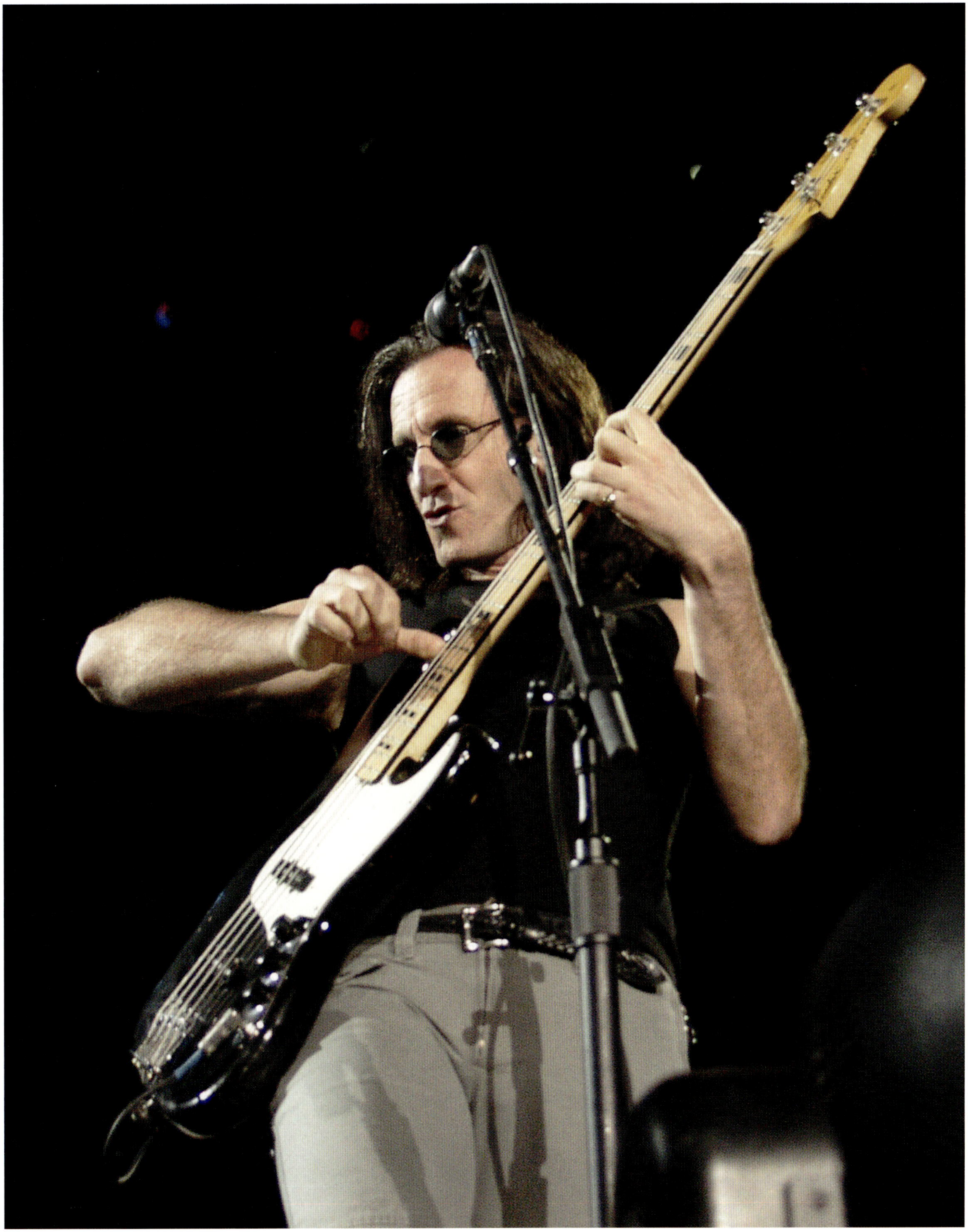

36

"HOLY SH*T, THIS IS RUSH!"

A performing entity comes roaring back to life

Geddy Lee tickles the ivories during the *Vapor Trails* tour.

Finishing *Vapor Trails* was a massive hurdle for Rush. Learning how to replicate the songs live for the tour was another. Lee, Lifeson, and Peart were world-class musicians, but there were still some lingering doubts as to whether the trio could really function the way they used to. It's one thing to come back, but staying is another.

Monitor engineer Brent Carpenter said that in the run-up to the tour, Lee, Lifeson, and Peart experienced a lot of difficulty getting their groove back. It initially seemed like a real uphill climb, if not a doomed effort entirely.

"The new record was so heavily layered," he said. "There was definitely some apprehension about how they were going to re-create it."

He said that Brad Madix, the band's front-of-house engineer from 2002 to 2015, observed the same trepidation pretty much from the moment rehearsals began.

"Most bands go in, do rehearsals, and maybe start with a song that they've done a thousand times," he said, citing "Working Man" as an ideal choice. Instead, the band started with "One Little Victory," setting themselves up for failure.

"It's got that crazy drumbeat at the beginning, then that droning guitar that Al plays, and they've got to figure out on the pedals where the background vocals are lying, where all the sound effects are that are in that song," he recalled.

It didn't work, and the whole day was a frustrating experience for all. When it was over, he and Madix discussed what they had just seen.

"I know what the band sounds like. I own all the records," he said. "What I heard that day was not the band. It was struggle and frustration, frustration with the technology of trying to re-create the tones."

The pair came back determined to get the band off square one. Carpenter said it was as simple as Madix just asking them to "play something."

"They turn around and two, three, four, and they go into 'Tom Sawyer,'" he said. "There's the keyboard, there's the intro sound, there's the drums, there's the guitar. I'm standing there, and I'm like, 'Holy sh*t, this is Rush!'"

Geddy Lee and Neil Peart during the *Vapor Trails* tour on October 13, 2002, at the Philips Arena in Atlanta. Or "Hot 'Lanta," if you're in the know.

FIVE: THE TIME IS NOW AGAIN / 119

Above: He's still got it! Geddy Lee demonstrates his most piercing shriek during the *Vapor Trails* tour at Shoreline Amphitheater in Mountain View, California, on September 20, 2002.

Opposite: Alex Lifeson being the most criminally underrated rock guitarist on earth during the *Vapor Trails* tour.

It made all the difference. While it still took some time to blow away all the cobwebs, this was when they remembered who they were and started becoming a band again.

"It was like, 'Okay, now we're getting somewhere,'" Carpenter said. "They started relaxing and started digging into, 'Okay, how the hell are we going to play these songs?' That was the first two days. But they went into 'Tom Sawyer' and played it like they had just gotten offstage last night."

Rehearsing the *Vapor Trails* material remained a bit of a struggle, but they eventually got the new songs into fighting shape. They did so by rehearsing them in a way that's unique to this particular Canadian power trio.

"They'd get halfway through the song," Carpenter said. "If something's wrong, Ged would give me the hairy eyeball, and I would make a note of something to fix, or he would just tell the keyboard programmer, Jim Burgess, what to fix. . . . Once they got through the song the first time, then every time they would do it again, they would go through it and through it before it was perfected. I've never seen a band work like that before."

Madix said that one of the more significant challenges was mixing Peart's kit now that his style had changed thanks to his lessons with Freddie Gruber. He had come to the tour thinking of Peart as a hard rock drummer but quickly learned that wasn't the case anymore.

"Neil's a jazz drummer," Madix said. "I didn't really work with him before he reinvented his playing style. I went into it thinking, 'Rock drums, rock drums, rock drums.' But the truth is, he was really a jazz drummer, and once you understood that's what you were mixing, then it was really eye-opening. You're not mixing Neil Peart from 1978."

He said that even though the band were returning from a long hiatus, they took their return to the stage as seriously as ever and didn't want to be perceived by their audience as needing training wheels. They wanted to come back as strong as they were when they stepped offstage from the final show of the *Test for Echo* tour, and they put in the time and the work to make that happen.

"They were like craftsmen, and this was their craft," Madix said. "The rehearsals would go on for weeks, and we never went into the first show of a tour feeling unprepared. You always felt like the band had put hours and hours and hours into getting it to this point, and I can't say that about everybody."

FIVE: THE TIME IS NOW AGAIN /121

37

RECORDING IN RIO

Rush endure a grade-A Charlie Foxtrot

After the hiatus of 1997–2002, Rush began to change up their schedule of studio album and live album releases. Rather than release four studio albums in succession, followed by a live album summing up the era, the decision was made to record a new live album right after *Vapor Trails*.

The concert they recorded was at Maracanã Stadium in Rio de Janeiro on November 23, 2002. It was the last night of the tour and the final show of three in Brazil. The evening before, they had played to sixty thousand in São Paulo, their largest audience ever as headliners. It was also their first trip to South America as a band.

"We had been told we were fairly popular there," Peart wrote in the *Rush in Rio* liner notes. "No one was more surprised than this humble Canadian rock trio when we played to more than 125,000 people over those three shows, way beyond any numbers we had attracted before, anywhere."

Before that, the largest crowd they had ever played to as headliners was twenty thousand at the Gorge in Washington State on May 17, 1997. Rio was the second-largest crowd they had ever played for, and between that and the fact that the evening was being recorded for a live album, everything needed to go off without a hitch. As it turned out, it was a day full of nothing but hitches. Monitor engineer Brent Carpenter said that getting from São Paulo to Rio de Janeiro was simply the first infuriating problem of many.

"Instead of getting up at 6:30 in the morning after the São Paulo show, they decided to put us on a passenger bus leaving São Paulo at 3:30 or 4:00 in the morning to drive to Rio," he said. "Nobody does this."

Monitors did not begin to appear onstage until 3:30 in the afternoon. For those who don't know how these things are usually supposed to go, suffice it to say that's very late. It was so late, in fact, that corners needed to be cut to start the show on time.

"This is the first show where they didn't do a sound check, because by the time we got set up and ready, it was 8:15 at night, and the audience was already coming in," Carpenter said.

Brad Madix, the band's front-of-house engineer, agreed that everything was gearing up for the night to be an unmitigated disaster.

"We did a line check through headphones," he said. "I've never done that with those guys."

Alex Lifeson, Neil Peart, and Geddy Lee demonstrate the importance of doing laundry in a timely fashion on the *Vapor Trails* tour.

The problems didn't stop there. Carpenter said the local authorities had decided the band didn't need to eat. They held up the caterers and took all the food away, so anyone hoping to carbo-load before going onstage was out of luck.

"Nobody ate dinner," he said. "The show got held for an hour or something like that. We were supposed to go on at 8:30, and we ended up going on at 9:30."

The *Rush in Rio* liner notes say that all the songs on the album come from the Rio de Janeiro concert except the last two songs: "Between Sun and Moon," recorded in Phoenix, and "Vital Signs," recorded in Quebec City. Carpenter said that, according to certain accounts, that's up for debate.

Those accounts allege that the album uses audio from the previous night's show in São Paulo to patch holes in the Rio de Janeiro recording. The São Paulo concert had been recorded so there would be a safety copy in case anything went wrong the next night, and as it turned out, the Pro Tools system used to record the Rio de Janeiro show stopped working during the performance. The album was said to be assembled from a combination of the São Paulo recording, the ADAT recording of the Rio de Janeiro performance, and whatever parts of the Rio concert had been successfully captured on Pro Tools before the system crapped out.

Whether the allegation is accurate or not, it's not exactly a secret that most live albums undergo extensive cosmetic surgery to hide all the flaws, even when the equipment behaves itself. That includes albums recorded by Rush, such as *Exit . . . Stage Left*. In this specific case, however, one thing is absolutely true: Everything that could have gone wrong that night went wrong, and a triumphant live album resulted anyway.

"The minute they started, that show was magic," Madix said. "It was one of those shows where a couple of songs into it, I was going, 'Wow, this is really good.'"

Once the show ended, the external nuisances plaguing Rush's crew resumed. The moment loadout began, it started raining—and it wasn't a light drizzle either.

"We spent the next four or five hours loading out in a downpour," Madix said. "Everything about that loadout was awful. One of our sound guys fell off the truck and broke his hand. Everything about that day was horrible, except the two and a half hours of the show."

Alex Lifeson during the *Vapor Trails* tour. Would it kill him to shave before he walks onstage?

Geddy Lee plays an extra loud note on September 28, 2002, at the Verizon Wireless Amphitheater in Irvine, California, just in case there are any haters in the parking lot who need to be antagonized.

FIVE: THE TIME IS NOW AGAIN / 125

38
A ROUGH NIGHT FOR AGORAPHOBES
The Rio crowd sings all the lyrics to "YYZ"

With thirty-one songs clocking in at almost three hours, *Rush in Rio* was the band's most comprehensive live album up to that point. It covers Rush's entire history, reaching back as far as "Working Man" and featuring four selections from their current album, *Vapor Trails*. The crowd's excitement is palpable throughout the whole thing and never lets up for a second. In fact, there are moments when they almost overshadow the band they've come to see.

It opens with excellent performances of songs like "Tom Sawyer," "Distant Early Warning," and "Earthshine," but the absolute highlight takes place six songs and less than half an hour in. You have to see the video to appreciate the full effect, so please fire up that *Rush in Rio* DVD and pay close attention when Peart starts playing the ride cymbal intro to "YYZ."

After the intro, the meat of the song begins, and the entire audience of forty thousand jumps up and down in time with the music, a jaw-dropping spectacle the likes of which you just don't see at many concerts. In fact, people watching the footage can be forgiven for thinking some kind of civil unrest is in progress—from a distance, it looks like forty thousand people in the middle of a full-scale riot. The difference is that everyone is smiling and laughing, and there's no tear gas.

The entire crowd then starts singing along with the guitar melody. It's worth stressing that "YYZ" is an instrumental, so to most people, there's nothing to sing along with. That's not a problem for this crowd, who clearly never got the memo.

All the performances on *Rush in Rio* are uniformly excellent, but unfortunately, as with *Vapor Trails*, there were some gripes on the part of the fans about the sound quality. They're not wrong—the mix is noisy and clangy and falls well short of audiophile quality. On the other hand, the crowd's energy is explosive, and you can feel the connection between them and the band. This was clearly an extraordinary night, and luckily it was documented.

That mysterious quality that makes most Rush live albums so good is fully on display here. In the live footage, it's easy to see that the trio know it's an unusually good night. They recognize their connection with the audience as it unfolds. One must also imagine that any professional musician would kill to be embraced this warmly by an audience—*any* audience—and that simply doesn't happen except in the most exceptional cases.

Rush would go on to perform at other venues for more than a decade afterward, and you'd have a hard time finding anyone who said the band didn't put on a fantastic show those nights. But monitor engineer Brent Carpenter said the audience singing along to "YYZ" stayed with the trio long after they left Maracanã Stadium.

"They talked about that in later years," he said. "How often do you hear a crowd sing along to a song without lyrics?"

Alex Lifeson, Neil Peart, and Geddy Lee during the *Vapor Trails* tour, their first time back on the road in the new millennium.

LIVE TRIPLE CD SET INCLUDES WORKING MAN, TOM SAWYER AND ONE LITTLE VICTORY

OUT NOW

THE 2-DISC DVD CONCERT, "RUSH IN RIO", WHICH COMES WITH A 45-MINUTE DOCUMENTARY, WILL BE RELEASED BY SANCTUARY VISUAL ENTERTAINMENT ON 24TH NOVEMBER.

WWW.RUSH.COM

FIVE: THE TIME IS NOW AGAIN / 127

Geddy Lee demonstrates his "Oh!" face at Sound Advice Amphitheater in West Palm Beach, Florida, on July 29, 2004.

39

FOR WHAT IT'S WORTH

The band's first EP and least essential release

In the annals of Rush history, few fans likely said, "You know what I'd really like to hear them do? I'd like to hear them cover eight psychedelic hits that influenced them as young musicians."

In the absence of such fans, the band went ahead and did it anyway. *Feedback* is the group's only EP, and it's entertaining enough the first time you listen to it. You are highly unlikely to listen to it a second time, though.

Some of the group's less essential releases, such as *Hold Your Fire* or *Test for Echo*, reward repeat listens, and hearing them for the first time is different from hearing them for the third time. You may not be won over, but you'll conclude there was more to those records than you first thought. *Feedback*, meanwhile, reveals everything the first time you play it, and once the novelty of Rush playing these crusty old songs is over, there's no reason to ever play it again.

The song selections and performances are all good, although if the EP was meant to recapture the youthful exuberance of a local band aspiring to acid rock glory, it doesn't do that. Instead, what you have here are competently executed, note-perfect versions of other people's music, and few Rush fans in 2004 wanted that.

The guys were all in their fifties when *Feedback* was released, so expecting the songs to convey brash youthfulness is unrealistic. It's also unrealistic to expect the raucous energy of the John Rutsey era to suddenly turn up again after thirty years. The band nonetheless turns in good performances of "Heart Full of Soul," "For What It's Worth," and "Mr. Soul."

"Summertime Blues" and "Seven and Seven Is" come perilously close to inspiring energetic head-nodding in the listener, if not headbanging. The trio also let off a few groovy psychedelic sounds during "Seven and Seven Is," which gives it some attitude. But for the most part, these are all exact replicas of the originals.

Some people gave this EP high praise. In fact, Thom Jurek of AllMusic gave it four stars out of five in a review that waxed ecstatic. "None of these tunes are done with an ounce of camp," he wrote. "They indulge in the hero-worship and dream roots of the garage band that eventually became Rush."

Rush certainly recorded worse things than *Feedback*, and at twenty-seven minutes in length, it's clear they didn't intend for it to be anything but good, clean fun. But the final analysis is that this didn't need to be made. *Hold Your Fire* may have been toothless, and *Test for Echo* may have been a muddle, but both had unique ideas and songs that revealed more of themselves to the listener over time. *Feedback*, meanwhile, is just kind of *there*, and while it may be more immediate than those two albums, it doesn't pay off down the road. Worse yet, there's a strong likelihood listeners will deem these versions no improvement on the originals and go back to "Summertime Blues" as performed by Blue Cheer.

FIVE: THE TIME IS NOW AGAIN / 129

40

HAPPY BIRTHDAY TO YOU

What do you get for the band that have everything?

Rush had observed their tenth and twentieth anniversaries with little fanfare, treating them as they would any other year in which they had a new album to promote. While the thirtieth anniversary coincided with the release of the *Feedback* EP, the band's official website treated that as a secondary consideration when announcing the upcoming tour.

"The 'R30: 30th Anniversary Tour' celebrated the 30th anniversary of the band's definitive formation in July 1974 after Neil Peart replaced original drummer John Rutsey," the website said. "It was also in support of the cover EP *Feedback*."

The tour lasted from May to October 2004, and the September 24 date in Frankfurt, Germany, was recorded for a live album and DVD. Consistent with *Rush in Rio*, it was an attempt to present a single night of the band's tour, and the set list was just as sprawling as it had been two years earlier.

The sound quality is a significant upgrade from that of *Rush in Rio*. If the sound quality on *R30* is meant to act as a sonic apology to fans for the rough sound on the previous live album, then apology accepted. Really though, the likelihood is that the band simply had enough time and resources to make the recording turn out the way they intended, and this was the result.

The set opens with the "R30 Overture," an instrumental medley containing snippets of "Finding My Way," "Anthem," "Bastille Day," "A Passage to Bangkok," and both books of "Cygnus X-1." Lifeson said in the liner notes that it was intended to help the band settle in for the three-hour performance. It also made older fans happy.

"They haven't heard those songs in a zillion years," Lifeson said.

The set list saw the band go deep into its history with songs that audiences probably didn't expect to hear, such as "Force Ten," "Between the Wheels," and approximately 60 percent of "Xanadu." These selections conveyed that the trio still considered their entire catalog relevant. The gesture may have also been meant to throw a bone to their loyal longtime fans, who had stuck with the band through everything.

The only time *R30* gets a little bogged down is when the songs from *Feedback* get an airing. Half of them are spread throughout the set list (this was the tour to promote it, after all), but they're a little jarring in the context of the overall performance. Those cover versions may have only added up to ten or fifteen minutes of the entire set, but it's hard not to imagine what they could have done with those minutes, like play the other 40 percent of "Xanadu." But who's counting?

R30 was released in 2005, and the Rush faithful dutifully reported to the record store to buy it. The liner notes contained a special dedication to the segment of the Rush audience that had hosted the concert: "A personal thank you from Rush to our long-neglected European fans, for their patience and dedication."

A young Geddy Lee watches over the proceedings during the *R30* tour stop at London's Wembley Stadium on September 9, 2004.

Neil Peart looks on as Geddy Lee does a Pete Townshend leap on May 4, 2008, at Concord Pavilion in California.

41

MIDDLE EAST, MIDDLE WEST
Another unique entry in the Rush catalog

When Rush last went five years between studio albums, it was because of a back-to-back set of tragedies that threatened to end the band. The next time it happened, it was just because they had been busy. *Snakes & Arrows* landed on store shelves in 2007, a full five years since the release of *Vapor Trails*, and even for a band that never made the same album twice, it was very different from its predecessor.

Anyone hoping the band would continue in the glum and noisy vein of the 2002 album was probably disappointed to hear the sparkling production on the new album. But overall, the fans were happy to get something more up to their sonic standards. Furthermore, the songs were really good, and unlike on *Feedback*, the band had written them all.

Most importantly, *Snakes & Arrows* was something made outside of the shadow of Peart's late-1990s family tragedies. He would certainly never "get over" the loss of his daughter and first wife, but the varied textures and lyrics on the new record contrasted with the despairing, monochromatic crunch of *Vapor Trails*. It suggested that even if he never fully recovered from those experiences, he had at least moved on to a life with more creativity and less pain. He might just pull through after all.

Regardless of what anyone in the band were going through, there was no debating that the new album, *Snakes & Arrows*, was excellent. It spends much of its duration in waltz time, giving it a lot of back-and-forth sway and swing. It's also very melodically astute and dynamic. In the British sense of the word, it seems like a "proper" Rush album.

One highlight is Lifeson's acoustic guitar, which turns up quite a bit in these songs and even gets its own two-minute solo spot on "Hope." The guitarist said the increased use of the instrument in unamplified form resulted from a suggestion by Pink Floyd's David Gilmour.

"I was playing a lot of acoustic guitars before we started the record," Lifeson said. "I had a meeting with David, and he was a very engaging, charming guy. We talked a lot about the power of the acoustic in terms of writing. It doesn't lie. It tells you straight up whether an idea has merit."

Snakes & Arrows feels less labored over than *Vapor Trails* partly because of the *Feedback* EP. The band had enjoyed the more straightforward recording of the cover songs, all of which took one month to record instead of fourteen. "In some ways, it reset us," Lee told the *National Post* in 2007.

They decided to approach the recording of their 2007 album in the same way. Nick Raskulinecz, who had worked with the Foo Fighters and Velvet Revolver, approached the band directly for the

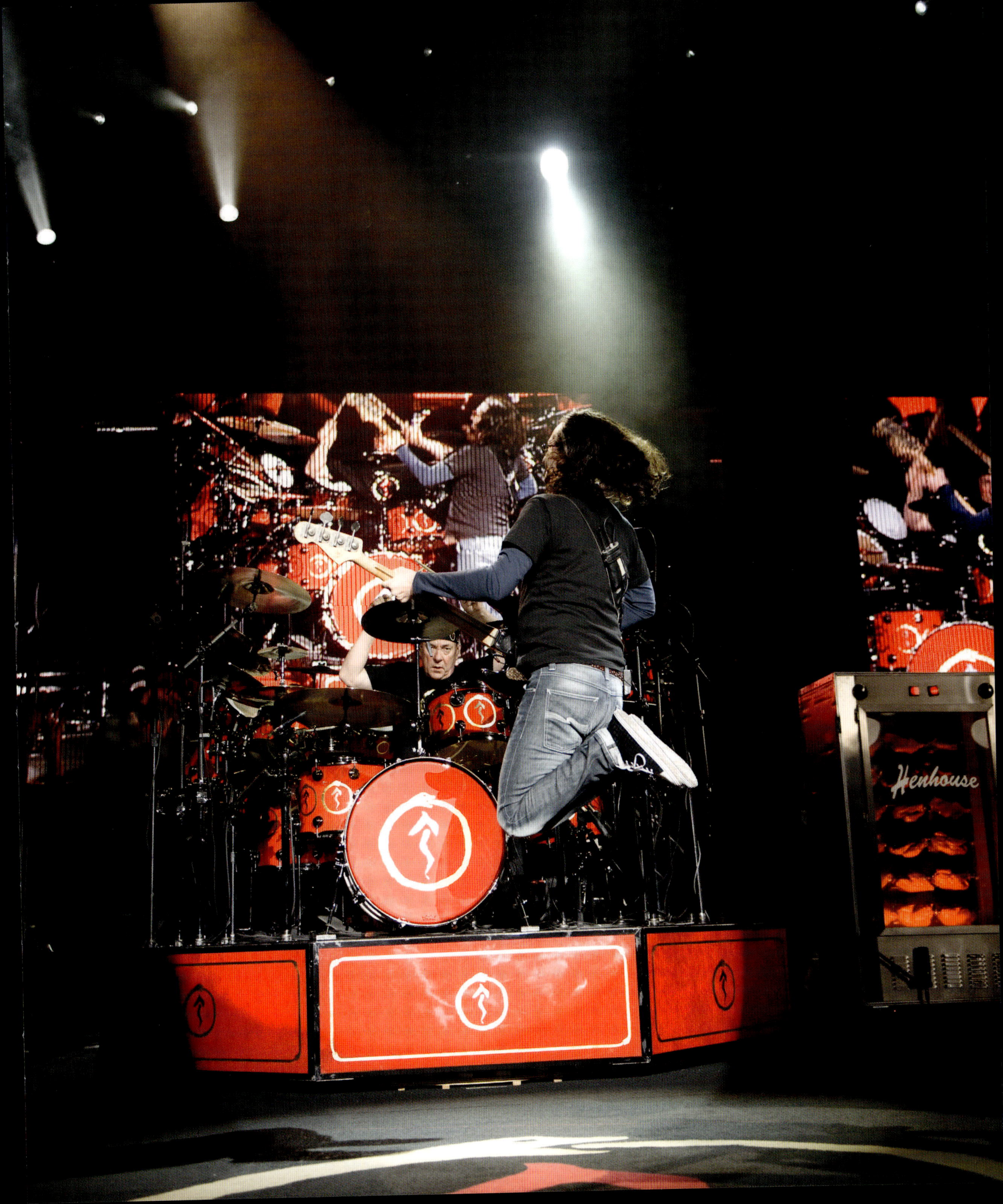
Henhouse

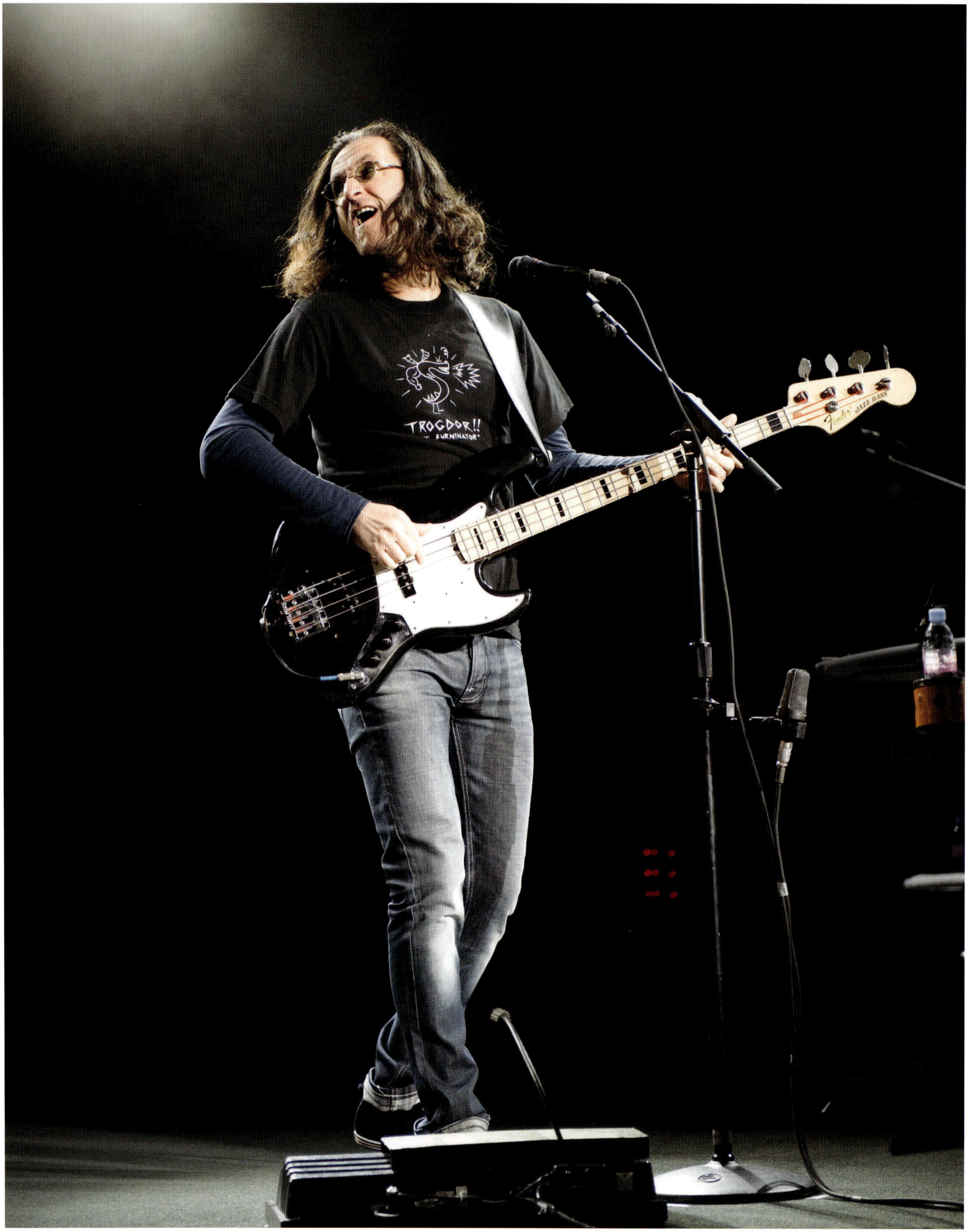
TROGDOR!!
Fender JAZZ BASS

Opposite: Bassist, vocalist, keyboard player, and pedal-stomper Geddy Lee multitasks at the Concord Pavilion in 2008.

Alex Lifeson defies arthritis at California's Concord Pavilion on May 4, 2008, gamely playing through the pain. This would get harder for him in the coming years.

job of co-producing *Snakes & Arrows*. He was almost twenty years younger than the band members and was also a fan, and they found his energy and enthusiasm refreshing. He might have been born around the time the band formed, but he was the right person for the job.

There are no weak tracks on *Snakes & Arrows*, and even the three instrumentals are essential. As with *Vapor Trails*, they had come up with over an hour of very engaging music with no weak spots at all, and whatever weirdness had plagued the 2002 album's original mix is absent here.

Picking the best songs on the album is difficult, partly because everything is consistently good and also because there's an interconnectedness to the music, making everything essential. Removing any of the tracks, even the two-minute "Hope," would diminish it. However, if forced at gunpoint to choose the album's highlights, it would be hard to go wrong with "Far Cry," which opens the album, the eerie "Spindrift," and the topical "The Way the Wind Blows," which is pretty clearly about U.S. military involvement in Iraq.

The instrumental "The Main Monkey Business" is also essential, whether you listen to it individually or as the lead-in to "The Way the Wind Blows." Honestly, this whole record seems to go by in five minutes. As anyone would expect from this trio, it's complex but is accessible and never drags.

If *Vapor Trails* was the sound of these three musicians coming back together and learning how to be a band again, *Snakes & Arrows* shows that they had cracked the code and were back in business. If you were still concerned about Peart's emotional state, this album showed that he was coping and in a better place in his life. It was a relief, and fans were happy to hear it.

Perhaps following his guitarist's example, Neil Peart shrugs off tendonitis at the Concord Pavilion on May 4, 2008. This would get harder for him, too.

FIVE: THE TIME IS NOW AGAIN / 135

42
NEW WORLD MEN
Pop acceptance on the thirty-five-year plan

On June 25, 2010, Rush receive a star on the Hollywood Walk of Fame in a location with convenient ATM access.

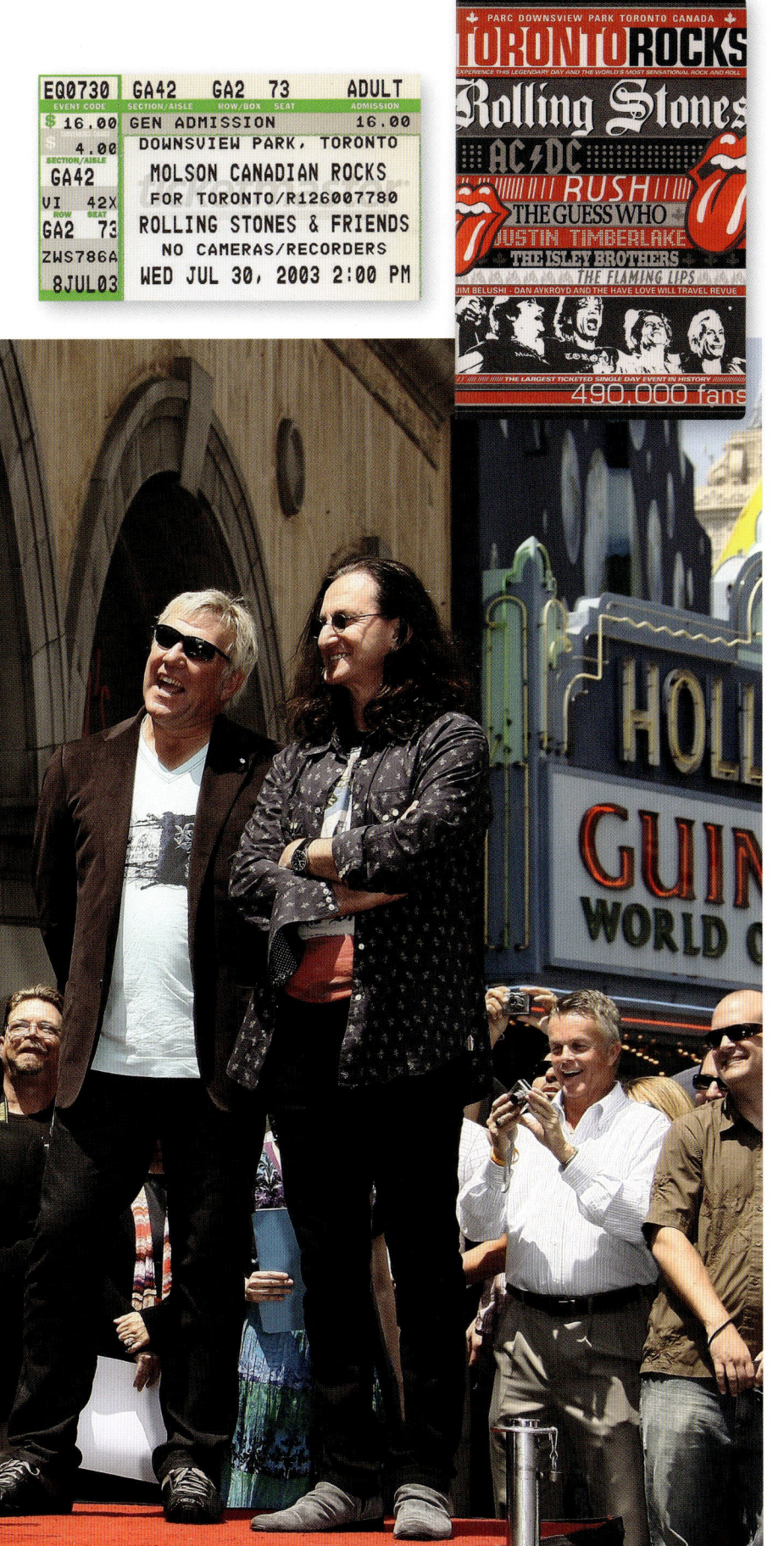

When Neil Peart started talking about returning to Rush in 2000, he may have believed they would pick up where they left off. As Lee said in the 2010 documentary *Rush: Beyond the Lighted Stage*, they had been "the world's biggest cult band" for decades, and there was no reason to believe that would change much upon the drummer's return.

Not only did they come back to find they had lost not one fan, but something even stranger was happening. People who were too young to have been fans during the 1970s—or even the 1980s—were showing up at their concerts and buying their records. Furthermore, the concerts were getting to be well attended by women.

According to popular wisdom, all women hate Rush and would never be caught dead at one of their concerts. Now they were showing up in force, they knew how to do all the air-drumming (including fills), and they didn't even look like their boyfriends had dragged them there.

It got weirder. Some of these Rush fans started having families, and when their kids got to be around eleven or twelve, they began showing up at the concerts with their parents. Rush concerts, previously believed to be the exclusive province of angry teenage boys, now had much broader appeal. You could almost say they had gone mainstream, and the band had never lifted a finger to achieve that.

The hits kept on coming. In 2003, they performed at Molson Canadian Rock for Toronto, better known as SARSStock. The audience numbered half a million people, although, to be fair, The Rolling Stones, AC/DC, and Justin Timberlake were performing, too, so credit for that turnout must be spread equally.

In 2008, they appeared on *The Colbert Report* on Comedy Central, their first U.S. television appearance since *Don Kirschner's Rock Concert* in 1975. The host asked them such questions as, "Have you ever written a song so epic that, by the end of the song, you were actually being influenced by yourself at the beginning of the song?"

They appeared in the 2009 comedy *I Love You, Man*, starring Paul Rudd and Jason Segel. After the 2010 release of the documentary *Rush: Beyond the Lighted Stage*, they received a star on the Hollywood Walk of Fame and then won the Living Legends Award at the Marshall Classic Rock Roll of Honour ceremony.

It was a lot of recognition all in rapid succession for a band that had been frozen out of stuff like that for decades. The band had endured years of hostility and were hated by most of the rock intelligentsia, but no matter what, the fans never went away, and Lee told the *National Post* that the group loved every air-drumming, air-guitaring, and air-singing one of them.

"I love those guys, and they're really good," Lee said. "You can't help but watch them all night and see if they miss anything. And you know, we miss more than they miss."

He said the only way he knew the band could start losing fans would be for them to start playing badly and writing terrible music. Changing their sound and writing songs not about black holes had already proven ineffective at repelling them.

"I don't know what they're going to like when we make a record," he said. "I'm certainly shocked they've stayed with us all these years."

FIVE: THE TIME IS NOW AGAIN / 137

WRETCHED EXCESS

Yeah, but did they ever drive a car into a swimming pool?

Rush are many things, but one of the things they never were was destructive rock star assholes. Most books about rock musicians are packed to the rafters with anecdotes about arrests, heroin overdoses, and violating groupies with mud sharks, but this particular tome is free of such tales, mainly because they don't exist. So, if you're looking for stories about Geddy Lee throwing a television out the window of a Holiday Inn in Akron, Ohio, please accept our sincerest apologies.

Lee, for his part, has admitted to smoking a ton of pot in his younger days and dabbling in cocaine, both of which he gave up decades ago. Today, his only real contact with mind-altering substances comes from being an avid wine collector.

The bassist said in a 2022 interview with CBC Radio 2's *House of Strombo* that the band had used cocaine in their earlier days, primarily so that they could keep up with the demands of touring.

"There was one leg of one tour that we did twenty-three one-nighters in a row," he said. "You're operating on fumes; you're doing whatever it takes to get through to the next show."

In 2023, he told *Rolling Stone* that in "the cocaine years"—the late 1970s and early 1980s—disco dust was so prevalent it was hard to get away from, and he indulged. Even then, he always prioritized the band's performance. "I really didn't do any coke before a gig because I could feel it in my throat, and that was hard on my voice," he said.

What he *really* didn't like, though, was how the drug could quickly go viral within a band and its crew. A tour could conceivably start with one or two people using cocaine, and by the end, it was an entire band and its crew doing it. He didn't say he

he used in the 1990s. He even convinced his wife, Charlene, to join him despite her lack of appetite for drugs.

"We cranked the music and we were dancing, and then we talked for hours about deep personal stuff for what seemed like the first time, even though we'd been married for years," he said. "We were going through a bit of a difficult time in our relationship, and that opened up a lot of doors."

The only time Rush and substances collided violently enough to play out in public was on New Year's Eve in 2003. Lifeson, his daughter-in-law Michelle, and his son Justin were arrested at a hotel in Naples, Florida, after his son got into an altercation with police. Lifeson had intervened on his son's behalf and was accused of drunkenly assaulting an officer.

The guitarist emerged with a broken nose, courtesy of Naples police, who had also tased him and his son multiple times. The matter played out in the courts for years, eventually ending with a confidential out-of-court settlement in 2008.

Peart told *Rolling Stone* in 2015 that along with his bandmates he too had enjoyed using certain substances from time to time. He also said he moved on from using them, just like his bandmates. He credited Lee and Lifeson with keeping him tethered to reality, a service he said they all performed for one another many times.

"We were lucky we had each other to ground us a little bit," he said. "If anybody got out of control, they would be sniped at. But we all went through all that together and just kept going and moved beyond it."

And that, dear readers, is the entire history of Rush as it pertains to sex, drugs, and rock 'n' roll. Mostly, they were well-behaved lads who didn't get into much destructive partying. If you're wondering what their secret was to not letting that stuff sideline them, Peart told *Rolling Stone* in 2015 what his formula was for staying mostly sober over forty-plus years of being a rock star.

"Drinking and drugs just made me throw up," he said. "So that's a pretty good way to keep yourself in line."

Former pot smoker and

FIVE: THE TIME IS NOW AGAIN / 139

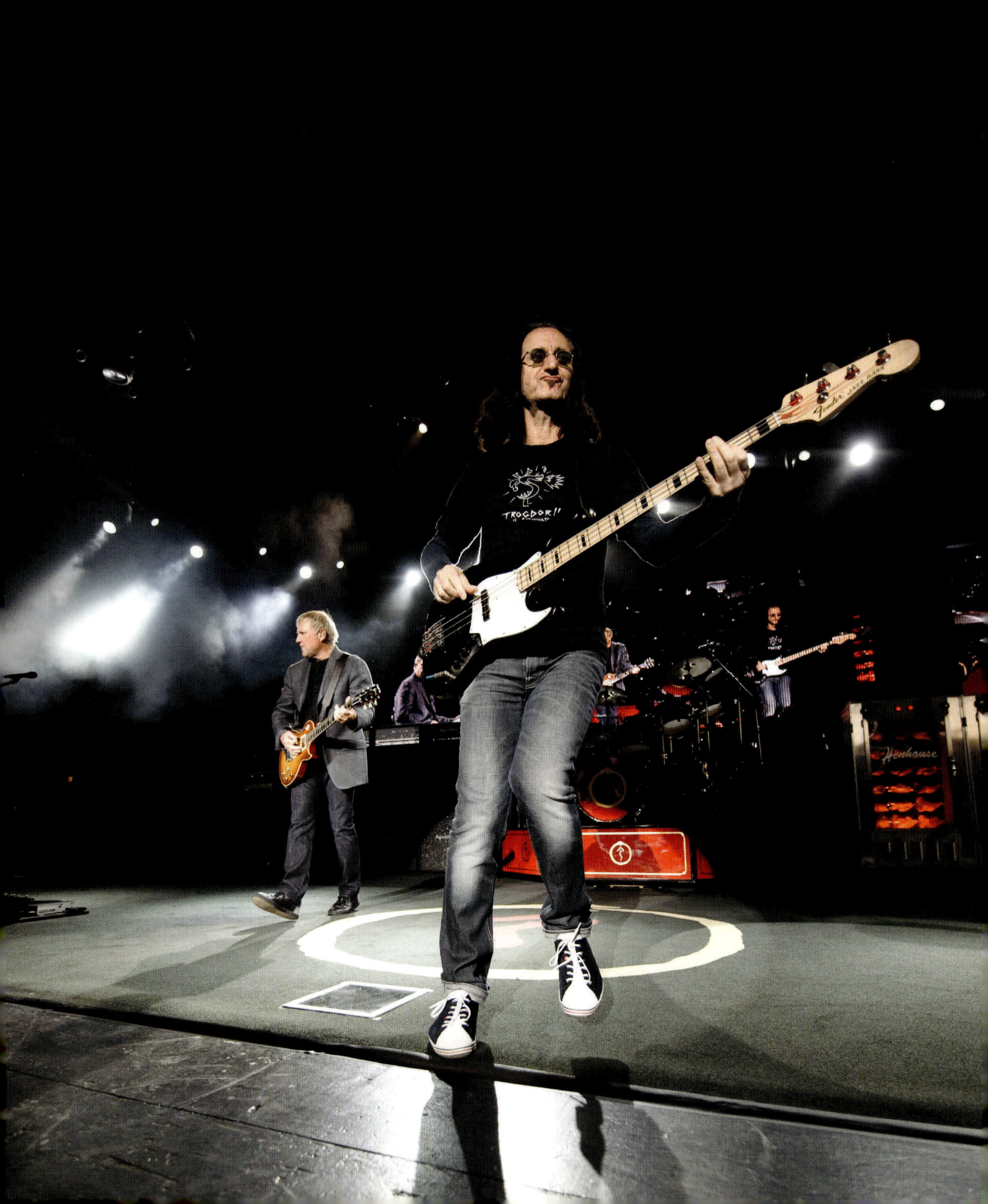
TROGDOR!!
Fender
Henhouse

SIX
TURN AROUND AND SAY GOODBYE

Alex Lifeson strikes an E major chord on the *Snakes & Arrows* tour at the Sound Advice Amphitheater in West Palm Beach, Florida, on June 15, 2007.

43
"THEY LOVED SOUND CHECKING"
Another live album, yet again

In 2008, Rush put out another live souvenir of their most recent tour, *Snakes & Arrows Live*. While their studio-to-live album ratio in the twentieth century was 4:1, the twenty-first century was shaping up to offer a new ratio of 1:1.

Not that anyone was complaining, mind you. *Snakes & Arrows Live* is a solid outing that covers all the bases of the Rush discography, so there wasn't much of an argument to be had with it.

Recorded on October 16 and 17, 2007, at the Ahoy Arena in Rotterdam, the album spans two discs, two and a half hours, and twenty-seven songs. The very generous track list includes some surprises, such as "Entre Nous" and "A Passage to Bangkok," the latter of which had been demoted to medley snippet status at the *R30* concerts.

The most surprising choice is "Circumstances," which the band had never performed live before. Those hoping for a spotless replica of the original didn't get one. The band had to drastically transpose it to a much lower key so Lee could still sing it, and while it's not bad, it doesn't beat the original. The down-tuning is so severe, in fact, that it's not really the same song anymore.

While the set stretches back as far as *2112*, the priority is promoting *Snakes & Arrows*—and boy, do they ever! Nine of the album's thirteen songs get an airing here, and those songs get the most enthusiastic performances of the set. The trio are clearly proud of the material and happy to showcase it to the faithful.

Monitor engineer Brent Carpenter said that when it came to choosing the set list, all three members had to agree on every song unanimously or it didn't get performed. Rush didn't perform "Closer to the Heart" on this tour because Peart didn't want to, and it was as simple as that.

This page: Geddy Lee in 2008, the year he donated six hundred autographed baseballs from his own collection to the Negro League Baseball Museum in Kansas City.

Opposite: Alex Lifeson, Geddy Lee, and Neil Peart in 2008, the same year they appeared on *The Colbert Report*, their first time on American television in thirty-three years.

SIX: TURN AROUND AND SAY GOODBYE / 143

Alex Lifeson in 2008, a long way from the $25 Kent acoustic guitar his parents bought him when he was twelve.

144 / RUSH AT 50

"Neil said no, and that's one-third," he said. "That's how they did it."

He said that at this point, technology had advanced to the point where the group could record their rehearsals with a multitrack console, making it possible for the band to play it back and ask for specific adjustments to what they heard through their monitors. This allowed them to fine-tune the performance to a degree that had never been possible before, and the whole band embraced it, Peart especially.

"Neil would come to me after rehearsals and say, 'During this song, I would really like for the guitar to go away during this section completely, but I need it back in for that section,'" he said. What the drummer had asked for was easily programmable in Pro Tools, so the engineer could make that one adjustment, and it would happen every night of the upcoming tour.

The new equipment didn't help with every technological issue the band faced onstage. They still had to figure out which member should trigger which sample, an ongoing job throughout the entire performance.

"There's an acoustic guitar sample in 'The Larger Bowl' that lasts for four bars," Carpenter said. "Alex couldn't play it because he's doing something with his feet. Ged couldn't do it because he's doing something with his feet. So, we moved the guitar sample into the drum world so that Neil could trigger it."

Sound checking was also a unique process. Peart was always the first to take the stage and start playing, then he would be joined a few minutes later by Lee. They would start improvising together, and a few minutes later, Lifeson would join in. All of this happened without the band saying one word to one another or even making eye contact.

"Suddenly, they're playing some esoteric, jazzy, King Crimson kind of thing, but they're all playing together, and they haven't said a word to each other yet," Carpenter said. "Still to this day, I haven't seen a band that can do that."

Hopefully, those jams were getting recorded and will make a very large and expensive box set one day. Not only would most of the die-hard Rush fans probably buy it, but it would shed some light on what the band were capable of when let entirely off the chain.

"They loved sound checking," Carpenter said.

In general, the way the band worked made Carpenter's job very different from how it usually went with other artists he had worked with. He said that for most bands, there's one member that the monitor engineer works with more closely than the others. Not so with this band. While he may have spent a little more of his time working with Lee, he said that the other members required an almost equal amount of his attention. There were no slouches and no passengers in this group.

"With Rush, it's completely egalitarian," Carpenter said. "Equals across the board."

Per his guitarist's description, Neil Peart pounds the crap out of the drums in 2008 on the *Snakes & Arrows* tour.

44
PLANET OLIVIA
Peart becomes a father again

On June 1, 2009, Peart posted an update to his official blog called "Under the Marine Layer," in which he expounded at length about a boat trip he had taken off the coast of Southern California with "a cargo of hikers, campers, kayakers, and birdwatchers" to see dolphins in their natural habitat.

The drummer had seriously buried the lede, so any readers who tapped out during the first twenty or so paragraphs of the blog post missed the big news. Carrie Nuttall was seven months pregnant, meaning Peart would be a father again. He confessed that the impending arrival was cause for both joy and trepidation. Considering what he had been through a decade earlier, that's not hard to understand.

Neil Peart at the Sarnia Bayfest on July 9, 2010, less than a year after the discovery of Planet Olivia.

"Our baby was growing and kicking, protected and insulated in its own oceanic fluid, its own marine layer," he wrote. "The anxious (not to say terrified) father kind of wished the baby could stay there, safe from harm, and not have to embark upon a life of menace and potential tragedy."

Still referring to himself in the third person, Peart talked plainly about his worries and anxieties. Again, few could blame him.

"He had lost before, and probably couldn't stand to lose again," he wrote. Returning to the parenting game was indeed a leap of faith for him, as it would be for anyone who lost a child.

When his first wife, Jackie, died in 1998, the drummer remarried two years later, which is not unusual—many widows and widowers will remarry after a year or two without anyone batting an eye. Meanwhile, it had been more than a decade since their daughter Selena's accident, and it was a matter of more than just having another kid. He was putting himself back into a very vulnerable position. The man who had once observed that "there is never love without pain" was risking pain again.

Once the baby was born, it was clear that he was glad he had taken the risk. All anyone had to do was read his May 1, 2010, blog post, which he called "Time Machines." It spent more than forty paragraphs on the topic of driving before getting to the latest baby news. Peart and Nuttall had welcomed a daughter the previous August and named her Olivia Louise. Now several months old, she caused her father to ruminate on having babies as a form of time travel.

"Humans don't really have a way to send ourselves into the future—with the sole exception of transmitting our DNA through the delightful medium of babies," he wrote. "Some might say creating something beautiful that endures is a kind of immortality, but even if a story or a song survives into the future, it can't take you with it. Baby can do that."

He referred to her as "Planet Olivia," a celestial body around which he and Nuttall now revolved perpetually. He characterized the effort as "a tempest, a whirlwind, a tornado," as everyone who has ever had a baby will know is the truth. If you've never had the privilege, it's like this: Human babies are very loud and expensive, they generate poop on a 24/7 basis, and they wake you up every two hours to be fed. Every other consideration in life takes a back seat while you acclimate to the new reality and prioritize that. And somehow, you don't mind one bit.

"We all revolved around Planet Olivia, orbiting like weather and communications satellites, fixed by her gravity, and by her radiance," he wrote.

Calling the blog post "Time Machines" was also fitting because Rush were gearing up to go out on their *Time Machine* tour. While Peart was back behind the kit and a husband and father again, he still preferred not to discuss his dark period in the late 1990s, when everything had been taken away from him. It was part of why the drummer never did the meet-and-greet events that Lee and Lifeson did before concerts. He simply didn't want to field those questions from fans or anyone else, no matter how sincerely well intended they might have been.

Be that as it may, the drummer had a question about that period sprung upon him during a 2010 interview with John Roberts of CNN. The journalist didn't press Peart for any details about the "dark times" but asked him what compelled him to end the five-year hiatus and return to the band.

While Peart had not wanted to answer any questions about that time in his life, he didn't angrily tear off his microphone and storm out of the interview, as much as he might have wanted to. Instead, he answered Roberts with a succinct response that summed it all up perfectly.

"Eventually, what you love trumps what you hate," he said.

Next page: Rush at the Sarnia Bayfest in Ontario on July 9, 2010, during the *Time Machine* tour, which saw the band perform the *Moving Pictures* album in its entirety.

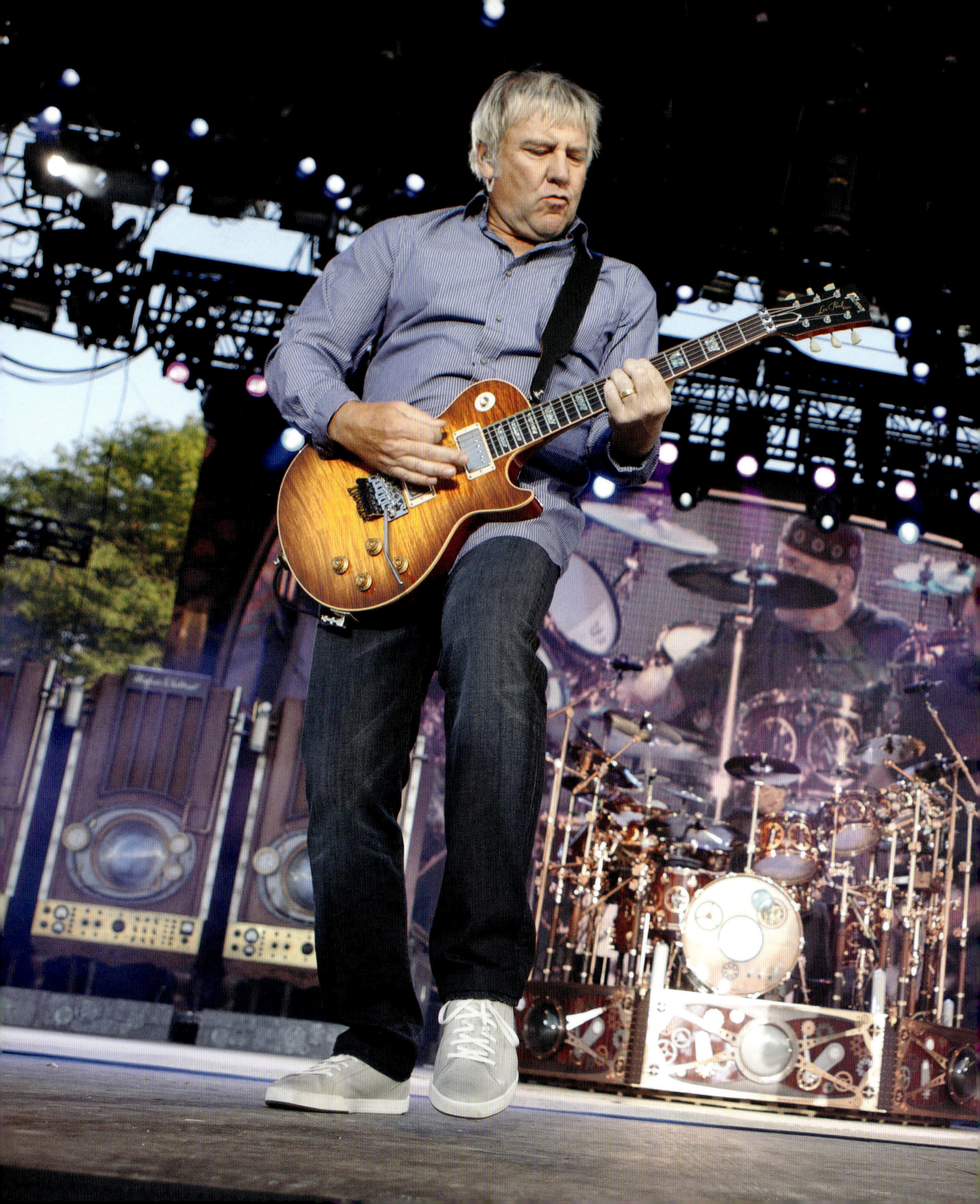

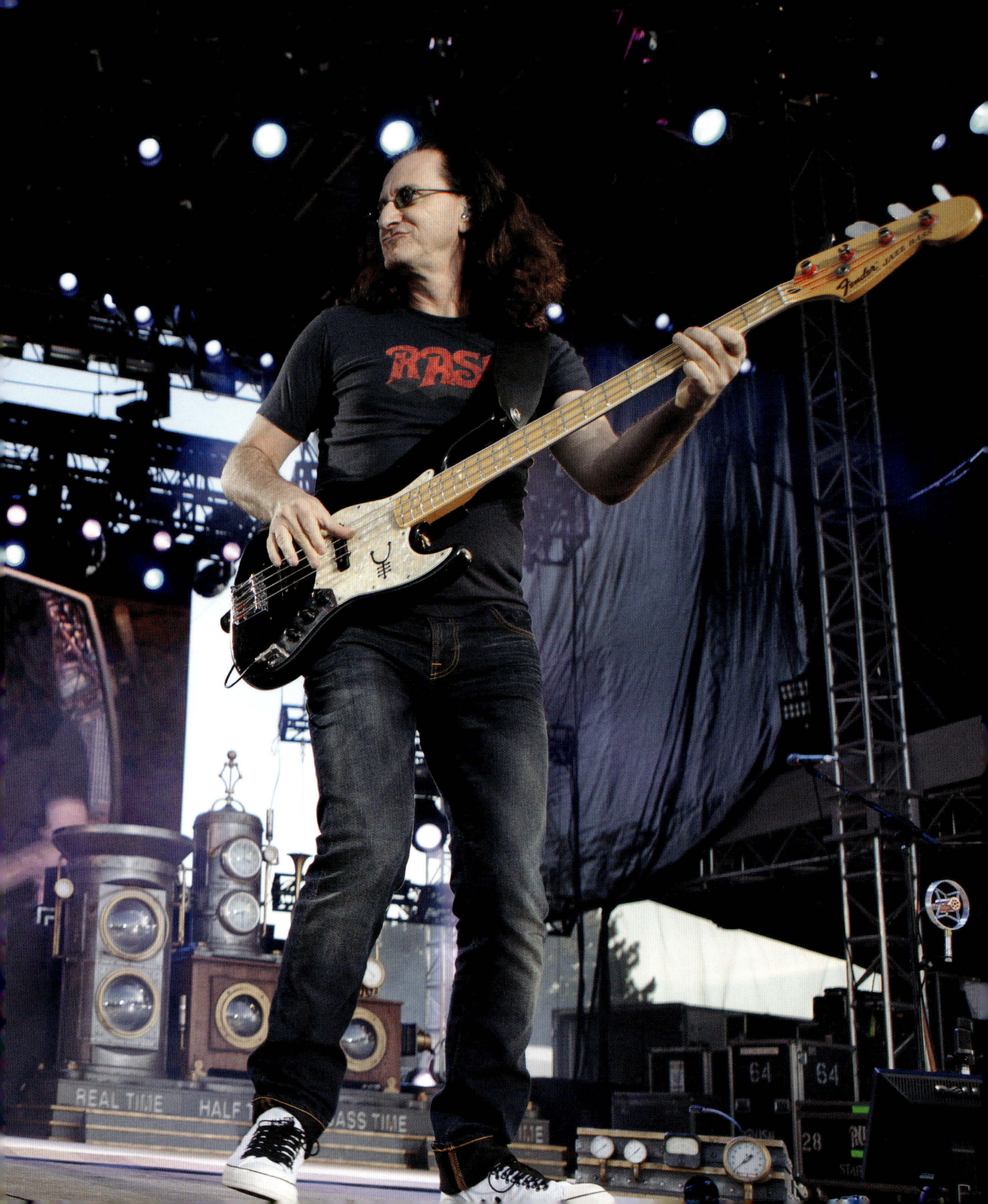
REAL TIME
64
64
28

45
A BOUT OF NOSTALGIA
Rush take a glorious look backward

In 2011, Rush violated the 1:1 studio-to-live album ratio they had followed since *Vapor Trails*. The band had recorded and released two songs, "Caravan" and "BU2B," but rather than record ten more songs and release everything as a new studio album, they went back out on tour. The studio-to-live ratio now stood at 0.16:1.

The resulting live album, *Time Machine 2011: Live in Cleveland*, is notable for three reasons. First, it was recorded in Cleveland, home of radio station WMMS, which had jump-started their career in 1974. Recording a concert in that city was a classy way for the band to honor the place that had been pivotal to their success.

The album is also notable for featuring every song on *Moving Pictures* in sequence. While audiences were happy to hear "Caravan" and "BU2B" performed, seeing their most popular album re-created live and in real time was bucket-list material for most of them.

Sadly, the third reason *Time Machine 2011* is notable is that Lee's singing voice shows the first real noticeable signs of wear and tear. The guy deserves a break, considering that he was now pushing sixty and had sung in the stadiums of the world for close to forty years—time had simply taken its toll. The wearing away of his voice doesn't ruin the performance, but it does provide a realistic picture of what happens to the human singing voice over a few decades, even when you take care of it.

The passage of time also became a consideration when it came to much of the band's gear. A good portion of it was vintage and irreplaceable, so if a Taurus pedal crapped out in the middle of a song, it would have been a real problem. At the same time, getting a warm analog sound out of a digital sample was not always a guaranteed success. The order of the day became balancing reliability with authenticity.

"We were trying to re-create sounds from twenty years prior but do it in a way that was true to the sound, and also do it on a platform that we were confident would work on a daily basis," front-of-house engineer Brad Madix said.

The band gave vinyl fans a treat by giving the *Moving Pictures* portion of the concert its own stand-alone release, *Moving Pictures: Live 2011*. Like the rest of the show from which it was culled, the performance is spotless, and it's neat to hear a song like "The Camera Eye" get dusted off and performed after decades of storage in the musty attic.

Time Machine 2011 is a museum piece for longtime fans and an interesting release for a band that never wanted to look backward. Despite their commitment to musical progression, Rush could, at this point, afford to indulge in a bit of nostalgia, and those who were there to work the concerts knew they were seeing something special. Madix characterized being part of the *Moving Pictures* performance night after night as something he felt lucky to participate in.

"I really, really was honored to have been a part of that," he said.

SIX: TURN AROUND AND SAY GOODBYE / 151

46

"I DO BELIEVE IT'S OUR BEST WORK"
Rush make their favorite album

In 2018, Lee was interviewed by *The Guardian*. He made a bold statement about their 2012 studio album, *Clockwork Angels*.

"I do believe it's our best work," he said.

Of course, most recording artists will say that about whatever their most recent album is, but in this case, Lee meant it. It was Rush's first and only concept album, which is kind of mind-blowing, considering they had a long stretch of sci-fi–obsessed albums that could have easily been turned into "concepts" with minimal effort.

As befits a band like Rush, their decision to make a concept album would have to consist of more than just ensuring every song had at least one mention of "Kilroy" or "Ziggy." Peart had very high artistic goals for this one, as he told *Prog* magazine in 2011. "I intend it to be my highest achievement lyrically and drumming-wise," he said.

He added that coproducer Nick Raskulinecz was actively trying to prod the trio into doing musical things they hadn't done in decades. He wanted Peart to be the same drummer who had auditioned for the band in 1974 or as close to it as possible.

"He wants us to be more Rush than we are," the drummer said. "In the middle of 'Caravan' there's a ridiculous fill, and it was Nick who wanted me to go all the way down the toms and back up again."

According to *Rolling Stone*, Raskulinecz wanted Lee to go back to singing in his highest register, too. It likely wouldn't have happened if Lee's weather-beaten vocal on *Time Machine 2011* is any indication. Still, the coproducer succeeded in getting an album out of them that was incredibly thoughtful and musically heavy as hell.

Clockwork Angels is consistent with the other studio albums made since Peart's return to the group. It not only rocks pretty damn hard but also shows the band as a trio with nothing left to prove. It was the sound of the group being themselves.

As for the story, it's complicated. Kevin J. Anderson, an author who was also Peart's longtime friend, had been interested in collaborating on some sort of ambitious, large-scale creative project with the drummer as far back as the 1980s. In 2012, Anderson revealed on his official Facebook page that it was finally going to happen.

"I'm writing the novelization of Rush's forthcoming album *Clockwork Angels*, their first new CD in five years," he wrote. He provided a synopsis of the epic story, somehow condensing its expansive concept into two sentences.

"In a young man's quest to follow his dreams, he is caught between the grandiose forces of order and chaos," Anderson wrote. "He travels across a lavish and colorful world of steampunk and alchemy, with lost cities, pirates, anarchists, exotic carnivals, and a rigid Watchmaker who imposes precision on every aspect of daily life."

The novel was released in September 2012, followed by a sequel, *Clockwork Lives*, in 2015. A graphic novel followed in 2018. The drummer told *Rolling Stone* that he would have also liked to see the *Clockwork Angels* story adapted for the movie screen,

Neil Peart in 2012 on the *Clockwork Angels* tour. His kit was set up in close proximity to the Clockwork Angels String Ensemble, all of whom had to have their instruments modified in order to be heard over him.

SIX: TURN AROUND AND SAY GOODBYE / 153

Alex Lifeson in 2012, one hundred years shy of the collectivist police state depicted on the band's fourth studio album.

Alex Lifeson, Neil Peart, and Geddy Lee in 2012 on the *Clockwork Angels* tour. Lee would call that album the band's "finest work."

calling it a great "semi-retirement project" for the trio. Sadly, that didn't pan out.

People who didn't want to follow the story (or couldn't) had their hands full with the music anyway. It wasn't quite as out there as *Caress of Steel* or *Hemispheres*, but it's without question a capital "P" prog album with lots of twists and turns, none so intricately complex that they bog down the proceedings. *Clockwork Angels* manages the neat trick of having all the idiosyncrasies of progressive rock while still feeling accessible, so it avoids Mahavishnu Orchestra syndrome.

All the songs are strong, but the album closer, "The Garden," is the best one on the record and hits an emotional note that appears nowhere else in their catalog. They may not have intended *Clockwork Angels* to be their final studio album when they recorded it, but the music has the bittersweet sound of a summing up of the band's career. The lyrics, written by a man whose life had been marked by both painful endings and joyful renewals, suggest an end is coming: "The way you live, the gifts that you give/In the fullness of time/It's the only return that you expect."

It's a sentiment very different from the one Peart expressed in "Anthem." That song said, "Live for yourself, there's no one else more worth living for." The lyrics to "The Garden" seem to push back on that and say that our connections and interactions with others are the most valuable things we have in life. The lyrics indicate that he had learned a lot from his pain and joy and was looking forward to whatever came next.

SIX: TURN AROUND AND SAY GOODBYE / 155

47

DIFFERENT STRINGS
Why add one member when you can add nine?

Throughout their history, Rush toyed with the idea of adding another musician to their touring lineup. If someone could have been drafted to replicate his keyboard parts in concert, it certainly would have simplified Lee's life as the man with the most to do onstage.

Ultimately, the group rejected the idea. They were a trio, they would always be a trio, and upsetting the apple cart by letting someone else trigger samples was not how they did business. Every sound coming from the stage at a Rush concert would come from Lee, Lifeson, Peart, and no one else.

Having said that, if you're going to smash a decades-old prohibition, go hard. That's exactly what Rush did when they repealed their long-standing ban on live backing musicians.

The predictable thing would have been to hire a keyboard player to perform offstage, but Rush never did the predictable thing, nor did they do the "small potatoes" version of anything. This is why, when they finally decided to break with tradition and enlist other musicians on their *Clockwork Angels* tour, they got a string section to back them up, with a conductor and everything.

Dubbed the Clockwork Angels String Ensemble, the new addition consisted of nine musicians. They were cellists Adele Stein and Jacob Szekely and violinists Mario De Leon, Joel Derouin, Jonathan Dinklage (yes, the brother of the actor who plays Tyrion Lannister), Gerry Hilera, Audrey Solomon, Hiroko Taguchi, and Entcho Todorov. They were led by conductor David Campbell.

The *Clockwork Angels* tour spanned seventy-three dates during 2012 and 2013, and the string section figured into it prominently. Front-of-house engineer Brad Madix said that he had mixed live string sections before but never in the context of a rock band. Still, he thought he had a handle on it—Lee would play the same string samples that appear on the album, and the ensemble would double those same parts. Easy peasy.

"If you mix real strings and the sample strings, it sounds pretty realistic," he said.

Campbell wrote the arrangements for the string section, and contrary to what everyone expected, he didn't replicate the parts on the record. Instead, he went rogue and wrote new arrangements for the ensemble that complemented the samples instead of just copying them.

All parties involved loved the new arrangements, but they created a problem. A selection of densely arranged songs had become much more challenging to mix for a live audience, to say nothing of recording them for the intended live album.

Neil Peart in 2012 on the *Clockwork Angels* tour. Being away from his family on this tour was a major factor in his 2015 decision to retire.

SIX: TURN AROUND AND SAY GOODBYE / 157

158 / RUSH AT 50

The string players would now need to be heard loud and clear for everything to work correctly. If the ensemble had only been meant to double the album arrangements, it didn't need the microphones to pick up what they played with 100 percent fidelity. Now, they were going to have to be heard at an equal level with the band, and they were standing onstage right behind the drums, which were played by a man who pounded the crap out of them. This meant the musicians would need a more radical solution to capturing their performances with a microphone.

Madix thought about the possibility of having pickups incorporated into the string instruments. Despite expecting them to say no, he asked the ensemble if they would agree to have their violins and cellos modified that way.

"They were really open to the idea," he said. "They were super cooperative, and they started rehearsing again a couple of days later with these things in place."

With that problem solved, there was now a new one. Live string sections have such a dramatic and all-encompassing sound that they make string synthesizers sound like shrill, pathetic crap by comparison. The song immediately following the *Clockwork Angels* portion of the show was "YYZ," which has a string synthesizer in the introduction. It paled in comparison to the real thing.

Campbell took it upon himself to get around the problem by writing new string arrangements for that song. He even did another for "Red Sector A," which made the *Grace Under Pressure* song sound much more poignant than its studio counterpart, which is pretty poignant as it is.

The November 28, 2012, concert date in Dallas was recorded and released as *Clockwork Angels Tour* in 2013, a title as creative as *Grace Under Pressure: 1984 Tour*. Speaking of the 1980s, the set list contains such Reagan-era deep cuts as "Grand Designs," "The Body Electric," and "Territories," all surprising to hear at that point. The real highlight, though, is the second disc, which features the string section. You can hear the violinists and cellists as clear as a bell thanks to Madix, who appreciated that when you want someone to modify their $100,000 instrument, there's a right way and a wrong way to ask.

"You can't just say, 'I'm going to drill a hole in your violin,'" he said.

Geddy Lee in 2012 on the steampunk-inspired stage set used during the *Clockwork Angels* tour.

48
LIFE BEGINS AT FORTY
10-4, good buddy, over and out

In 2015, the members of Rush had to face a harsh reality. They may have been young on the inside, but the outside was a different story. Simply put, they were getting too old for this.

Lifeson laid it out for *Classic Rock* in 2015. He had battled arthritis for years, but now it was getting much harder to tolerate. He also said that Peart had tendonitis in one arm, which could be crippling to any drummer, no matter who it was.

"I don't know how he gets through playing the way he does, being in that sort of discomfort and pain," the guitarist said.

More than the physical pain, what was really starting to make Peart want to leave touring behind was his new family. The darkest period of his life had ebbed, and while he was happy to be playing and creating, he wanted to focus on his life with Carrie and Olivia. He had talked about retiring from touring decades earlier but prioritized being an active musician. Now, his family was his priority.

The band decided to undertake another major tour, this time to celebrate forty years together. No one referred to it officially as a farewell tour, but it had that vibe.

The maybe-farewell tour can be enjoyed in all its glory on the *R40 Live* CD and DVD sets. Culled from two June 2015 shows in Toronto, *R40 Live* features twenty-nine songs that the band played in reverse chronological order, starting with "The Anarchist" from *Clockwork Angels* and winding its way to "Working Man" from the debut. There were numerous songs that didn't get played a lot during the band's career in the set list, such as "How It Is,"

This page: Alex Lifeson in 2015 on the very emotional *R40* tour. After forty-one years as a band, he would go on to say, "It was enough."

Opposite: A televised Alex Lifeson looms large behind Geddy Lee during 2015's *R40* tour. There were a lot of valid reasons why the band called it quits afterward, but if they had continued touring, the fans would have kept showing up.

SIX: TURN AROUND AND SAY GOODBYE

Neil Peart in 2015 on the *R40* tour, looking forward to the next chapter of his life as a family man.

The last hurrah. Geddy Lee in 2015 on the *R40* tour, wishing the road would go on forever.

"Losing It," and the prelude to "Cygnus X-1 Book II." They added to the "it's now or never" feel of the overall set.

The final tour date was August 1, 2015, at the Forum in Los Angeles. They played a marathon set, and according to everyone who was there to see it, they played their rear ends off. After the final encore, "Working Man," two things happened that could only be interpreted as signs that Rush were really and truly done.

One concerned the drummer's gear. Whenever the band finished a tour, their equipment would be shipped back to their Toronto warehouse. At the end of the *R40* tour, the drummer sent everything to his personal storage locker in Los Angeles.

The second indication that Peart was finished was something more casual fans wouldn't have noticed. When the trio were done playing their final song in Los Angeles, the drummer got up from behind his kit, walked to the front of the stage, and took a bow with his bandmates, something he had never done in forty-one years. With that gesture, many people in the band's orbit knew it was over, from the crew to the die-hard fans. Front-of-house engineer Brad Madix was upset to see it, but he wasn't surprised.

"It was getting harder and harder for him to play those songs," he said. "He wanted to do it to their standard of quality, and I think it just hurt to play like that."

From that moment on, Rush as it had existed for forty-one years came to an end, and with it a triumphant career that had spanned nineteen albums, one EP, and endless, grueling world tours beyond counting. So, what was next?

Lifeson told *Rolling Stone* in 2015 that he wanted to deal with his health issues and spend more time with his grandchildren. Peart said he wanted to spend more time with his family, too, but unlike scandal-plagued members of Congress who say that when forced to resign from office, the drummer really and truly wanted to spend more time with his family. Being away from Planet Olivia had been the deciding factor.

"I realized on the last tour that it's good for her when I'm there, and it's really bad for her when I'm not," he said.

Former WMMS radio music director Donna Halper, recalling a discussion she'd had with him in 2010, also knew he meant to dedicate this next chapter of his life to Carrie and Olivia. He had always regretted being on the road for so much of his first family's life, something he could never make up to them now that they were gone. He wasn't about to squander this opportunity.

"He felt like his second marriage was like a second chance," she said. "He wanted to be sure he could be there for Olivia."

With the *R40* tour complete, Peart and his gear made their way to California, and Rush were over. Not long after, Lifeson confirmed to the *Toronto Globe and Mail* what a lot of people had hoped was not true: "We have no plans to tour or record anymore," he said. "We're basically done. After forty-one years, we felt it was enough."

SIX: TURN AROUND AND SAY GOODBYE / 163

49
IN PRAISE OF NEIL ELLWOOD PEART (1952–2020)
"I miss him even to this day"

In 2019, former WMMS radio music director Donna Halper visited Toronto and had lunch with Pegi Cecconi, vice president at SRO/Anthem. While catching up, Halper said, "I'm not hearing anything from Neil. How's he doing?"

Cecconi begged off the question. The following year, Halper found out why.

"I was on the phone talking to a friend of mine when the bulletin came across the wire that he had passed," Halper said. "I had no idea he was that sick. It broke my heart."

As it turned out, very few people knew. The drummer had been diagnosed with glioblastoma, an aggressive form of brain cancer. The handful of people who knew about it didn't mention it to anyone, because he had asked them not to.

"Neil did not want anyone other than very, very close family to know how sick he was," she said.

Peart passed away on January 7, 2020. Nothing was said publicly until three days later, on January 10, when Rush sent out a statement disclosing the news:

"It is with broken hearts and the deepest sadness that we must share the terrible news that on Tuesday our friend, soul brother and bandmate of over 45 years, Neil, has lost his incredibly brave three and a half year battle with brain cancer (Glioblastoma). We ask that friends, fans, and media alike understandably respect the family's need for privacy and peace at this extremely painful and difficult time. Those wishing to express their condolences can choose a cancer research group or charity of their choice and make a donation in Neil Peart's name. Rest in peace brother." Neil Peart September 12, 1952–January 7, 2020.

According to those who knew him, the intensely private drummer wasn't the sort of person who would disclose to the world that he was terminally ill. Halper surmised that there were other reasons he kept the news under wraps.

"The moment people know that you're ill, they want to come visit," she said. "They're all well meaning, but you may just feel like garbage and don't want to see people."

Furthermore, she believed Peart wanted to be remembered as he was, not as an object of pity. She also thought he was trying to protect his family from the circus that would likely ensue if the news got out.

"He had every right to keep his health private," she said.

Front-of-house engineer Brad Madix said that before Peart's passing, rumors had circulated among the core crew that the drummer had been ill. He said that the fact that the news didn't get out until it was supposed to said a lot about the band, their organization, and the people around them.

"That news would have leaked in a lot of camps, but because this was Rush, everybody respected the fact that they did not want everybody to know about this," he said.

Keeping news like that under wraps for nearly four years surely took a significant emotional toll on Lee and Lifeson. Monitor engineer Brent Carpenter said he wasn't surprised they chose to carry that burden as long as they did, as painful as it was. They were friends first and members of Rush second, and he mentioned a story to demonstrate his point that dated back to the band's earliest days with Peart. Their manager, Ray Danniels, had asked them how they wanted their publishing money split up.

"They said, 'Split it three ways equally and promise that we never have to have this discussion again,'" Carpenter said.

Royalties aside, the most striking thing about the trio was their lack of pretense. All that distinguished them from the general population was their musical talent, which they made the primary feature of the group beyond anything else. They may have been rock musicians, but they would never be rock stars, and they conducted themselves without ego the entire time they were together. Carpenter said they preferred it that way, Peart especially.

Neil Peart in 1978, just a few years after leaving the farm equipment business for bigger and better things.

SIX: TURN AROUND AND SAY GOODBYE

A view from the back line during the *Hemispheres* tour at London's Hammersmith Odeon in May 1979. If you were Neil Peart, this is what you saw every night of your life as a touring musician.

"On the *Snakes & Arrows* tour, a kid named Anson worked on the crew," he said. "Neil went outside for a smoke, and Anson did, too."

The drummer and the crew member introduced themselves to each other. Anson asked his new smoking buddy what he did for a living.

"Neil looks at him and goes, 'I'm a drummer,'" Carpenter said. "Anson goes, 'Cool,' puts his cigarette out, and walks back in. Neil loved the fact that Anson had no clue who he was."

Peart's death was made worse by the fact that two months later, the COVID-19 pandemic started. Large gatherings where people could share their grief couldn't happen due to social distancing requirements, so there could be no "Concert for Neil" where tens of thousands could come together and celebrate him. Instead, the whole world shut down, interfering with the grieving process for anyone who had only found out he had been sick on January 10, 2020.

Once the pandemic ended, the tributes began. While they helped some people start to come to terms with their grief, the people who knew him still felt a void, and it's still there.

"I miss him even to this day," Halper said.

Neil Peart, the Professor, the youngest person ever to win the *Modern Drummer* Readers Poll Hall of Fame, and the greatest drummer who ever lived.

Neil Peart gives a master class in percussion to the audience at New York City's Palladium on May 10, 1980.

SIX: TURN AROUND AND SAY GOODBYE / 167

50
EPILOGUE
"It's what we do"

Geddy Lee and Alex Lifeson on April 7, 2017, at the Rock & Roll Hall of Fame Induction Ceremony at Barclays Center in New York City. That night, Lee played bass with Yes in place of one of his idols, the late Chris Squire.

Despite Rush ending their career on a very high note with the *R40* tour, a feeling of unfinished business had persisted since January 10, 2020. Many Rush fans wanted Lee and Lifeson to carry on, usually naming very technical drummers who could conceivably take Peart's place.

That's a tall order, and not just because Neil Peart was the greatest drummer who ever lived. He was also the band's lyricist, a job he performed like no one else before or since.

Besides that, would the fans accept someone who tried to step into those shoes? Most drummers probably would not want to find out. In general, it's a losing proposition being the person who steps into the void left by a beloved band member, especially when that band member has passed away. The fans are just unlikely to accept you.

At the same time, there was a desire to complete whatever work Peart had left unfinished. With the approval of Carrie Nuttall, Kevin J. Anderson completed the third and final novel in the *Clockwork Angels* series, *Clockwork Destiny*, which was published in 2022. That same year, Lifeson released an album with a new band called Envy of None, whose music was atmospheric, largely instrumental, and sounded nothing like Rush at all.

Lee, meanwhile, struggled with moving on. Unlike Lifeson and Peart, he had not been plagued by painful health issues that put his performances at risk, and he was still raring to go when the *R40* tour finished. He released a book in 2018, *Geddy Lee's Big Beautiful Book of Bass*, and played with various musicians in one-off capacities, but he had taken the end of the band very hard. It had been a kind of death in itself, really.

In 2023, he released the memoir *My Effin' Life*. While promoting it, the question of his musical future kept coming up. He told *Rolling Stone* that the 2022 tribute concert for the Foo Fighters' Taylor Hawkins at Wembley Arena was the first time he had really felt good about playing since leaving the Los Angeles Forum in 2015. It reminded him why he was in the business in the first place.

"The atmosphere at that gig was just magic," he said. "I know it sounds corny, but there really was so much love in that building at Wembley. It was the most special gig I think I've ever done in my life, in that regard."

Lee said the concert had been a restorative experience for him, one that reminded him why he had become a musician in the first place. Simply put, he loved to play, he loved being onstage, and he loved the company of other musicians. He said that performing

Geddy Lee at the *South Park* 25th Anniversary Concert at Red Rocks Amphitheater in Morrison, Colorado, on August 10, 2022.

SIX: TURN AROUND AND SAY GOODBYE / 169

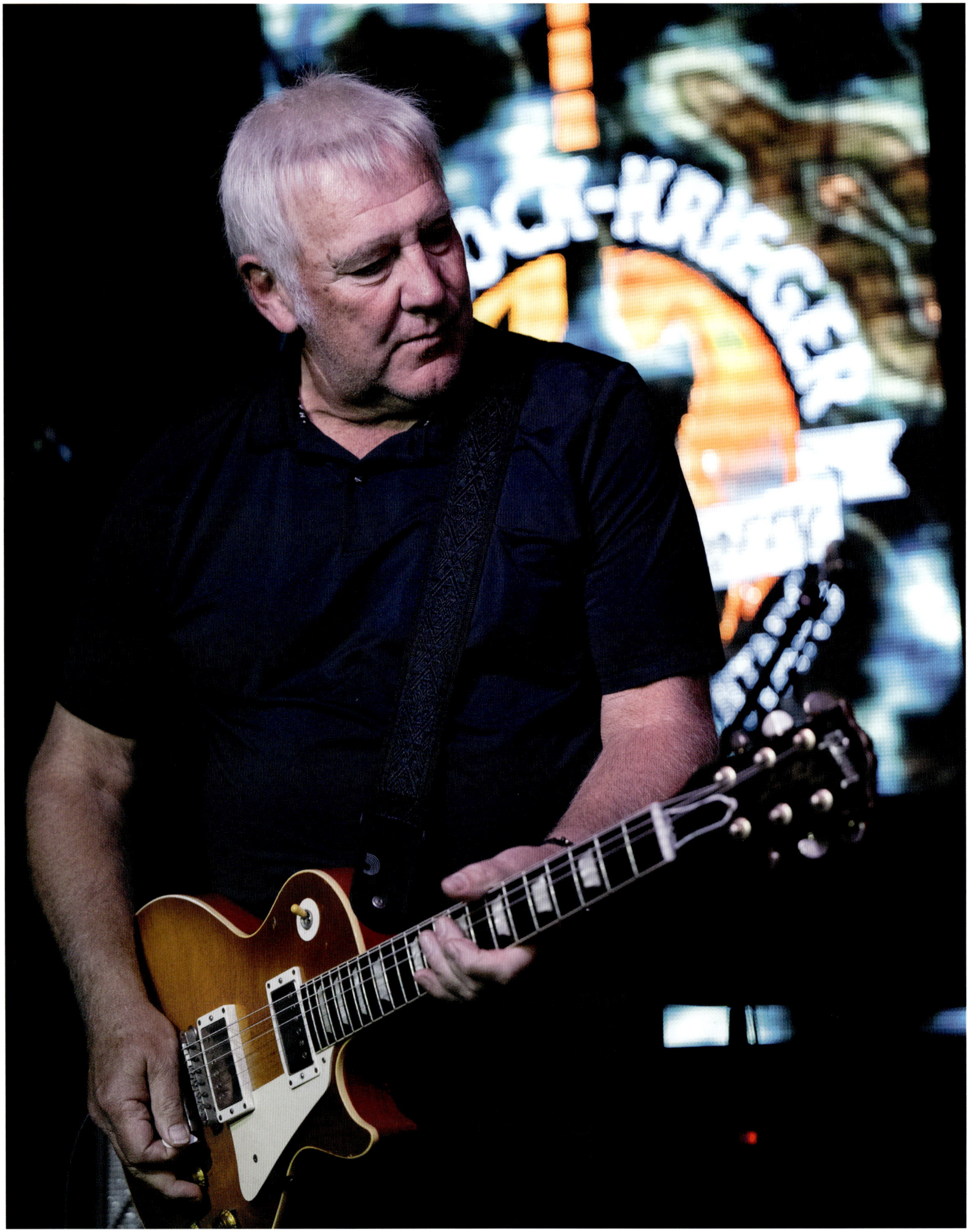

This page: On December 17, 2023, during the book tour for Geddy Lee's memoir *My Effin' Life*, Alex Lifeson was a special effin' guest.

Opposite: Alex Lifeson performs at Bogie's on October 24, 2022, in Westlake Village, California, at a 2022 tribute concert for artist Scott Medlock.

at the tribute concert made him understand that his *shiva*—the traditional Jewish period of mourning—needed to pass.

"The grief has to end, and something else has to replace it," he said. "What do you replace it with? Remembrance, respect, and homage."

After performing a few Rush songs with Lifeson at the tribute, Lee said that he could see teaming up with the guitarist again at some point under the "Rush" name. The fans summarily went crazy and took this as a sign that the two schoolmates would draft a new drummer, put on kimonos, and go out and perform "Xanadu" again. Lee had to walk the comment back, saying that he was simply observing that the possibility existed. He was not saying the band were getting back together, just that they *could*.

Still, the tantalizing possibility of Lee and Lifeson suiting up again for the road wouldn't go away. No less a luminary than Paul McCartney told Lee and Lifeson that they should get back out on the road again. They were musicians, and not using their gift when the public still wanted it was a waste.

"He was very emphatic, talking about, 'You know what Ringo always says: 'It's what we do,'" Lee said.

He also stressed that he was speaking hypothetically when he said that he and Lifeson could team up again and call it "Rush."

"I don't know how comfortable we would be doing that, calling ourselves Rush," he said. "But we could always call ourselves some other stupid name, or Rash."

He was, however, emphatic that if they were to start playing together again—whatever they called it—they would not choose a name that stunk of a nostalgia effort designed to fleece Boomers and Gen Xers of their hard-earned money as they attempted to relive the past. That meant that if they decided to go through with it and get back out there again, "Lee and Lifeson Play the Songs of Rush" would not be what they called it.

"That really sounds like an old-fart eighties band," he said.

SIX: TURN AROUND AND SAY GOODBYE / 171

BLAH, BLAH, BLAH

A boisterous induction into the RRHOF

Alex Lifeson gives a sincere and well-thought-out speech at Rush's induction into the Rock & Roll Hall of Fame on April 13, 2013.

Rush were first nominated for the Rock & Roll Hall of Fame in 1998. Fifteen years later, they got in. If you're wondering why it took so long, people close to the band can answer that with two words: Jann Wenner.

The co-founder of both *Rolling Stone* magazine and the Rock & Roll Hall of Fame, Wenner has been said not to enjoy the band's music overly much. Lifeson told the *Hamilton Spectator* in 2013 that the publisher had said Rush would never, ever get into the Rock & Roll Hall of Fame while he still drew breath.

"We kind of wore it as a badge of honor that there was a core inside the committee that did not want us in there," he said. "Some said, 'Over my dead body,' literally, 'before Rush gets in here.'"

Well, they got in there, and when Wenner was at the induction ceremony, he was alive.

Former WMMS radio music director Donna Halper said Wenner hadn't necessarily changed his mind about the trio. Rather, the culture at the Rock & Roll Hall of Fame had changed. Many of the judges from the old guard had stepped down, and the younger ones who replaced them did not share their predecessors' hostility toward the Canadian trio. The band had outlasted the deranged hatred they once received from critics.

The passage of time was only one factor. Rush fans were relentless in their efforts to get the band inducted, and combined with the changing culture at the Hall, the situation tilted in the band's favor.

"We had done everything short of lighting ourselves on fire," Halper said. "We petitioned, we wrote letters. I did everything legally possible that I could do. We never gave up."

The trio recognized that their very persistent fans had put them over the top. Ironically, the publication in which Lee explained that was none other than *Rolling Stone*.

"I appreciated how much it meant to our fan base," he said. "It was kind of a cause they championed."

He also identified another reason why the band were being inducted. All three members were roughly sixty years old at that time, putting them in the age bracket where people who once talked all kinds of smack about you will suddenly start handing you trophies.

"It's the life achievement period of your career," Lee said.

The trio may have been polite folk who wanted to collect their statuettes without fanfare, but that became impossible when Wenner took to the lectern to announce the evening's inductees. In each case, he announced the city where the artist being inducted was from, then gave the artist's name.

"All he said was, 'And from Toronto . . .' and the whole room exploded," Lee told *Toronto Life*.

Wenner gave his prepared comments to a deafening roar of boos. To his credit, he stayed up there and finished his speech, perhaps finally aware that Rush fans will burst through brick walls if it means being of some small assistance to their heroes.

Halper was one of the people booing, but she said she never suspected Wenner of anything nefarious in keeping Rush out of the Hall. He just didn't like their music.

"He couldn't understand why people liked them, because *he* didn't like them," she said.

The trio came to the stage, and both Lee and Peart gave what one would call traditional acceptance speeches. Then Lifeson, who had written and attempted to memorize a prepared speech, came to the microphone and said, "Blah, blah, blah," over and over again for several minutes.

Some who saw it thought the guitarist was engaged in an edgy act of performance art whose subtext was that the Rock & Roll Hall of Fame is a bunch of hooey. He told *Rolling Stone* that was not the case at all. Instead, before the ceremony, he had told his wife Charlene that he would be unable to remember everything he had written and would go up there and say, "Blah, blah, blah." Just before Rush's induction, honoree Quincy Jones gave a very long speech, prompting Charlene to ask her husband of many years if he was still going to get up there and say, "Blah blah blah."

"When we were walking up onstage, that was really when I committed to it," the guitarist said.

While it was true that there had been systemic changes at the Hall that played in the group's favor, there was no question that the band got in because the fans got them in. Despite being part of that campaign, Halper bore Wenner no personal animosity, since his whole reason for opposing the band as long as he did was because he didn't like their music.

"He's entitled to his opinion," she said. "But that opinion, if I may say, is wicked stupid."

SIX: TURN AROUND AND SAY GOODBYE / 173

DISCOGRAPHY

The Rush discography consists of nineteen studio albums, one EP, and eleven live albums. Only those original, official albums appear here, so no bootlegs, compilations, home videos, singles, box sets, or reissues. *R30: 30th Anniversary World Tour* and *R40 Live* are hybrid video/audio releases, but for those, we've listed the audio portion only.

To reduce redundancy, many corners have been cut. Rush's most frequent songwriting credit is "Music by Geddy Lee and Alex Lifeson, lyrics by Neil Peart," per the official website. Assume that for everything unless otherwise indicated in "Notes."

The lineup is Geddy Lee (lead vocals, bass), Alex Lifeson (guitar), and Neil Peart (percussion). Assume all that, too, unless there's something in "Notes" that says otherwise. Some album credits show Peart playing "crotales," "cymbals," "electronic percussion," and so on. All of that is filed under "percussion." Same with guitars, basses, and lead vocals. It was tempting to include "synthesizers" as something you can assume is being played by Lee, but it's not that simple, so it goes in "Notes."

All deviations outlined in "Notes" are only listed once, so the *Moving Pictures* entry says the lyrics to "Tom Sawyer" were written by Neil Peart and Pye Dubois, but that is not restated in the *Exit . . . Stage Left* entry. Also, Rush coproduced the majority of their albums, so I'm only listing coproducers unless Rush or someone else alone acted in that capacity. Some of the live packages don't list an outside producer, so those are credited to Rush alone.

Albums have their tracks enumerated in a single list, like on a compact disc, digital download, or streaming platform. Multidisc sets have track lists displayed by each disc. Finally, if a track has subsections marked by Roman numerals, that gets one mention.

All information comes from the official Rush website and the fan sites Cygnus-X1.net and 2112.net. U.S. catalog numbers come from Discogs.com and designate the original U.S. pressing. Great care has been taken to ensure veracity, but if I've made a mistake in a book about Rush, I'm sure someone from the fan community will be happy to let me know.

STUDIO ALBUMS

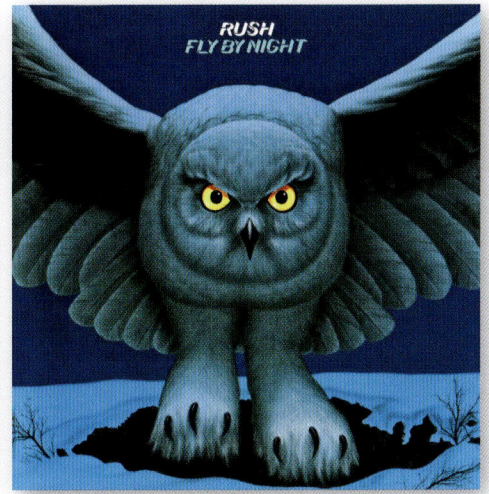

RUSH

Released March 18, 1974. Moon. MN 100.

Recorded March 1973 at Eastern Sound, Toronto; November 1973 at Toronto Sound, Toronto.

Produced by Rush.

1. Finding My Way (5:06)
2. Need Some Love (2:19)
3. Take a Friend (4:24)
4. Here Again (7:35)
5. What You're Doing (4:22)
6. In the Mood (3:34)
7. Before and After (5:34)
8. Working Man (7:10)

Notes: Lyrics by Geddy Lee and Alex Lifeson except "In the Mood," by Geddy Lee. Drums and backing vocals by John Rutsey.

FLY BY NIGHT

Released February 15, 1975. Mercury. SRM-1-1023.

Recorded December 1974 at Toronto Sound.

Coproduced by Terry Brown.

1. Anthem (4:22)
2. Best I Can (3:25)
3. Beneath, Between, and Behind (3:02)
4. By-Tor and the Snow Dog (8:37)
   I. At the Tobes of Hades
   II. Across the Styx
   III. The Battle
   IV. Epilogue
5. Fly by Night (3:21)
6. Making Memories (2:58)
7. Rivendell (4:57)
8. In the End (6:47)

Notes: "Best I Can," "Fly by Night," and "Rivendell" music by Geddy Lee. "Beneath, Between, and Behind" music by Alex Lifeson. "Best I Can" lyrics by Geddy Lee. "In the End" lyrics by Geddy Lee and Alex Lifeson.

DISCOGRAPHY / 175

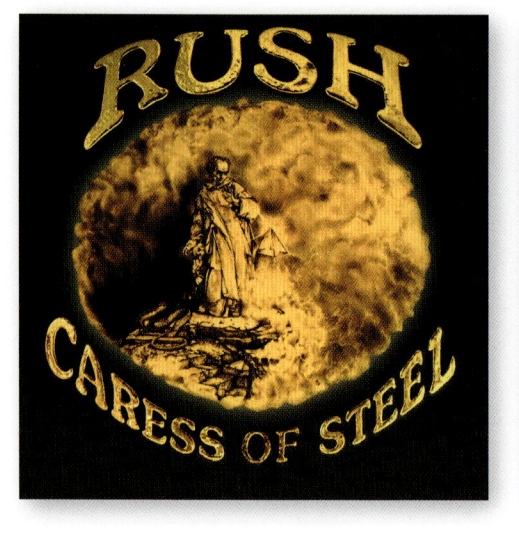

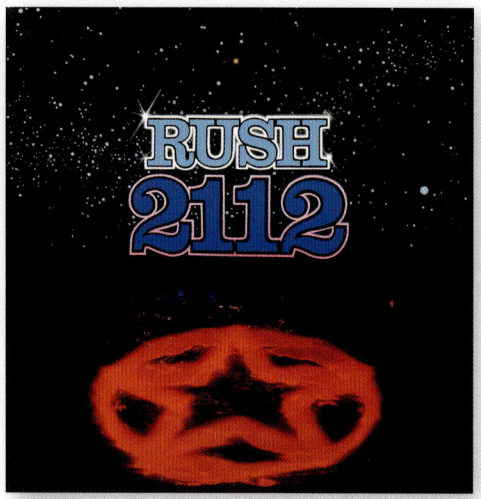

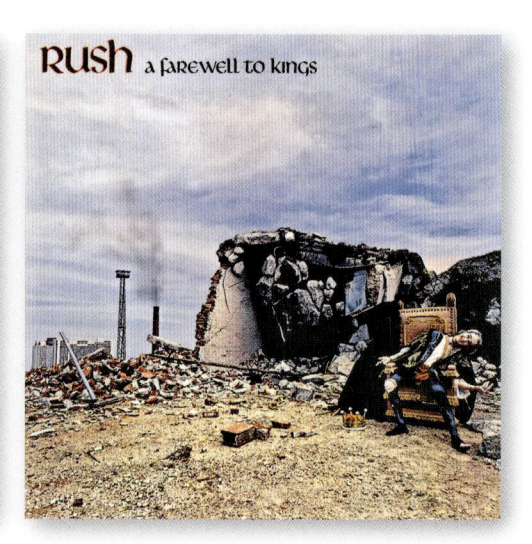

CARESS OF STEEL

Released September 24, 1975. Mercury. SRM-1-1046.

Recorded July 1975 at Toronto Sound.

Coproduced by Terry Brown.

1. Bastille Day (4:37)
2. I Think I'm Going Bald (3:37)
3. Lakeside Park (4:08)
4. The Necromancer (12:30)
  I. Into Darkness
  II. Under the Shadow
  III. Return of the Prince
5. The Fountain of Lamneth (19:59)
  I. In the Valley
  II. Didacts and Narpets
  III. No One at the Bridge
  IV. Panacea
  V. Bacchus Plateau
  VI. The Fountain

2112

Released April 1, 1976. Mercury. SRM-1-1079.

Recorded February 1976 at Toronto Sound.

Coproduced by Terry Brown.

1. 2112 (20:34)
  I. Overture
  II. Temples of Syrinx
  III. Discovery
  IV. Presentation
  V. Oracle: The Dream
  VI. Soliloquy
  VII. The Grand Finale
2. A Passage to Bangkok (3:34)
3. The Twilight Zone (3:17)
4. Lessons (3:51)
5. Tears (3:31)
6. Something for Nothing (3:59)

Notes: ARP Odyssey synthesizer, synth guitar, and Mellotron by Hugh Syme.

A FAREWELL TO KINGS

Released August 29, 1977. Mercury. SRM-1-1184.

Recorded June 1977 at Rockfield Studios, Rockfield, Wales.

Coproduced by Terry Brown.

1. A Farewell to Kings (5:51)
2. Xanadu (11:08)
3. Closer to the Heart (2:53)
4. Cinderella Man (4:21)
5. Madrigal (2:35)
6. Cygnus X-1 Book I: The Voyage (10:25)

Notes: "Closer to the Heart" lyrics by Neil Peart and Peter Talbot. "Cinderella Man" lyrics by Geddy Lee.

HEMISPHERES

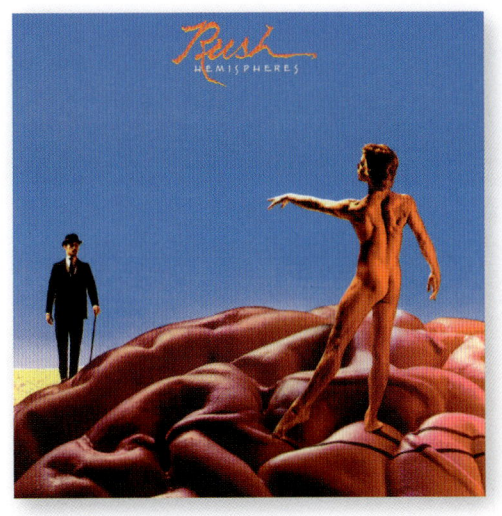

Released October 24, 1978. Mercury. SRM-1-3743.

Recorded June–July 1978 at Rockfield Studios and Advision Studios, London.

Coproduced by Terry Brown.

1. Cygnus X-1 Book II: Hemispheres (18:05)

I. Prelude

II. Apollo: Bringer of Wisdom

III. Dionysus: Bringer of Love

IV. Armageddon: The Battle of Heart and Mind

V. Cygnus: Bringer of Balance

VI. The Sphere: A Kind of Dream

2. Circumstances (3:41)

3. The Trees (4:46)

4. La Villa Strangiato (An Exercise in Self-Indulgence) (9:35)

I. Buenas Noches, Mein Froinds!

II. To Sleep, Perchance to Dream . . .

III. Strangiato Theme

IV. A Lerxst in Wonderland

V. Monsters!

VI. Danforth and Pape

VII. The Waltz of the Shreves

VIII. Never Turn Your Back on a Monster!

IX. Monsters! (Reprise)

X. Strangiato Theme (Reprise)

XI. A Farewell to Things

Notes: "La Villa Strangiato" music by Geddy Lee, Alex Lifeson, and Neil Peart. Mini-Moog, Oberheim polyphonic, and Taurus pedals by Geddy Lee. Roland guitar synthesizer and Taurus pedals by Alex Lifeson.

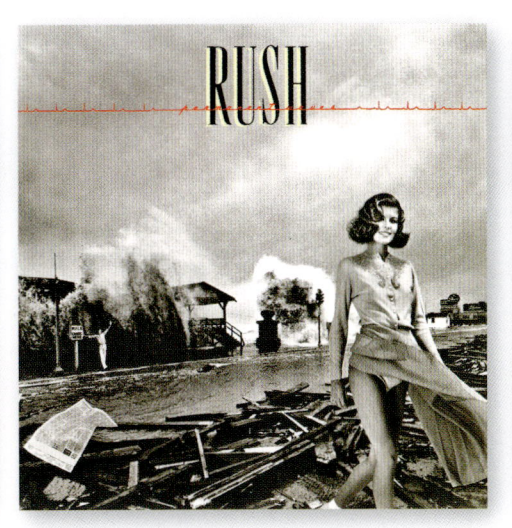

PERMANENT WAVES

Released January 14, 1980. Mercury. SRM-1-4001.

Recorded September–October 1979 at Le Studio, Morin-Heights, Quebec.

Coproduced by Terry Brown.

1. The Spirit of Radio (4:57)

2. Freewill (5:23)

3. Jacob's Ladder (7:28)

4. Entre Nous (4:37)

5. Different Strings (3:49)

6. Natural Science (9:16)

I. Tide Pools

II. Hyperspace

III. Permanent Waves

Notes: "Different Strings" lyrics by Geddy Lee. Oberheim polyphonic, OB-1, Mini-Moog, and Taurus pedal synthesizers by Geddy Lee. Taurus pedals by Alex Lifeson.

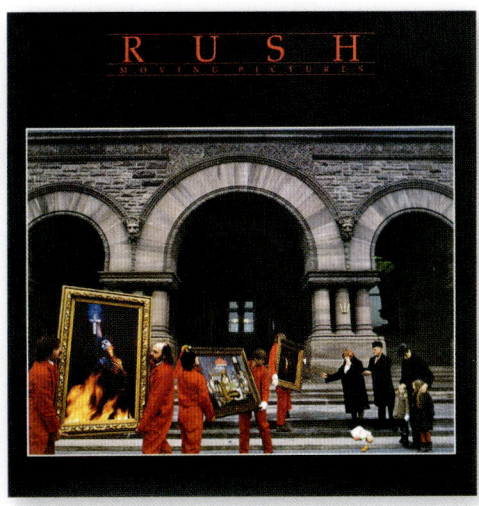

MOVING PICTURES

Released February 12, 1981. Mercury. SRM-1-4013.

Recorded October–November 1980 at Le Studio.

Coproduced by Terry Brown.

1. Tom Sawyer (4:33)

2. Red Barchetta (6:06)

3. YYZ (4:24)

4. Limelight (4:19)

5. The Camera Eye (10:56)

6. Witch Hunt (Part III of Fear) (4:43)

7. Vital Signs (4:43)

Notes: "YYZ" music by Geddy Lee and Neil Peart. "Tom Sawyer" lyrics by Neil Peart and Pye Dubois. Oberheim polyphonic, OB-X, Mini-Moog, and Taurus pedal synthesizers by Geddy Lee. Taurus pedals by Alex Lifeson. Synthesizers by Hugh Syme.

SIGNALS

Released September 9, 1982. Mercury. SRM-1-4063.

Recorded April–July 1982 at Le Studio.

Coproduced by Terry Brown.

1. Subdivisions (5:33)
2. The Analog Kid (4:46)
3. Chemistry (4:56)
4. Digital Man (6:20)
5. The Weapon (Part II of Fear) (6:22)
6. New World Man (3:41)
7. Losing It (4:51)
8. Countdown (5:49)

Notes: "Chemistry" lyrics by Geddy Lee, Alex Lifeson, and Neil Peart. Synthesizers by Geddy Lee. Taurus pedals by Alex Lifeson. Electric violin by Ben Mink.

GRACE UNDER PRESSURE

Released April 12, 1984. Mercury. 818 476-4 M-1.

Recorded November 1983–March 1984 at Le Studio.

Coproduced by Peter Henderson.

1. Distant Early Warning (4:59)
2. Afterimage (5:04)
3. Red Sector A (5:10)
4. The Enemy Within (Part I of Fear) (4:34)
5. The Body Electric (5:00)
6. Kid Gloves (4:18)
7. Red Lenses (4:42)
8. Between the Wheels (5:44)

Notes: Synthesizers by Geddy Lee.

POWER WINDOWS

Released October 21, 1985. Mercury. 826 098-4 M-1.

Recorded April–August 1985 at the Manor Studio, Oxfordshire; AIR Studios, Montserrat.

Coproduced by Peter Collins.

1. The Big Money (5:36)
2. Grand Designs (5:05)
3. Manhattan Project (5:05)
4. Marathon (6:09)
5. Territories (6:19)
6. Middletown Dreams (5:15)
7. Emotion Detector (5:10)
8. Mystic Rhythms (5:54)

Notes: Synthesizers and bass pedals by Geddy Lee.

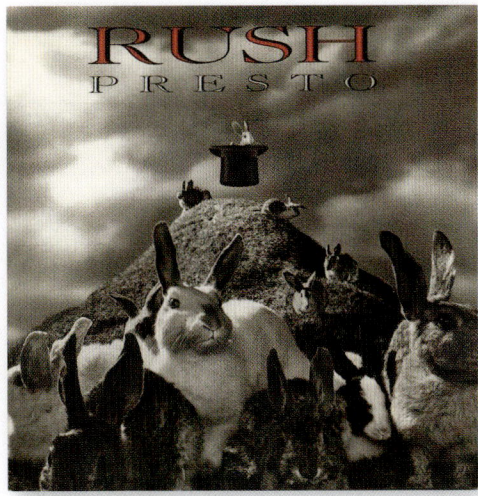

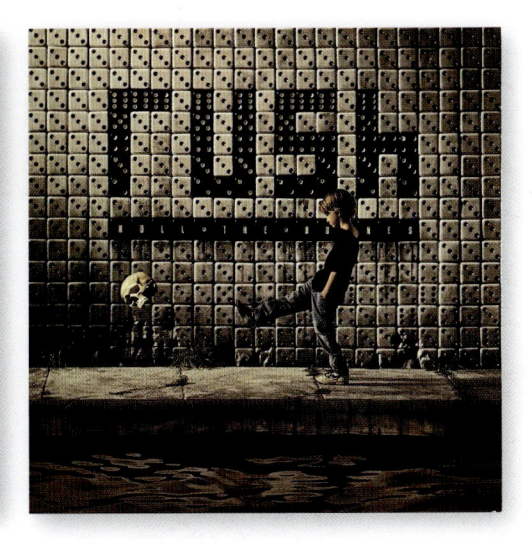

HOLD YOUR FIRE

Released September 8, 1987. Mercury. 832 464-1.

Recorded January–April 1987 at the Manor Studio; Ridge Farm Studio, Surrey; AIR Studios; McClear Place, Toronto; Lerxst Mobile.

Coproduced by Peter Collins.

1. Force Ten (4:28)
2. Time Stand Still (5:07)
3. Open Secrets (5:37)
4. Second Nature (4:35)
5. Prime Mover (5:19)
6. Lock and Key (5:08)
7. Mission (5:15)
8. Turn the Page (4:53)
9. Tai Shan (4:14)
10. High Water (5:32)

Notes: "Force Ten" lyrics by Neil Peart and Pye Dubois. Synthesizers by Geddy Lee. Additional vocals by Aimee Mann.

PRESTO

Released November 21, 1989. Atlantic. A1-82040.

Recorded June–August 1989 at Le Studio; McClear Place.

Coproduced by Rupert Hine.

1. Show Don't Tell (5:01)
2. Chain Lightning (4:33)
3. The Pass (4:51)
4. War Paint (5:24)
5. Scars (4:07)
6. Presto (5:45)
7. Superconductor (4:47)
8. Anagram (for Mongo) (4:00)
9. Red Tide (4:29)
10. Hand Over Fist (4:11)
11. Available Light (5:03)

Notes: Synthesizers by Geddy Lee.

ROLL THE BONES

Released September 3, 1991. Atlantic. 7 82293-2.

Recorded February–May 1991 at Le Studio; McClear Place.

Coproduced by Rupert Hine.

1. Dreamline (4:38)
2. Bravado (4:56)
3. Roll the Bones (5:30)
4. Face Up (3:54)
5. Where's My Thing? (Part IV, "Gangster of Boats" Trilogy) (3:49)
6. The Big Wheel (5:15)
7. Heresy (5:26)
8. Ghost of a Chance (5:19)
9. Neurotica (4:40)
10. You Bet Your Life (5:00)

Notes: Synthesizers by Geddy Lee. Backing vocals by Alex Lifeson.

COUNTERPARTS

Released October 19, 1993. Atlantic. 82528 2.

Recorded April–June 1993 at Le Studio; McClear Pathé, Toronto.

Coproduced by Peter Collins.

1. Animate (6:03)
2. Stick It Out (4:30)
3. Cut to the Chase (4:48)
4. Nobody's Hero (4:54)
5. Between Sun and Moon (4:37)
6. Alien Shore (5:45)
7. Speed of Love (5:02)
8. Double Agent (4:51)
9. Leave That Thing Alone (4:05)
10. Cold Fire (4:26)
11. Everyday Glory (5:11)

Notes: "Between Sun and Moon" lyrics by Neil Peart and Pye Dubois. Synthesizers by Geddy Lee.

TEST FOR ECHO

Released September 10, 1996. Atlantic. 82925 2.

Recorded January–April 1996 at Bearsville Studios, Bearsville; Reaction Studios, Toronto.

Coproduced by Peter Collins.

1. Test for Echo (5:56)
2. Driven (4:27)
3. Half the World (3:43)
4. The Color of Right (4:49)
5. Time and Motion (5:01)
6. Totem (4:58)
7. Dog Years (4:55)
8. Virtuality (5:44)
9. Resist (4:24)
10. Limbo (5:29)
11. Carve Away the Stone (4:05)

Notes: "Limbo" music by Geddy Lee, Alex Lifeson, and Neil Peart. "Test for Echo" lyrics by Neil Peart and Pye Dubois. Synthesizers by Geddy Lee. Mandola by Alex Lifeson.

VAPOR TRAILS

Released May 14, 2002. Atlantic. 83531-2.

Recorded August–December 2001 at Reaction Studios.

Coproduced by Paul Northfield.

1. One Little Victory (5:08)
2. Ceiling Unlimited (5:28)
3. Ghost Rider (5:41)
4. Peaceable Kingdom (5:23)
5. The Stars Look Down (4:28)
6. How It Is (4:05)
7. Vapor Trail (4:57)
8. Secret Touch (6:34)
9. Earthshine (5:38)
10. Sweet Miracle (3:40)
11. Nocturne (4:49)
12. Freeze (Part IV of Fear) (6:21)
13. Out of the Cradle (5:03)

Notes: Mandola by Alex Lifeson.

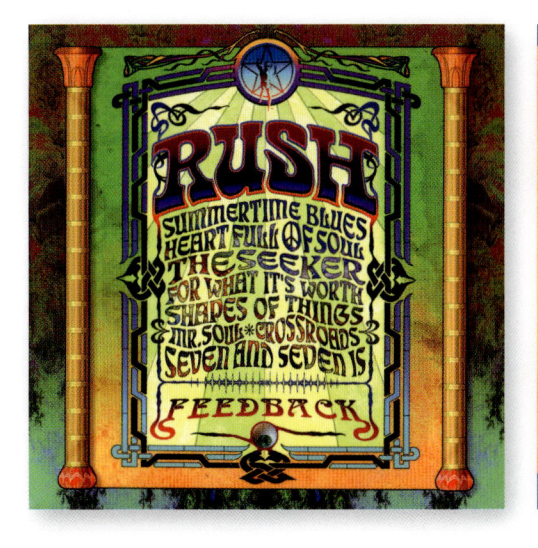

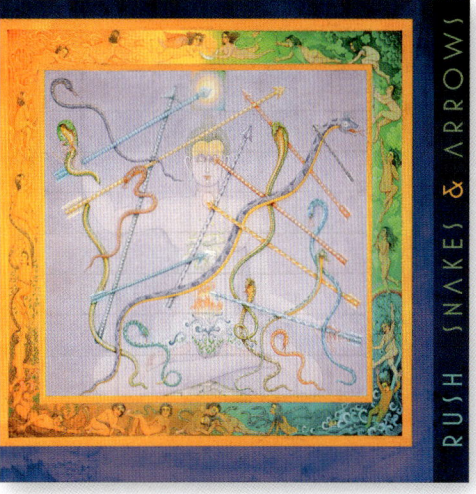

FEEDBACK

Released June 29, 2004. Atlantic. 83728-2.

Recorded March–April 2004 at Phase One Studios, Toronto.

Coproduced by David Leonard.

1. Summertime Blues (3:52)
2. Heart Full of Soul (2:52)
3. For What It's Worth (3:30)
4. The Seeker (3:27)
5. Mr. Soul (3:51)
6. Seven and Seven Is (2:53)
7. Shapes of Things (3:16)
8. Crossroads (3:27)

Notes: "Summertime Blues" by Eddie Cochran and Jerry Capehart. "Heart Full of Soul" by Graham Gouldman. "For What It's Worth" by Stephen Stills. "The Seeker" by Pete Townshend. "Mr. Soul" by Neil Young. "Seven and Seven Is" by Arthur Lee. "Shapes of Things" by Paul Samwell-Smith, Keith Relf, and Jim McCarty. "Crossroads" by Robert Johnson. Mandola by Alex Lifeson.

SNAKES & ARROWS

Released May 1, 2007. Atlantic. 135484-2.

Recorded November–December 2006 at Allaire Studios, Shokan.

Coproduced by Nick Raskulinecz.

1. Far Cry (5:21)
2. Armor and Sword (6:36)
3. Workin' Them Angels (4:47)
4. The Larger Bowl (4:07)
5. Spindrift (5:24)
6. The Main Monkey Business (6:01)
7. The Way the Wind Blows (6:28)
8. Hope (2:02)
9. Faithless (5:31)
10. Bravest Face (5:12)
11. Good News First (4:51)
12. Malignant Narcissism (2:17)
13. We Hold On (4:13)

Notes: "Hope" music by Alex Lifeson. Keyboards and Mellotron by Geddy Lee. Mandola, mandolin, and bouzouki by Alex Lifeson. Strings by Ben Mink.

CLOCKWORK ANGELS

Released June 12, 2012. Roadrunner. RR 7656-2.

Recorded October–December 2011 at Revolution Recording, Toronto; except "Caravan" and "BU2B," recorded April 2010 at Blackbird Studios, Nashville; strings recorded January 18, 2012, at Ocean Way Recording, Los Angeles.

Coproduced by Nick Raskulinecz.

1. Caravan (5:40)
2. BU2B (5:10)
3. Clockwork Angels (7:31)
4. The Anarchist (6:52)
5. Carnies (4:52)
6. Halo Effect (3:14)
7. Seven Cities of Gold (6:32)
8. The Wreckers (5:01)
9. Headlong Flight (7:20)
10. BU2B2 (1:28)
11. Wish Them Well (5:25)
12. The Garden (6:59)

Notes: Keyboards and bass pedals by Geddy Lee. Keyboards by Alex Lifeson. Piano by Jason Sniderman.

B. LIVE ALBUMS

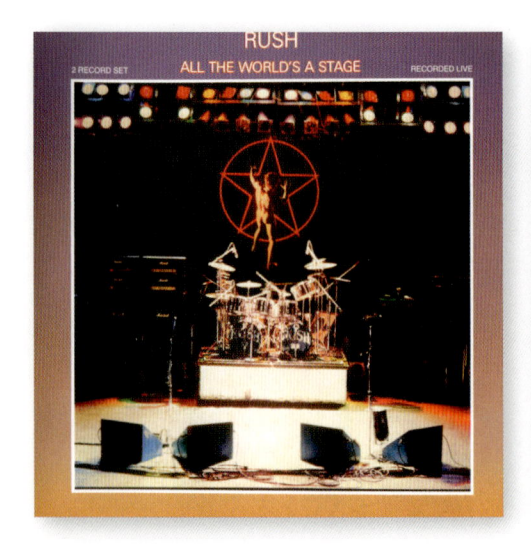

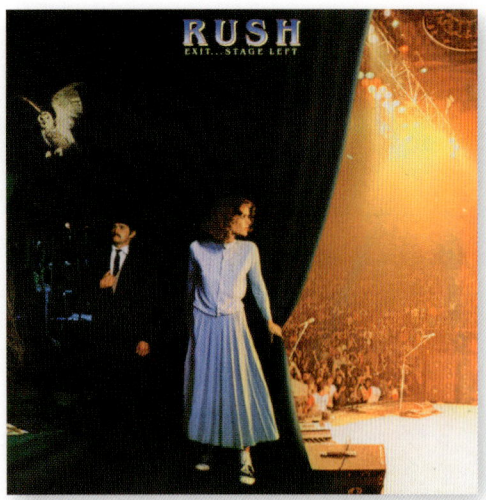

ALL THE WORLD'S A STAGE

Released September 29, 1976. Mercury. SRM-2-7508.

Recorded June 11–13, 1976, at Massey Hall, Toronto.

Coproduced by Terry Brown.

1. Bastille Day (4:59)
2. Anthem (4:57)
3. Fly by Night / In the Mood (4:05)
4. Something for Nothing (4:04)
5. Lakeside Park (5:06)
6. 2112 (16:51)
7. By-Tor and the Snow Dog (12:01)
8. In the End (7:15)
9. Working Man / Finding My Way (14:20)
10. What You're Doing (5:41)

EXIT... STAGE LEFT

Released October 29, 1981. Mercury. SRM-2-7001.

Recorded June 10–11, 1980, at the Apollo, Glasgow; March 27, 1981, at the Forum, Montreal.

Produced by Terry Brown.

1. The Spirit of Radio (5:12)
2. Red Barchetta (6:48)
3. YYZ (7:44)
4. A Passage to Bangkok (3:47)
5. Closer to the Heart (3:09)
6. Beneath, Between, and Behind (2:34)
7. Jacob's Ladder (8:47)
8. Broon's Bane (1:37)
9. The Trees (5:50)
10. Xanadu (12:10)
11. Freewill (5:33)
12. Tom Sawyer (5:01)
13. La Villa Strangiato (9:38)

Notes: "Broon's Bane" music by Alex Lifeson. Synthesizers, bass pedal synthesizer, and occasional rhythm guitar by Geddy Lee. Bass pedal synthesizer by Alex Lifeson.

A SHOW OF HANDS

Released January 10, 1989. Mercury. 836 346-1.

Recorded March 31 and April 1, 1986, at Meadowlands Arena, East Rutherford; January 27, 1988, at Lakefront Arena, New Orleans; February 1, 1988, at Veterans Memorial Coliseum, Phoenix; February 3, 1988, at the Sports Arena, San Diego; April 21–24, 1988, at the National Exhibition Centre, Birmingham.

Produced by Rush.

1. Intro (0:53)
2. The Big Money (5:52)
3. Subdivisions (5:19)
4. Marathon (6:32)
5. Turn the Page (4:40)
6. Manhattan Project (5:00)
7. Mission (5:44)
8. Distant Early Warning (5:18)
9. Mystic Rhythms (5:32)
10. Witch Hunt (3:55)
11. The Rhythm Method (4:34)
12. Force Ten (4:50)
13. Time Stand Still (5:10)
14. Red Sector A (5:12)
15. Closer to the Heart (4:53)

Notes: Synthesizers by Geddy Lee. Synthesizers and backing vocals by Alex Lifeson.

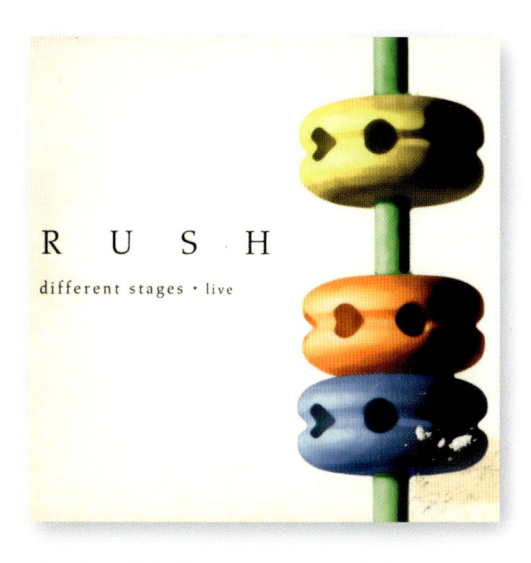

DIFFERENT STAGES

Released November 10, 1998; Atlantic. 83122-2.

Recorded February 20, 1978, at Hammersmith Odeon, London; February 27, 1994, at Miami Arena, Miami; April 30, 1994, at the Spectrum, Philadelphia; May 24, 1997, at Coca-Cola Starplex Amphitheater, Dallas; June 14, 1997, at World Music Theater, Tinley Park; June 23, 1997, at Great Woods Center, Mansfield; July 2, 1997, at Molson Amphitheater, Toronto.

Produced by Geddy Lee and Paul Northfield.

Disc 1

1. Dreamline (5:34)
2. Limelight (4:32)
3. Driven (5:16)
4. Bravado (6:23)
5. Animate (5:29)
6. Show Don't Tell (5:29)
7. The Trees (5:28)
8. Nobody's Hero (5:01)
9. Closer to the Heart (5:13)
10. 2112: I. Overture (4:32)
11. 2112: II. The Temples of Syrinx (2:20)
12. 2112: III. Discovery (4:17)
13. 2112: IV. Presentation (3:40)
14. 2112: V. Oracle: The Dream (1:49)
15. 2112: VI. Soliloquy (2:07)
16. 2112: VII. Grand Finale (2:39)

Disc 2

1. Test for Echo (6:15)
2. The Analog Kid (5:14)
3. Freewill (5:36)
4. Roll the Bones (5:58)
5. Stick It Out (4:42)
6. Resist (4:27)
7. Leave That Thing Alone (4:46)
8. The Rhythm Method (8:19)
9. Natural Science (8:05)
10. The Spirit of Radio (5:00)
11. Tom Sawyer (5:18)
12. YYZ (5:25)

Disc 3

1. Bastille Day (5:07)
2. By-Tor and the Snow Dog (4:59)
3. Xanadu (12:32)
4. A Farewell to Kings (5:53)
5. Something for Nothing (4:01)
6. Cygnus X-1 (10:23)
7. Anthem (4:47)
8. Working Man (4:00)
9. Fly by Night (2:04)
10. In the Mood (3:34)
11. Cinderella Man (5:09)

Notes: Synthesizers by Geddy Lee and Alex Lifeson.

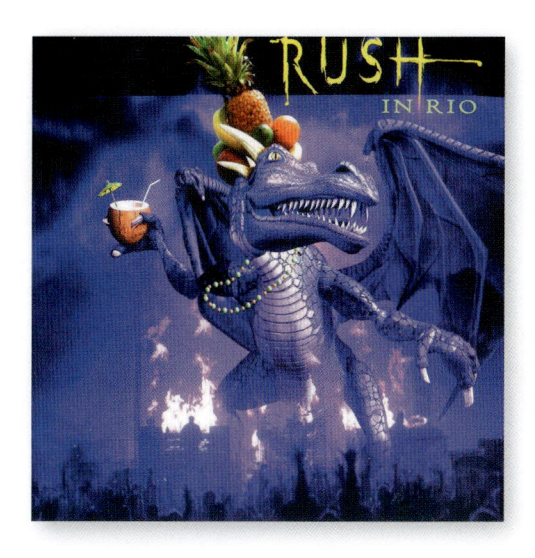

RUSH IN RIO

Released October 21, 2003. Atlantic. 83672-2.

Recorded November 23, 2002, at Maracanã Stadium, Rio de Janeiro; September 27, 2002, at Cricket Pavilion, Phoenix; October 19, 2002, at Colisée Pepsi Arena, Quebec City.

Produced by Alex Lifeson and James "Jimbo" Barton.

Disc 1

1. Tom Sawyer (5:10)
2. Distant Early Warning (4:48)
3. New World Man (4:03)
4. Roll the Bones (6:03)
5. Earthshine (5:42)
6. YYZ (4:35)
7. The Pass (4:50)
8. Bravado (6:15)
9. The Big Money (5:58)
10. The Trees (5:07)
11. Freewill (5:32)
12. Closer to the Heart (3:01)
13. Natural Science (8:34)

Disc 2

1. One Little Victory (5:32)
2. Driven (5:05)
3. Ghost Rider (5:36)
4. Secret Touch (7:00)
5. Dreamline (5:04)
6. Red Sector A (5:12)
7. Leave That Thing Alone! (4:59)
8. O Baterista (8:18)
9. Resist (4:24)
10. 2112: Overture / The Temples of Syrinx (6:52)

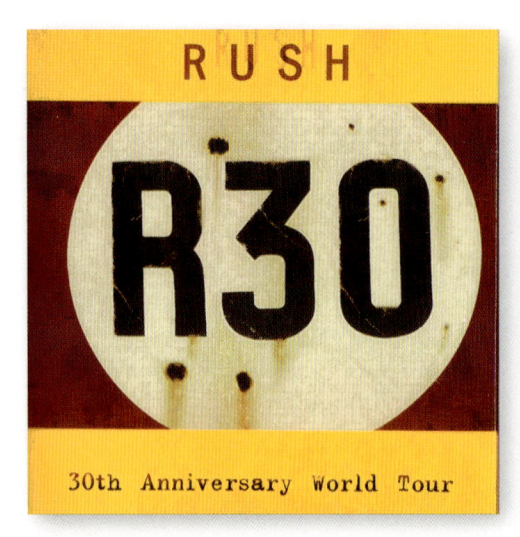

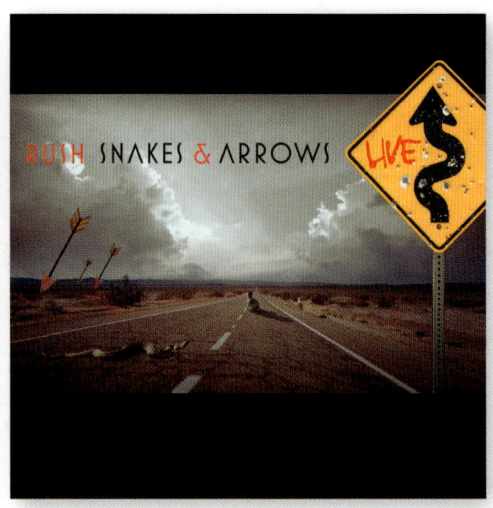

Disc 3

1. Limelight (4:24)
2. La Villa Strangiato (10:05)
3. The Spirit of Radio (4:59)
4. By-Tor and the Snow Dog (4:35)
5. Cygnus X-1: Prologue (3:12)
6. Working Man (5:35)
7. Between Sun and Moon (4:48)
8. Vital Signs (4:59)

Notes: Synthesizers by Geddy Lee.

R30: 30TH ANNIVERSARY WORLD TOUR

Released November 22, 2005. Anthem. 01143-1082-9.
Recorded September 24, 2004, at Festhalle, Frankfurt.
Produced by Rush.

Disc 1

1. R30 Overture (6:42)
2. The Spirit of Radio (5:05)
3. Force Ten (4:49)
4. Animate (5:49)
5. Subdivisions (6:09)
6. Earthshine (5:41)
7. Red Barchetta (6:49)
8. Roll the Bones (6:22)
9. The Seeker (3:27)
10. Tom Sawyer (5:00)
11. Dreamline (5:20)

Disc 2

1. Between the Wheels (6:17)
2. Mystic Rhythms (5:22)
3. Der Trommler (9:01)
4. Resist (4:33)
5. Heart Full Of Soul (2:44)
6. 2112: Overture / The Temples of Syrinx / Grand Finale (8:23)
7. Xanadu (6:43)
8. Working Man (6:13)
9. Summertime Blues (3:41)
10. Crossroads (3:13)
11. Limelight (4:57)

Notes: Keyboards by Geddy Lee. Bass pedal synth by Alex Lifeson.

SNAKES & ARROWS LIVE

Released April 15, 2008. Atlantic. 442620-2.
Recorded October 16 and 17, 2007, at Ahoy Arena, Rotterdam.
Produced by Rush.

Disc 1

1. Limelight (4:48)
2. Digital Man (6:57)
3. Entre Nous (5:18)
4. Mission (5:39)
5. Freewill (6:02)
6. The Main Monkey Business (6:06)
7. The Larger Bowl (4:21)
8. Secret Touch (7:45)
9. Circumstances (3:47)
10. Between the Wheels (6:01)
11. Dreamline (5:16)
12. Far Cry (5:20)
13. Workin' Them Angels (4:49)
14. Armor and Sword (6:57)

Disc 2

1. Spindrift (5:46)
2. The Way the Wind Blows (6:25)
3. Subdivisions (5:43)
4. Natural Science (8:34)
5. Witch Hunt (4:49)
6. Malignant Narcissism / De Slagwerker (10:42)
7. Hope (2:21)
8. Distant Early Warning (4:54)
9. The Spirit of Radio (5:03)
10. Tom Sawyer (5:49)
11. One Little Victory (5:27)
12. A Passage to Bangkok (3:57)
13. YYZ (5:17)

Notes: Synthesizers by Geddy Lee. Bass pedal synth by Alex Lifeson.

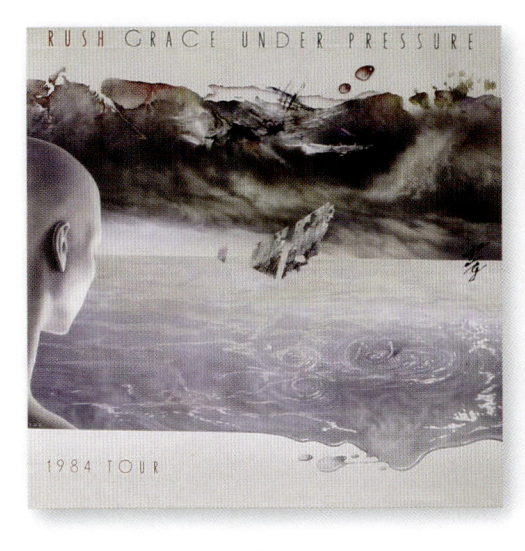

GRACE UNDER PRESSURE: 1984 TOUR

Released August 11, 2009. Mercury. B0013252-02.

Recorded September 20–22, 1984, at Maple Leaf Gardens, Toronto.

Produced by Rush.

1. Intro (Three Stooges) (0:57)
2. The Spirit of Radio (4:54)
3. The Enemy Within (4:48)
4. The Weapon (7:42)
5. Witch Hunt (4:41)
6. New World Man (3:59)
7. Distant Early Warnings (6:11)
8. Red Sector A (5:23)
9. Closer to the Heart (3:35)
10. Medley: YYZ / The Temples of Syrinx / Tom Sawyer (9:41)
11. Vital Signs (4:56)
12. Medley: Finding My Way / In the Mood (3:35)

Notes: Synthesizers by Geddy Lee.

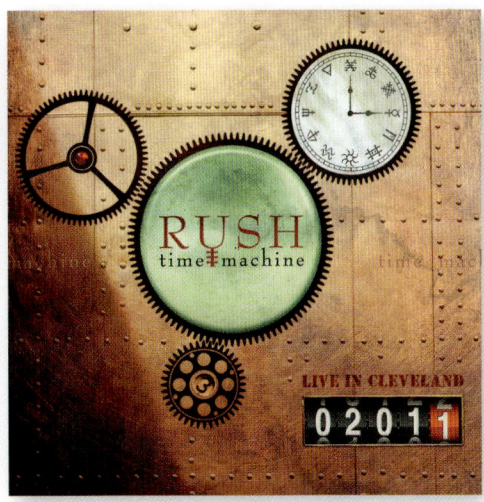

TIME MACHINE 2011: LIVE IN CLEVELAND

Released November 8, 2011. Roadrunner. 1686-176655.

Recorded April 15, 2011, at Quicken Loans Arena, Cleveland.

Produced by Rush.

Disc 1

1. The Spirit of Radio (5:02)
2. Time Stand Still (5:17)
3. Presto (6:33)
4. Stick It Out (4:22)
5. Workin' Them Angels (4:44)
6. Leave That Thing Alone (5:14)
7. Faithless (5:47)
8. BU2B (4:24)
9. Freewill (5:29)
10. Marathon (6:29)
11. Subdivisions (5:30)
12. Tom Sawyer (4:53)
13. Red Barchetta (6:55)
14. YYZ (4:33)
15. Limelight (4:31)

Disc 2

1. The Camera Eye (10:10)
2. Witch Hunt (4:42)
3. Vital Signs (5:28)
4. Caravan (5:37)
5. Moto Perpetuo (8:23)
6. O'Malley's Break (1:34)
7. Closer to the Heart (3:28)
8. 2112: Overture / The Temples of Syrinx (7:10)
9. Far Cry (6:23)
10. La Villa Strangiato (7:40)
11. Working Man (6:41)

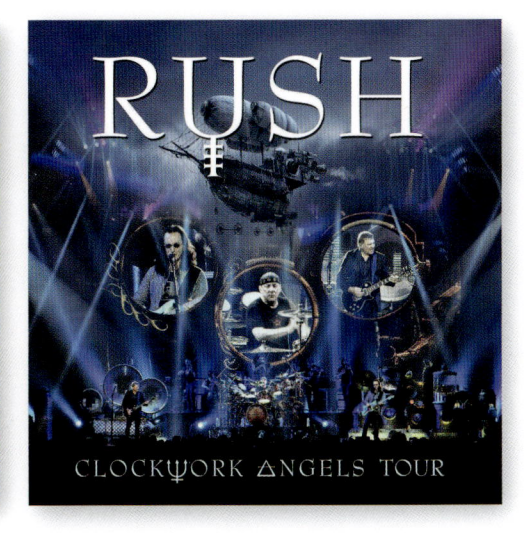

CLOCKWORK ANGELS TOUR

Released November 19, 2013. Roadrunner. 1686-175982.

Recorded November 25, 2012, at US Airways Center, Phoenix; November 28, 2012, at American Airlines Center, Dallas; November 30, 2012, at AT&T Center, San Antonio.

Produced by Rush.

Disc 1

1. Subdivisions (5:39)
2. The Big Money (6:02)
3. Force Ten (5:35)
4. Grand Designs (5:15)
5. The Body Electric (4:52)
6. Territories (6:46)
7. The Analog Kid (5:24)
8. Bravado (5:46)
9. Where's My Thing? / Here It Is! (8:23)
10. Far Cry (5:33)

Disc 2

1. Caravan (5:42)
2. Clockwork Angels (8:12)
3. The Anarchist (6:59)
4. Carnies (5:16)
5. The Wreckers (5:27)
6. Headlong Flight / Drumbastica (8:17)
7. Peke's Repose / Halo Effect (5:15)
9. Seven Cities of Gold (6:24)
10. Wish Them Well (6:41)
11. The Garden (7:14)

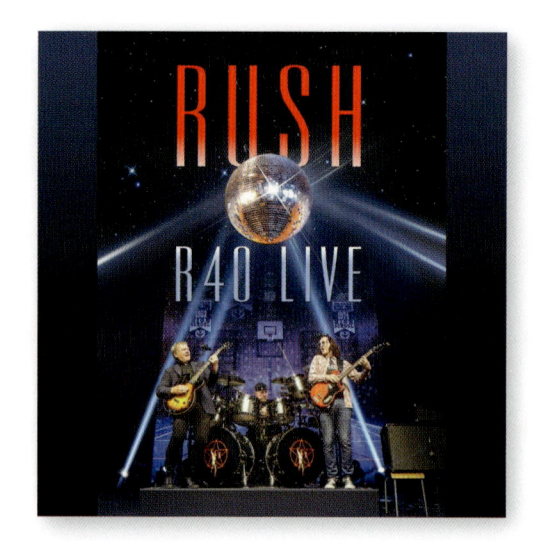

R40 LIVE

Released November 20, 2015. Roadrunner. 1686-175982.

Recorded June 17 and 19, 2015, at Air Canada Centre, Toronto.

Produced by David Bottrill.

Disc 1
1. The World Is . . . The World Is . . . (2:11)
2. The Anarchist (7:07)
3. Headlong Flight (8:46)
4. Far Cry (5:31)
5. The Main Monkey Business (6:08)
6. How It Is (4:45)
7. Animate (6:15)
8. Roll the Bones (6:05)
9. Between the Wheels (5:58)
10. Losing It (5:55)
11. Subdivisions (5:49)

Disc 2
1. Tom Sawyer (5:00)
2. YYZ (4:32)
3. The Spirit of Radio (5:03)
4. Natural Science (8:32)
5. Jacob's Ladder (7:34)
6. Cygnus X-1 Book II: Prelude (4:19)
7. Cygnus X-1 / The Story So Far (9:21)
8. Closer to the Heart (3:08)
9. Xanadu (10:40)
10. 2112 (12:15)

Disc 3
1. Mel's Rockpile (1:36)
2. Lakeside Park / Anthem (5:29)
3. What You're Doing / Working Man (9:35)
4. One Little Victory (5:47)
5. Distant Early Warning (5:24)
6. Red Barchetta (7:09)
7. Clockwork Angels (7:46)
8. The Wreckers (5:39)
9. The Camera Eye (10:22)
10. Losing It (6:13)

Notes: Vocals by Alex Lifeson. Violin by Ben Mink (Disc 1). Violin by Jonathan Dinklage (Disc 3).

Disc 3
1. Dreamline (5:19)
2. The Percussor (3:10)
3. Red Sector A (5:21)
4. YYZ (4:52)
5. The Spirit of Radio (6:28)
6. Tom Sawyer (5:56)
7. 2112 (8:19)
8. Limelight (4:42)
9. Middletown Dreams (5:20)
10. The Pass (5:03)
11. Manhattan Project (5:18)

Notes: David Campbell, Conductor. Cello by Adele Stein and Jacob Szekely. Violin by Audrey Solomon, Entcho Todorov, Gerry Hilera, Hiroko Taguchi, Joel Derouin, Jonathan Dinklage, and Mario De Leon.

BIBLIOGRAPHY

BOOK

Lemieux, Patrick. *The Rush Chronology*. Across the Board Books, 2015.

ARTICLES

Altaf, Rodrigo. "World-Renowned Music Producer Terry Brown Remembers His Storied Career in 25 Questions: 'The Way Rush Sounded Was Unique, I'd Never Heard Anything Like It!'" sonicperspectives.com, April 5, 2022.

Anderson, Kevin J. "Author Kevin J. Anderson to write novelization of Rush's upcoming *Clockwork Angels* album," rushisaband.com, February 9, 2012.

Azerrad, Michael. "*A Show of Hands* Album Review," *Rolling Stone*, April 20, 1989.

Beaulieu, Paul. "Terry Brown: Differed with Band on Electronics," rushvault.com, December 27, 2011.

Begrand, Adrien. "All the Gifts of Life: 40 Years of Rush's '2112,'" npr.org, April 30, 2016.

Blenn, John. "Geddy Lee: Entering Different Stages," *Long Island Entertainment*, October 1998.

Boone, Brian. "The Tragic Real-Life Story of Rush," grunge.com, March 4, 2020.

Brannigan, Paul. "'Someone said that I sounded like the damned howling in Hades': Geddy Lee on why Rush shunned their record label and management's wishes that they'd become the next Led Zeppelin or Bad Company," *Louder*, November 20, 2023.

Bullock, Scott. "A Rebel and a Drummer," *Liberty*, September 1997.

Cantin, Paul. "Geddy Lee on the Rush Reunion," *Jam!Showbiz*, January 12, 2001.

Childers, Chad. "How a Robert Plant Phone Call Sparked Rush's Post-2000 Return," loudwire.com, May 21, 2021.

Cohen, Scott. "The Rush Tapes, Part 1: Neil Peart Sizes Up 'Farewell to Kings,' The Latest Canadian Rock Opus," *Circus*, October 13, 1977.

Dafoe, Chris. "Rush Looks Back with Cold, Critical Eyes," *Toronto Star*, May 11, 1990.

Daly, Skip. "Alex Lifeson Interview," *Modern Guitars*, January 23, 2009.

Daly, Skip. "Ian Grandy Interview: Rush's First Roadie," guitarinternational.com, September 16, 2009.

Diamond, Jonny. "How an iconic Canadian rock band lured angry teens to the dark arts of Ayn Rand," lithub.com, October 6, 2021.

Duffy, John. "It's still the Rush hour," lancasteronline.com, April 3, 2011.

Ebert, Roger. "North," *Chicago Sun-Times*, July 22, 1994.

Elliott, Paul. "The History of Rush by Geddy Lee & Alex Lifeson: From Rebirth to Retirement," *Classic Rock*, August 7, 2016.

Elliott, Paul. "The History of Rush by Geddy Lee & Alex Lifeson: *Moving Pictures* and the 1980s," *Classic Rock*, June 24, 2016.

Elliott, Paul. "The History of Rush by Geddy Lee & Alex Lifeson: The Early Years," *Classic Rock*, February 3, 2016.

Elliot, Paul. "The Magic Circle," *Sounds*, December 9, 1989.

Elliott, Paul. "Neil Peart: The ultimate interview," *Classic Rock*, June 2013.

Elliott, Paul. "Rush: 'We're coming towards the end,'" *Classic Rock*, May 15, 2015.

Elliott, Paul. "Rush Make *2112*, 1976," *Mojo*, March 2016.

Everley, Dave. "'They had their own code... They would communicate with each other via eye contact and head movements. It was amazing how many long, nuanced phrases they could play that way': How Rush made *Signals*," *Prog*, September 9, 2023.

Finulanu. "Twelve Things I'd Rather Hear Than Geddy Lee's Voice," rateyourmusic.com, April 10, 2022.

Flohil, Dick. "Rush: Millionaire Stars of High-Tech Rock," *Toronto Star's Today Magazine*, May 3, 1980.

Ford, Stephen. "Rush, Runaway Concert: Good Only as Advice," *Detroit News*, February 11, 1977.

Fricke, David. "*Permanent Waves* Album Review," *Rolling Stone*, May 1, 1980.

Fricke, David. "Power Windows," *Rolling Stone*, January 30, 1986.

Gallucci, Michael. "Geddy Lee Says He and Alex Lifeson Could Perform as Rush Again," ultimateclassicrock.com, November 10, 2023.

Garone, Anthony. "Alex Lifeson Interview," makeweirdmusic.com, January 30, 2021.

Graff, Gary. "Geddy Lee Talks New Rush Album," *Yahoo!Entertainment*, October 20, 2000.

Greene, Andy. "Geddy Lee on Rush's Rock and Roll Hall," *Rolling Stone*, December 11, 2012.

Greene, Andy. "Neil Peart on Rush's New LP and Being a 'Bleeding Heart Libertarian,'" *Rolling Stone*, June 12, 2012.

Gross, Michael. "Rush-BTO's Heavy Metal Challengers: Breaking into America, Canada's Answer to the New York Dolls?" *Circus Raves*, November 1975.

Grow, Kory. "Rush's Alex Lifeson on 40 Years of *2112*: 'It Was Our Protest Album,'" *Rolling Stone*, March 29, 2016.

Hann, Michael. "Geddy Lee on Rush's greatest songs: 'Even I can barely make sense of our concept albums,'" *The Guardian*, December 24, 2018.

Hann, Michael. "Rush: a band who sparked the teenage imagination like few others," *The Guardian*, January 25, 2018.

Harkinson, Josh. "Rand Paul Clashes with Rush Over 'Spirit of the Radio.'" *Mother Jones*, June 3, 2010.

Hiatt, Brian. "22 Things You Learn Hanging Out with Rush," *Rolling Stone*, June 30, 2015.

Hiatt, Brian. "'Coke Was Everywhere': Getting High during Neil Peart's Drum Solos, and More Geddy Lee Revelations," *Rolling Stone*, November 21, 2023.

Hiatt, Brian. "From Rush with Love,'" *Rolling Stone*, June 16, 2015.

Hiatt, Brian. "Geddy Lee Wants to Tour with Alex Lifeson: 'I Keep Working on Him,'" *Rolling Stone*, November 19, 2023.

Hicks, Graham. "*Hemispheres*: Shattered by Latest Rush Opus," *Music Express*, December 1978.

Hill, Doug. "*Moving Pictures*," *In the Studio with Redbeard*, January 2, 1989.

Hogan, Richard. "Vital Signs from Rush," *Circus*, December 30, 1981.

Hunt, Dennis. "At the Whisky: Rushing through the Looking Glass," *Los Angeles Times*, November 28, 1974.

Hunt, Dennis. "Rush Is in No Hurry to Call It Quits," *Los Angeles Times*, February 2, 1986.

Iero, Cheech. "Neil Peart," *Modern Drummer*, April–May 1980.

Ivie, Devon. "Relive the Glory of Rush and Neil Peart with This Rare, Resurfaced *Colbert Report* Interview," vulture.com, January 22, 2020.

Johnson, Howard. "'I was trying to get them laid'—what happened when Rush toured with Kiss," *Classic Rock*, January 5, 2022.

Jurek, Thom. "*Feedback* Review," allmusic.com, June 29, 2004.

Kielty, Martin. "How Rush Connected the Dots with *Snakes and Arrows*," ultimateclassicrock.com, May 1, 2017.

Kmetzko, Mark. "Live in Concert: Rush, Reign, The Agora, August 26," *Scene*, August 29–September 4, 1974.

Kordosh, John. "Rush: But Why Are They in Such a Hurry?" *CREEM*, June 1981.

Krewen, Nick. "Presto Change-O," *Canadian Musician*, April 1990.

Lee, Geddy; Lifeson, Alex; Peart, Neil. "The Story of '2112,'" *Live at Massey Hall Official Program*, June 11–13, 1976.

Loder, Kurt. "*Grace Under Pressure* Album Review," *Rolling Stone*, June 21, 1984.

Mack, Bob. "Confessions of a Rush Fan," *SPIN*, March 1992.

Mack, Bob. "Precious Metal," *SPIN*, October 1991.

Mendelssohn, John. "Rush: *Fly by Night*," *Phonograph Record*, March 1975.

Mercury Records. *Caress of Steel* Press Kit, August 29, 1975.

Miles, Barry. "Is Everybody Feelin' All RIGHT? (Geddit...?)," *New Musical Express*, March 4, 1978.

Milkowski, Bill. "Rush in Revolution," *Guitar World*, March 1990.

Mohr, Jay. "'Oh, God, Rush Hate Me.' Steve Lillywhite Talks *Grace Under Pressure*," *Mohr Talk*, July 5, 2013.

Niester, Alan. "There's a Need for This Kind of Music," *Toronto Globe and Mail*, November 17, 1998.

Noble, Douglas J. "Counter Attack," *Guitar Magazine (UK)*, November 1993.

Pareles, Jon. "Review/Rock; A 20-Year-Old Band with Some New Tricks," *New York Times*, March 10, 1994.

Peart, Neil. "Flying Down to Rio—Leaving Vapor Trails Behind," *Rush in Rio* Liner Notes, October 21, 2003.

Peart, Neil. "In Memoriam: Freddie Gruber," hudsonmusic.com, October 12, 2011.

Peart, Neil. "Neil Peart in His Own Words: Four Decades in the Studio with Rush," *Drum!*, November 15, 2016.

Peart, Neil. "*Personal Waves*—The Story of an Album," *Permanent Waves* Tour Book, 1980.

Peart, Neil. "A Port boy's story," *St. Catharines Standard*, June 24, 1994.

Peart, Neil. "Pressure Release," *Grace Under Pressure* Tour Book, 1984.

Peart, Neil. "Remembering Andrew: Andrew MacNaughtan, February 25, 1964–January 25, 2012," neilpeart.net, January 30, 2012.

Peart, Neil. "Starting Over," *Modern Drummer*, November 1995.

Peart, Neil. "Time Machines," neilpeart.net, May 1, 2010.

Peart, Neil. "Under the Marine Layer," neilpeart.net, June 1, 2009.

Pipher, Geneen. "Transcript: Alex Lifeson of Rush," cnn.com, June 3, 2002.

Roberts, John. "Rush on CNN: Geddy Lee, Neil Peart, and Alex Lifeson talk with John Roberts," cnn.com, October 2, 2010.

Rockingham, Graham. "Graciously BITTER," *Hamilton Spectator*, April 13, 2013.

"Rush, Unhurried," *National Post*, April 23, 2007.

Rusty, Brandon. "Rush's Alex Lifeson Recounts Graphic Details of Police Altercation," chartattack.com, June 10, 2005.

Salem, Jeff. "From Power Trio to Big Band: Neil Peart Talks about *Burning for Buddy*," *Canadian Musician*, December 1994.

Sculley, Alan. "Rush brings *Moving Pictures* to Toledo," *Toledo Free Press*, April 5, 2011.

Sharp, Keith. "The Weigh-In," *Music Express*, January 1989.

Shea, Courtney. "'There was a period when we were doing cocaine just to keep the energy up': A Q&A with Geddy Lee of Rush," *Toronto Life*, November 14, 2023.

Sheffield, Rob. "*2112*: Deluxe Edition," *Rolling Stone*, January 2, 2013.

Simon, Pam. "*Fly by Night*, Rush," *Statesville (North Carolina) Record & Landmark*, March 29, 1975.

Swenson, John. "Liner Notes," *Chronicles* Liner Notes, September 4, 1990.

Tannyan, Gary. "*Rush* (Moon MN-100)," *Saskatoon Star-Phoenix*, June 6, 1974.

Tattrie, Boyd. "Speeding Ahead," *RPM Weekly*, April 24, 1976.

Taylor, Peter. "Piccadilly Tube Feels the Rush August 21st," *RPM Weekly*, September 1, 1973.

Tepner, Stan. "Rush, *Caress of Steel* (Mercury)," *Kingston (Ontario) Whig-Standard*, November 21, 1975.

Thompson, Robert. "Original Rush Drummer John Rutsey Dies," *Billboard*, May 16, 2008.

Veitch, David. "In No Rush Band Gives Peart Time to Grieve," *Calgary Sun*, October 29, 1998.

Wilding, Philip. "The Meaning of Lifeson," *Kerrang!*, November 25, 1989.

Wilding, Philip. "Neil Peart interview: 'I never set out to be famous—I set out to be good,'" *Classic Rock*, June 3, 2020.

Woods, Scott. "Critical Collage: Rush vs. the Critics," rockcritics.com, March 5, 2013.

WEBSITES

2112.net
allmusic.com
billboard.com
blabbermouth.net
chartattack.com
cnn.com
cygnus-x1.net
drummagazine.com
grunge.com
guitarinternational.com
hudsonmusic.com
lancasteronline.com
lithub.com
loudersound.com
loudwire.com
makeweirdmusic.com
neilpeart.net
npr.org
rateyourmusic.com
rockcritics.com
rogerebert.com
rollingstone.com
rush.com
rushisaband.com
rushvault.com
songfacts.com
sonicperspectives.com
spin.com
theguardian.com
torontolife.com
ultimateclassicrock.com
vulture.com
yahoo.com

PHOTO CREDITS

B = bottom, L = left, M = moiddle, R = right, T = top

Alamy Stock Photos: 54, CBW; 55, Science History Images; 79T, Pictorial Press; 108, Michael Bush; 110B, Ross Pelton/Media Punch; 115, Chris McKay/Media Punch; 116TL, Chris McKay/Media Punch; 116B, Chris McKay/Media Punch; 117, Chris McKay/Media Punch; 118B, Chris McKay/Media Punch; 119, Chris McKay/Media Punch; 121, Chris McKay/Media Punch; 129, Michael Bush; 133, Jerome Brunet/ZUMA Press; 134, Jerome Brunet/ZUMA Press; 135TR, Jerome Brunet/ZUMA Press; 135BL, Jerome Brunet/ZUMA Press; 136–137, Allstar Picture Library Ltd.; 140, Jerome Brunet/ZUMA Press; 146–147, Gene Schilling/ZUMA Press; 148–149, Gene Schilling/ZUMA Press; 171, Anne-Marie Forker. **Robert Alford:** 2, 21, 51TL, 60, 62T, 63, 66, 67T. **Copyright Bruce Cole/PlumCom Inc.:** 8, 29. **Kevin Estrada:** 70TR, 70B, 71, 107, 142, 143, 144, 145, 151, 153, 154, 155T, 156–157, 158–159, 160, 161, 162, 163. **Rich Galbraith:** 17, 23. **Getty Images:** 2, Fin Costello/Redferns; 7, Fin Costello/Redferns; 11, Michael Ochs Archives; 13, Icon and Image/Michael Ochs Archives; 15, Icon and Image/Michael Ochs Archives; 25B, Chris Walter/WireImage; 27, Fin Costello/Redferns; 30, Fin Costello/Redferns; 33, Fin Costello/Redferns; 35T, Fin Costello/Redferns; 37B, Fin Costello/Redferns; 39T, Fin Costello/Redferns; 40T, Fin Costello/Redferns; 40B, Fin Costello/Redferns; 41, Fin Costello/Redferns; 42, Fin Costello/Redferns; 43T, Fin Costello/Redferns; 53T, Fin Costello/Redferns; 56, Brian Rasic/Hulton Archive; 65T, Fin Costello/Redferns; 74BR, Jim Steinfeldt/Michael Ochs Archives; 75T, Ebet Roberts/Redferns; 77, Ebet Roberts/Redferns; 80–81, Rob Verhorst/Redferns; Doug Griffin/Toronto Star; 84, Tim Mosenfelder/Hulton Archive; 89, John Atashian/Getty Images Entertainment; 91, Tim Mosenfelder/Hulton Archive; 95, Patti Ouderkirk/WireImage; 97, Patti Ouderkirk/WireImage; 99, Houston Chronicle/Hearst Newspapers; 100, Tim Mosenfelder/Archive Photos; 102, Peter Still/Redferns; 103, Peter Still/Redferns; 104, Ebet Roberts/Redferns; 105, Tim Mosenfelder/Hulton Archive; 113, Ethan Miller/Getty Images Entertainment; 114, Ethan Miller/Getty Images Entertainment; 120, Tim Mosenfelder/Archive Photos; 123, Annamaria DiSanto/WireImage; 124, Annamaria DiSanto/WireImage; 125, Annamaria DiSanto/WireImage; 127T, Annamaria DiSanto/WireImage; 131B, Brian Rasic/Getty Images Entertainment; 139, Fin Costello/Redferns; 165, Fin Costello/Redferns; 166, Fin Costello/Redferns; 167T, Mick Hutson/Redferns; 168, Jamie McCarthy/WireImage; 169, Kevin Mazur/Getty Images Entertainment; 170, Scott Dudelson/Getty Images Entertainment; 173, Kevin Winter/Getty Images Entertainment. **IconicPix:** 73B, MM Media; 76, George Bodnar Archive; 111, MM Media. **Bill O'Leary:** 6, 45TL, 45BR, 46TL, 46TR, 47, 49, 50, 51ML, 167B. **Photofest:** 19T. **Stephen W Tayler:** 86, 87TL, 87ML. **Frank White:** 59, 69T, 93, 101.

ACKNOWLEDGMENTS

I am deeply grateful to the following people, who worked alongside Rush and let me interview them:

Brent Carpenter, Rush monitor engineer, 2002–2015

Guy Charbonneau, recording engineer, Le Mobile

Donna L. Halper, Ph.D., music historian

Brad Madix, Rush front-of-house engineer, 2002–2015

Robert Scovill, multi-award-winning concert sound mixer and engineer

Hugh Syme, Rush album cover designer

Stephen W Tayler, music producer and mixer

Special thanks to award-winning cabaret singer Mardie Millit for her analysis of Geddy Lee's vocal technique and to musician Angie Scarpa for decoding the trickier time signatures for me. Additional thanks to Donna L. Halper, Ph.D., for keeping complete records of every bad review Rush ever received and sharing the particularly demented ones with me.

Thank you to Scott Marshall for being an early influence when I was getting into this band. I will never get tired of discussing with you what Neil is doing as Geddy sings "weary of the night" on the studio version of "Xanadu."

Thank you to John Kane, founder and cohost of the *Two Guys Talking Rush* podcast. We discussed the greatest music in the world and met a ton of cool people, some of whom I interviewed for this book. Every minute was a blast, and you deserve all the credit.

My utmost gratitude to Ina B. Ratner, M.D.; Kayane Hanna-Hindy, M.D.; and Rebecca Rhee, M.D., chief of colorectal surgery at Maimonides Medical Center. You were my all-female backing band, and I'll be writing more books in the future because of your combined expertise, albeit with a little less colon than I used to have.

Thank you to my parents, Albert and Joanna Bukszpan; my sister Claudia Rutherford; my mother-in-law Valborg Linn; and my ride-or-die lesbian work wife Constance Brinkley-Badgett for your ongoing and unwavering support while I see how this whole "writing" thing goes.

Thank you to Dennis Pernu of Quarto/Motorbooks for letting me take a crack at writing something of my own about this band. I've wanted this for years.

Thanks to my son, Roman, for keeping me grounded and performing the best version of "It's Not Unusual" in high school talent show history. Finally, thank you to my wife, Asia, the love of my life and the woman who made everything possible for me by loving me as I am. I love you and Roman more than anything in the world—even the guitar solo to "Freewill."

This book would have been much harder to write without the tireless efforts of these fan sites, which have kept voluminous records of everything related to Rush for years.

2112.net

cygnus-x1.net

rushisaband.com

Thank you also to the band's official website, rush.com, for keeping the discography and tour information tidy.

Most of all, thank you to Geddy Lee, Alex Lifeson, Neil Peart, and John Rutsey for making this music.

DEDICATION

This book is dedicated to all the future Rush fans and all the young people just discovering them today. You're going to keep this band's music and memory alive long after we're all gone, so here's their story.

ABOUT THE AUTHOR

Daniel Bukszpan is a writer with thirty years of experience. He is the author of *The Encyclopedia of Heavy Metal* (2003), *The Encyclopedia of New Wave* (2012), *The Art of Brütal Legend* (2013), *The Essential Wit of the World's Funniest People* (2017), *Woodstock: 50 Years of Peace and Music* (2019), and *Ozzy at 75* (Motorbooks, 2023).

INDEX

A
albums
2112, 24, 54, 96, 106
All the World's a Stage, 26, 53, 78
Caress of Steel, 20, 22, 24, 82, 115
Chronicles, 81
Clockwork Angels, 152–155, 160
Clockwork Angels Tour, 159
Counterparts, 91, 106, 112
Different Stages, 103–104
Exit . . . Stage Left, 52–53, 69, 78, 79, 123
A Farewell to Kings, 32, 34, 36, 53, 104
Feedback, 128, 130, 131, 132
Fly by Night, 18–19, 20, 54, 82, 112
Grace Under Pressure, 68–69, 115, 159
Grace Under Pressure Tour, 69
Hemispheres, 36, 38–39, 42, 81
Hold Your Fire, 74–75, 81, 128
Moving Pictures, 48–51, 150
Moving Pictures: Live 2011, 150
My Favorite Headache (Geddy Lee), 110
Permanent Waves, 44–47
Power Windows, 72–73, 81
Presto, 86
R30 Live, 130–131, 142
R40 Live, 160–163
Retrospective III, 115
Roll the Bones, 88
Rush, 10, 12, 14, 160
Rush in Rio, 122–123, 126, 130
A Show of Hands, 69, 78
Signals, 58–61, 64, 106
Snakes & Arrows, 132–135, 142
Snakes & Arrows Live, 142–145
Test for Echo, 92, 94, 128
Time Machine 2011: Live in Cleveland, 150, 152
Vapor Trails, 112–115, 119, 126, 132, 135
Vapor Trails Remixed, 115
Allen, Larry, 86
Anderson, Kevin J., 152, 169
Anson (crew member), 166
Atlantic Records, 86
Azerrad, Michael, 79

B
Bottrill, David, 115
Brown, Terry, 12, 18, 24, 32, 36, 38, 64–65, 66, 68
Bruford, Bill, 92
Burgess, Jim, 120
Burning for Buddy: A Tribute to the Music of Buddy Rich, 92

C
Campbell, David, 157, 159
Carpenter, Brent, 16, 48, 68, 119, 122–123, 126, 142–145, 164
Cecconi, Pegi, 164
Charbonneau, Guy, 53, 79
Chycki, Richard, 115
Clockwork Angels (Kevin J. Anderson), 152
Clockwork Angels String Ensemble, 157
Clockwork Destiny (Kevin J. Anderson), 169
Clockwork Lives (Kevin J. Anderson), 152
Coleridge, Samuel Taylor, 34
Collins, Peter, 72, 91, 94, 106

D
Danniels, Ray, 10, 12, 67, 164
De Leon, Mario, 157
Derouin, Joel, 157
Diamond, Jonny, 55
Dinklage, Jonathan, 157
Don Quixote (Cervantes), 34

E
Envy of None (band), 169

F
Farmer, Robert, 54
Ford, Stephen, 26
Fricke, David, 73

G
Geddy Lee's Big Beautiful Book of Bass (Geddy Lee), 169
Ghost Rider: Travels on the Healing Road (Neil Peart), 98
Grace Under Pressure, 68–69
Grandy, Ian, 28
Gruber, Freddie, 92, 120

H
Halper, Donna, 14, 17, 19, 28, 29, 38–39, 43, 47, 55, 81, 98, 106, 163, 164, 166, 172
Henderson, Peter, 67
Hilera, Gerry, 157
Hine, Rupert, 86, 88
Hollywood Walk of Fame, 137
Hush (band), 16

I
Ian Thomas Band, 20

J
J.R. Flood (band), 16
Jurek, Thom, 128

K
Kirke, Simon, 12
Kirschner, Don, 137
KISS (band), 22
Kmetzko, Mark, 18
Kordosh, John, 51
KSHE radio (St. Louis), 47
"Kubla Khan" (Samuel Taylor Coleridge), 34

L
Lakewoods Farm (Ontario), 43
Lee, Geddy
  childhood of, 10
  post-Rush career of, 163, 169, 171
  solo album, 110
  substance use of, 138
  vocals of, 82–83, 150, 152
Le Mobile studio, 79
Le Studio (Quebec), 43, 51, 68, 88
Lifeson, Alex
  childhood of, 10
  health of, 29, 160, 163, 169
  post-Rush career of, 169, 171
  retirement of, 163
  substance use of, 138
Lillywhite, Steve, 66–67
Living Legends Award, 137
Loder, Kurt, 69

M
Mack, Bob, 90
MacNaughtan, Andrew, 110–111
Madix, Brad, 14, 119, 120, 122, 123, 150, 157, 159, 163, 164
McCartney, Paul, 171
McNicol, Charlene, 138, 172
Mendelssohn, John, 19
Mercury Records, 14, 20, 22
Michaels, Bret, 28
Miles, Barry, 55
Millit, Mardie, 82–83
Mink, Ben, 61
Molson Canadian Rock for Toronto (SARSStock), 137
Moon Records, 10, 14
My Effin' Life (Geddy Lee), 169

N
Niester, Alan, 82
Northfield, Paul, 103
Nuttall, Carrie, 110–111, 146, 160, 163, 169

P
Pareles, Jon, 82
Paul, Rand, 54
Peart, Neil
  audition of, 16, 130, 152
  blog of, 146–147
  childhood of, 16
  death of, 164
  drum lessons of, 92, 120
  fatherhood of, 98, 103, 132, 146–147, 160, 163
  health of, 160, 164, 169
  in London, 16, 18, 38
  lyrics of, 17, 169
  marriage to Carrie, 110–111, 146, 160, 163
  marriage to Jackie, 98, 103, 132, 147
  rehearsal habits of, 86, 88
  retirement of, 163
  substance use of, 138
Peart, Olivia, 147, 160, 163
Peart, Selena, 98, 103, 132, 147
Pinkpop Festival (Holland), 42
Pond, Steve, 82

R

Rand, Ayn, 54–55
Raskulinecz, Nick, 132–135, 152
Richards, Andy, 72
Rich, Buddy, 92
Rich, Cathy, 92
Roach, Max, 92
Rockfield Studios, 32, 43
Rock & Roll Hall of Fame, 172
Roper, Bob, 14
Rudd, Paul, 137
Rush: Beyond the Lighted Stage (documentary), 137
Rush Replay 3X box set, 69
Rutsey, John, 10, 12, 14, 18, 28–29, 130

S

Scovill, Robert, 38, 86
Segel, Jason, 137
Sheffield, Rob, 24
Simmons, Gene, 22
Simon, Pam, 19, 82
Smith, Steve, 92
Solomon, Audrey, 157
songs
　"2112," 22, 26, 38, 54, 96, 104
　"Afterimage," 68
　"Alien Shore," 91
　"The Analog Kid," 58
　"The Anarchist," 160
　"Anthem," 18, 26, 54, 130, 155
　"Available Light," 86
　"Bastille Day," 20, 26, 130
　"Beneath, Between, and Behind," 18
　"Best I Can," 18
　"Between Sun and Moon," 123
　"Between the Wheels," 131
　"The Big Money," 72
　"The Body Electric," 68, 159
　"Broon's Bane," 52–53
　"BU2B," 150
　"By-Tor and the Snow Dog," 19
　"The Camera Eye," 150
　"Caravan," 150, 152
　"Chemistry," 58
　"Cinderella Man," 34
　"Circumstances," 38, 39, 142
　"Closer to the Heart," 34, 104, 142–145
　"The Color of Right," 94
　"Countdown," 61, 64
　"Cygnus X-1 Book I: The Voyage," 34, 130
　"Cygnus X-1 Book II: Hemispheres," 36, 38, 130, 163
　"Different Strings," 45
　"Digital Man," 58–61
　"Distant Early Warning," 68, 126
　"Dog Years," 94
　"Double Agent," 91
　"Dreamline," 88, 103
　"Driven," 94, 103
　"Earthshine," 112, 115, 126
　"Emotion Detector," 73
　"The Enemy Within (Part I of Fear)," 68
　"Entre Nous," 142
　"Far Cry," 135
　"Finding My Way," 12, 29, 130
　"Force Ten," 74, 131
　"For What It's Worth," 128
　"The Fountain of Lamneth," 20
　"Freewill," 44
　"The Garden," 155
　"Ghost of a Chance," 88
　"Ghost Rider," 112
　"Grand Designs," 159
　"Half the World," 94
　"Heart Full of Soul," 128
　"Here Again," 12
　"High Water," 75
　"Hope," 132, 135
　"How It Is," 160
　"In the End," 18
　"In the Mood," 12
　"Into Darkness," 20
　"I Think I'm Going Bald," 20
　"Jacob's Ladder," 44, 52
　"Lakeside Park," 20
　"The Larger Bowl," 145
　"La Villa Strangiato (An Exercise in Self-Indulgence)," 39, 53
　"Limbo," 94
　"Limelight," 48, 104
　"Lock and Key," 75
　"Losing It," 61, 163
　"The Main Monkey Business," 135
　"Manhattan Project," 72, 78
　"Marathon," 72, 78
　"Middletown Dreams," 73
　"Mission," 75
　"Mr. Soul," 128
　"Mystic Rhythms," 73, 78
　"Natural Science," 45
　"The Necromancer," 20
　"Need Some Love," 12
　"New World Man," 58
　"Not Fade Away," 10
　"One Little Victory," 115, 119
　"Open Secrets," 75
　"Overture," 24, 96
　"The Pass," 86
　"A Passage to Bangkok," 24, 130, 142
　"Prime Mover," 74
　"R30 Overture," 130
　"Red Barchetta," 48
　"Red Sector A," 159
　"Resist," 94
　"The Rhythm Method," 79
　"Rivendell," 19
　"Second Nature," 74
　"Secret Touch," 115
　"Seven and Seven Is," 128
　"Show Don't Tell," 86
　"Something for Nothing," 24
　"Spindrift," 135
　"The Spirit of Radio," 44, 45, 52, 54
　"The Stars Look Down," 112–115
　"Stick It Out," 91
　"Subdivisions," 58, 64, 73
　"Summertime Blues," 128
　"Tai Shan," 75
　"Tears," 24
　"The Temples of Syrinx," 96
　"Territories," 159
　"Time and Motion," 94
　"Time Stand Still," 75
　"Tom Sawyer," 48, 82, 119–120, 126
　"The Trees," 38–39, 53, 104
　"Turn the Page," 75, 78
　"The Twilight Zone," 24
　"Under the Shadow," 20
　"Vapor Trail," 112
　"Virtuality," 94
　"Vital Signs," 51, 123
　"The Way the Wind Blows," 135
　"The Weapon," 64
　"What You're Doing," 12
　"Witch Hunt (Part III of Fear)," 48–51, 78
　"Working Man," 12, 14, 28, 29, 119, 126, 160, 163
　"Xanadu," 34, 53, 131
　"You Can't Fight It," 10
　"YYZ," 126, 159
Stein, Adele, 157
Syme, Hugh, 20, 24, 51, 61, 64, 91, 111
Szekely, Jacob, 157

T

Taguchi, Hiroko, 157
Tannyan, Gary, 14, 82
Tattrie, Boyd, 24, 26
Tayler, Stephen W, 86, 88
Taylor, Jackie, 98, 147
Taylor, Peter, 10
Tepner, Stan, 20, 82
Todorov, Entcho, 157
tours
　All the World's a Stage, 32
　Caress of Steel, 22
　Clockwork Angels, 157–159
　Counterparts, 103
　An Evening with Rush, 96
　Grace Under Pressure, 66, 68
　Hemispheres, 42
　Permanent Waves, 42
　Power Windows, 96
　R30: 30th Anniversary Tour, 130–131
　R40: 40th Anniversary Tour, 160, 163, 169
　Rush, 16, 18
　Snakes & Arrows, 142–145, 166
　Test for Echo, 96, 103, 120
　Time Machine, 147, 150
　Vapor Trails, 119, 122

U

Ulrich, Lars, 90–91
Ungerleider, Howard, 64

W

Wenner, Jann, 172
Whelan, Paul, 68
Wilson, Vic, 10, 16
WMMR radio (Philadelphia), 47
WMMS radio (Cleveland), 14, 28, 47

/ 191

Quarto.com

© 2024 Quarto Publishing Group USA Inc.
Text © 2024 Daniel Bukszpan

First Published in 2024 by Motorbooks, an imprint of The Quarto Group,
100 Cummings Center, Suite 265-D, Beverly, MA 01915, USA.
T (978) 282-9590 F (978) 283-2742

All rights reserved. No part of this book may be reproduced in any form without written permission of the copyright owners. All images in this book have been reproduced with the knowledge and prior consent of the artists concerned, and no responsibility is accepted by producer, publisher, or printer for any infringement of copyright or otherwise, arising from the contents of this publication. Every effort has been made to ensure that credits accurately comply with information supplied. We apologize for any inaccuracies that may have occurred and will resolve inaccurate or missing information in a subsequent reprinting of the book.

Motorbooks titles are also available at discount for retail, wholesale, promotional, and bulk purchase. For details, contact the Special Sales Manager by email at specialsales@quarto.com or by mail at The Quarto Group, Attn: Special Sales Manager, 100 Cummings Center, Suite 265-D, Beverly, MA 01915, USA.

28 27 26 25 24   2 3 4 5

ISBN: 978-0-7603-8715-3

Digital edition published in 2024
eISBN: 978-0-7603-8716-0

Library of Congress Cataloging-in-Publication Data

Names: Bukszpan, Daniel, author.
Title: Rush at 50 / Daniel Bukszpan.
Description: Beverly, MA : Motorbooks, 2024. | Series: At 50 | Includes bibliographical references and index. | Summary: "Rush at 50 presents an authoritative and illustrated retrospective of one of rock's most beloved acts, as told through 50 landmark releases, career pivots, and professional associations"-- Provided by publisher.
Identifiers: LCCN 2024012594 | ISBN 9780760387153 (hardcover) | ISBN 9780760387160 (ebook)
Subjects: LCSH: Rush (Musical group) | Rock musicians--Canada--Biography.
Classification: LCC ML421.R87 B85 2024 | DDC 782.42166092/2--dc23/eng/20240319
LC record available at https://lccn.loc.gov/2024012594

Design and layout: Burge Agency

Cover Photograph: Fin Costello/Redferns/Getty Images

Back Cover Photographs: Frank White

Printed in China